TAXMANN'S

GST ACTS

TAXMANN®'S

GST Acts

Taxmann®

Price : ₹ 995

Law stated in this book is as amended by the Finance (No. 2) Act, 2024

Published by :
Taxmann Publications (P.) Ltd.

Sales & Marketing :
59/32, New Rohtak Road, New Delhi-110 005 India
Phone : +91-11-45562222
Website : www.taxmann.com
E-mail : sales@taxmann.com

Regd. Office :
21/35, West Punjabi Bagh, New Delhi-110 026 India

Printed at :
Tan Prints (India) Pvt. Ltd.
44 Km. Mile Stone, National Highway, Rohtak Road
Village Rohad, Distt. Jhajjar (Haryana) India
E-mail : sales@tanprints.com

9 789364 551649

Disclaimer

CONTENTS

PAGE

DIVISION ONE 1

Central Goods and Services Tax Act, 2017

DIVISION TWO 2

Integrated Goods and Services Tax Act, 2017

DIVISION THREE 3

Union Territory Goods and Services Tax Act, 2017

PAGE

DIVISION FOUR 4

Goods and Services Tax (Compensation to States) Act, 2017

DIVISION ONE

Central Goods and Services Tax Act, 2017

1

CENTRAL GOODS AND SERVICES TAX ACT, 2017

Arrangement of Sections

SECTIONS PAGE

SECTIONS PAGE

CHAPTER VIII

ACCOUNTS AND RECORDS

CHAPTER IX

RETURNS

SECTIONS PAGE

CHAPTER X

PAYMENT OF TAX

CHAPTER XI

REFUNDS

CHAPTER XII

ASSESSMENT

CHAPTER XIII

AUDIT

CHAPTER XIV

INSPECTION, SEARCH, SEIZURE AND ARREST

CHAPTER XV

DEMANDS AND RECOVERY

CHAPTER XVI

LIABILITY TO PAY IN CERTAIN CASES

CHAPTER XVII

ADVANCE RULING

CHAPTER XVIII

APPEALS AND REVISION

CHAPTER XIX

OFFENCES AND PENALTIES

CHAPTER XX

TRANSITIONAL PROVISIONS

CHAPTER XXI

MISCELLANEOUS

Central Goods and Services Tax Act, 2017

[12 OF 2017]*

An Act to make a provision for levy and collection of tax on intra-State supply of goods or services or both by the Central Government and for matters connected therewith or incidental thereto.

BE it enacted by Parliament in the Sixty-eighth Year of the Republic of India as follows:—

CHAPTER I

PRELIMINARY

Short title, extent and commencement.

1. (1) This Act may be called the Central Goods and Services Tax Act, 2017.

(2) It extends to the whole of India [1][***].

(3) It shall come into force on such date as the Central Government may, by notification in the Official Gazette, appoint:

Provided that different dates may be appointed for different provisions of this Act and any reference in any such provision to the commencement of this Act shall be construed as a reference to the coming into force of that provision.

Definitions.

2. In this Act, unless the context otherwise requires,—

* Assented by the President of India on 12-4-2017.

1. Words "except the State of Jammu and Kashmir" omitted by the Central Goods and Services Tax (Extension to Jammu and Kashmir) Act, 2017, w.r.e.f. 8-7-2017.

(*1*) "actionable claim" shall have the same meaning as assigned to it in section 3 of the Transfer of Property Act, 1882 (4 of 1882);

(*2*) "address of delivery" means the address of the recipient of goods or services or both indicated on the tax invoice issued by a registered person for delivery of such goods or services or both;

(*3*) "address on record" means the address of the recipient as available in the records of the supplier;

(*4*) "adjudicating authority" means any authority, appointed or authorised to pass any order or decision under this Act, but does not include the [2][Central Board of Indirect Taxes and Customs], the Revisional Authority, the Authority for Advance Ruling, the Appellate Authority for Advance Ruling, [3][*the National Appellate Authority for Advance Ruling*,] [4][the Appellate Authority, the Appellate Tribunal and the Authority referred to in sub-section (2) of section 171];

(*5*) "agent" means a person, including a factor, broker, commission agent, *arhatia, del credere* agent, an auctioneer or any other mercantile agent, by whatever name called, who carries on the business of supply or receipt of goods or services or both on behalf of another;

(*6*) "aggregate turnover" means the aggregate value of all taxable supplies (excluding the value of inward supplies on which tax is payable

---

2. Substituted for "Central Board of Excise and Customs" by the Central Goods and Services Tax (Amendment) Act, 2018, w.e.f. 1-2-2019.
3. Inserted by the Finance (No. 2) Act, 2019, with effect from a date yet to be notified.
4. Substituted for "the Appellate Authority and the Appellate Tribunal" by the Central Goods and Services Tax (Amendment) Act, 2018, w.e.f. 1-2-2019.

by a person on reverse charge basis), exempt supplies, exports of goods or services or both and inter-State supplies of persons having the same Permanent Account Number, to be computed on all India basis but excludes central tax, State tax, Union territory tax, integrated tax and cess;

(*7*) "agriculturist" means an individual or a Hindu Undivided Family who undertakes cultivation of land—

(*a*) by own labour, or

(*b*) by the labour of family, or

(*c*) by servants on wages payable in cash or kind or by hired labour under personal supervision or the personal supervision of any member of the family;

(*8*) "Appellate Authority" means an authority appointed or authorised to hear appeals as referred to in section 107;

(*9*) "Appellate Tribunal" means the Goods and Services Tax Appellate Tribunal constituted under section 109;

(*10*) "appointed day" means the date on which the provisions of this Act shall come into force;

(*11*) "assessment" means determination of tax liability under this Act and includes self-assessment, re-assessment, provisional assessment, summary assessment and best judgment assessment;

(*12*) "associated enterprises" shall have the same meaning as assigned to it in section 92A of the Income-tax Act, 1961 (43 of 1961);

(*13*) "audit" means the examination of records, returns and other documents maintained or furnished by the registered person under this Act or the rules made thereunder or under any other law for the time being in force to verify the correctness of turnover declared, taxes paid, refund claimed and input tax credit availed, and to assess his compliance with the provisions of this Act or the rules made thereunder;

(*14*) "authorised bank" shall mean a bank or a branch of a bank authorised by the Government to collect the tax or any other amount payable under this Act;

(*15*) "authorised representative" means the representative as referred to in section 116;

(*16*) "Board" means the [5][Central Board of Indirect Taxes & Customs] constituted under the Central Boards of Revenue Act, 1963 (54 of 1963);

(*17*) "business" includes—

(*a*) any trade, commerce, manufacture, profession, vocation, adventure, wager or any other similar activity, whether or not it is for a pecuniary benefit;

(*b*) any activity or transaction in connection with or incidental or ancillary to sub-clause (*a*);

(*c*) any activity or transaction in the nature of sub-clause (*a*), whether or not there is volume, frequency, continuity or regularity of such transaction;

(*d*) supply or acquisition of goods including capital goods and services in connection with commencement or closure of business;

(*e*) provision by a club, association, society, or any such body (for a subscrip-

5. Substituted for "Central Board of Excise and Customs" by the Finance Act, 2018, w.e.f. 29-3-2018.

tion or any other consideration) of the facilities or benefits to its members;

(*f*) admission, for a consideration, of persons to any premises;

(*g*) services supplied by a person as the holder of an office which has been accepted by him in the course or furtherance of his trade, profession or vocation;

[6][(*h*) activities of a race club including by way of totalisator or a license to book maker or activities of a licensed book maker in such club; and]

(*i*) any activity or transaction undertaken by the Central Government, a State Government or any local authority in which they are engaged as public authorities;

(*18*) [7][***]

(*19*) "capital goods" means goods, the value of which is capitalised in the books of account of the person claiming the input tax credit and which are used or intended to be used in the course or furtherance of business;

(*20*) "casual taxable person" means a person who occasionally undertakes transactions involving supply of goods or services or both in the course or furtherance of business, whether as principal, agent or in any other capacity, in a State or a Union territory where he has no fixed place of business;

(*21*) "central tax" means the central goods and services tax levied under section 9;

---

6. Substituted by the Central Goods and Services Tax (Amendment) Act, 2018, w.e.f. 1-2-2019.

7. Omitted, *ibid.*

(*22*) "cess" shall have the same meaning as assigned to it in the Goods and Services Tax (Compensation to States) Act;

(*23*) "chartered accountant" means a chartered accountant as defined in clause (*b*) of sub-section (1) of section 2 of the Chartered Accountants Act, 1949 (38 of 1949);

(*24*) "Commissioner" means the Commissioner of central tax and includes the Principal Commissioner of central tax appointed under section 3 and the Commissioner of integrated tax appointed under the Integrated Goods and Services Tax Act;

(*25*) "Commissioner in the Board" means the Commissioner referred to in section 168;

(*26*) "common portal" means the common goods and services tax electronic portal referred to in section 146;

(*27*) "common working days" in respect of a State or Union territory shall mean such days in succession which are not declared as gazetted holidays by the Central Government or the concerned State or Union territory Government;

(*28*) "company secretary" means a company secretary as defined in clause (*c*) of sub-section (1) of section 2 of the Company Secretaries Act, 1980 (56 of 1980);

(*29*) "competent authority" means such authority as may be notified by the Government;

(*30*) "composite supply" means a supply made by a taxable person to a recipient consisting of two or more taxable supplies of goods or services or both, or any combination thereof, which are naturally bundled and supplied in conjunction with each other in the ordinary course of business, one of which is a principal supply.

Illustration: Where goods are packed and transported with insurance, the supply of goods, packing materials, transport and insurance is a composite supply and supply of goods is a principal supply;

(*31*) "consideration" in relation to the supply of goods or services or both includes—

(*a*) any payment made or to be made, whether in money or otherwise, in respect of, in response to, or for the inducement of, the supply of goods or services or both, whether by the recipient or by any other person but shall not include any subsidy given by the Central Government or a State Government;

(*b*) the monetary value of any act or forbearance, in respect of, in response to, or for the inducement of, the supply of goods or services or both, whether by the recipient or by any other person but shall not include any subsidy given by the Central Government or a State Government:

Provided that a deposit given in respect of the supply of goods or services or both shall not be considered as payment made for such supply unless the supplier applies such deposit as consideration for the said supply;

(*32*) "continuous supply of goods" means a supply of goods which is provided, or agreed to be provided, continuously or on recurrent basis, under a contract, whether or not by means of a wire, cable, pipeline or other conduit, and for which the supplier invoices the recipient on a regular or periodic basis and includes supply of such goods as the Government may, subject to such conditions, as it may, by notification, specify;

(*33*) "continuous supply of services" means a supply of services which is provided, or agreed to be provided, continuously or on recurrent basis, under a contract, for a period exceeding three months with periodic payment obligations and includes supply of such services as the Government may, subject to such conditions, as it may, by notification, specify;

(*34*) "conveyance" includes a vessel, an aircraft and a vehicle;

(*35*) "cost accountant" means a cost accountant as defined in [8][clause (*b*)] of sub-section (1) of section 2 of the Cost and Works Accountants Act, 1959 (23 of 1959);

(*36*) "Council" means the Goods and Services Tax Council established under article 279A of the Constitution;

(*37*) "credit note" means a document issued by a registered person under sub-section (1) of section 34;

(*38*) "debit note" means a document issued by a registered person under sub-section (3) of section 34;

(*39*) "deemed exports" means such supplies of goods as may be notified under section 147;

(*40*) "designated authority" means such authority as may be notified by the Board;

(*41*) "document" includes written or printed record of any sort and electronic record as defined in clause (*t*) of sub-section (1) of section 2 of the Information Technology Act, 2000 (21 of 2000);

(*42*) "drawback" in relation to any goods manufactured in India and exported, means the

8. Substituted for "clause (*c*)" by the Central Goods and Services Tax (Amendment) Act, 2018, w.e.f. 1-2-2019.

rebate of duty, tax or cess chargeable on any imported inputs or on any domestic inputs or input services used in the manufacture of such goods;

(*43*) "electronic cash ledger" means the electronic cash ledger referred to in sub-section (1) of section 49;

(*44*) "electronic commerce" means the supply of goods or services or both, including digital products over digital or electronic network;

(*45*) "electronic commerce operator" means any person who owns, operates or manages digital or electronic facility or platform for electronic commerce;

(*46*) "electronic credit ledger" means the electronic credit ledger referred to in sub-section (2) of section 49;

(*47*) "exempt supply" means supply of any goods or services or both which attracts *nil* rate of tax or which may be wholly exempt from tax under section 11, or under section 6 of the Integrated Goods and Services Tax Act, and includes non-taxable supply;

(*48*) "existing law" means any law, notification, order, rule or regulation relating to levy and collection of duty or tax on goods or services or both passed or made before the commencement of this Act by Parliament or any Authority or person having the power to make such law, notification, order, rule or regulation;

(*49*) "family" means,—

(*i*) the spouse and children of the person, and

(*ii*) the parents, grand-parents, brothers and sisters of the person if they are wholly or mainly dependent on the said person;

(*50*) "fixed establishment" means a place (other than the registered place of business) which is characterised by a sufficient degree of permanence and suitable structure in terms of human and technical resources to supply services, or to receive and use services for its own needs;

(*51*) "Fund" means the Consumer Welfare Fund established under section 57;

(*52*) "goods" means every kind of movable property other than money and securities but includes actionable claim, growing crops, grass and things attached to or forming part of the land which are agreed to be severed before supply or under a contract of supply;

(*53*) "Government" means the Central Government;

(*54*) "Goods and Services Tax (Compensation to States) Act" means the Goods and Services Tax (Compensation to States) Act, 2017;

(*55*) "goods and services tax practitioner" means any person who has been approved under section 48 to act as such practitioner;

(*56*) "India" means the territory of India as referred to in article 1 of the Constitution, its territorial waters, seabed and sub-soil underlying such waters, continental shelf, exclusive economic zone or any other maritime zone as referred to in the Territorial Waters, Continental Shelf, Exclusive Economic Zone and other Maritime Zones Act, 1976 (80 of 1976), and the air space above its territory and territorial waters;

(*57*) "Integrated Goods and Services Tax Act" means the Integrated Goods and Services Tax Act, 2017;

(*58*) "integrated tax" means the integrated goods and services tax levied under the Integrated Goods and Services Tax Act;

(*59*) "input" means any goods other than capital goods used or intended to be used by a supplier in the course or furtherance of business;

(*60*) "input service" means any service used or intended to be used by a supplier in the course or furtherance of business;

[9]**[**(*61*) *"Input Service Distributor" means an office of the supplier of goods or services or both which receives tax invoices towards the receipt of input services, including invoices in respect of services liable to tax under sub-section (3) or sub-section (4) of section 9, for or on behalf of distinct persons referred to in section 25, and liable to distribute the input tax credit in respect of such invoices in the manner provided in section 20;***]**

(*62*) "input tax" in relation to a registered person, means the central tax, State tax, integrated tax or Union territory tax charged on any supply of goods or services or both made to him and includes—

(*a*) the integrated goods and services tax charged on import of goods;

(*b*) the tax payable under the provisions of sub-sections (3) and (4) of section 9;

(*c*) the tax payable under the provisions of sub-sections (3) and (4) of section 5 of the Integrated Goods and Services Tax Act;

(*d*) the tax payable under the provisions of sub-sections (3) and (4) of section 9 of the respective State Goods and Services Tax Act; or

(*e*) the tax payable under the provisions of sub-sections (3) and (4) of section

9. Substituted by the Finance Act, 2024, w.e.f. **1-4-2025**.

7 of the Union Territory Goods and Services Tax Act,

but does not include the tax paid under the composition levy;

(*63*) "input tax credit" means the credit of input tax;

(*64*) "intra-State supply of goods" shall have the same meaning as assigned to it in section 8 of the Integrated Goods and Services Tax Act;

(*65*) "intra-State supply of services" shall have the same meaning as assigned to it in section 8 of the Integrated Goods and Services Tax Act;

(*66*) "invoice" or "tax invoice" means the tax invoice referred to in section 31;

(*67*) "inward supply" in relation to a person, shall mean receipt of goods or services or both whether by purchase, acquisition or any other means with or without consideration;

(*68*) "job work" means any treatment or process undertaken by a person on goods belonging to another registered person and the expression "job worker" shall be construed accordingly;

(*69*) "local authority" means—

(*a*) a "Panchayat" as defined in clause (*d*) of article 243 of the Constitution;

(*b*) a "Municipality" as defined in clause (*e*) of article 243P of the Constitution;

(*c*) a Municipal Committee, a Zilla Parishad, a District Board, and any other authority legally entitled to, or entrusted by the Central Government or any State Government with the control or management of a municipal or local fund;

(*d*) a Cantonment Board as defined in section 3 of the Cantonments Act, 2006 (41 of 2006);

(*e*) a Regional Council or a District Council constituted under the Sixth Schedule to the Constitution;

(*f*) a Development Board constituted under article 371 [10][and article 371J] of the Constitution; or

(*g*) a Regional Council constituted under article 371A of the Constitution;

(*70*) "location of the recipient of services" means,—

(*a*) where a supply is received at a place of business for which the registration has been obtained, the location of such place of business;

(*b*) where a supply is received at a place other than the place of business for which registration has been obtained (a fixed establishment elsewhere), the location of such fixed establishment;

(*c*) where a supply is received at more than one establishment, whether the place of business or fixed establishment, the location of the establishment most directly concerned with the receipt of the supply; and

(*d*) in absence of such places, the location of the usual place of residence of the recipient;

(*71*) "location of the supplier of services" means,—

(*a*) where a supply is made from a place of business for which the registration has been obtained, the location of such place of business;

(*b*) where a supply is made from a place other than the place of business for which registration has been obtained

10. Inserted by the Central Goods and Services Tax (Amendment) Act, 2018, w.e.f. 1-2-2019.

(a fixed establishment elsewhere), the location of such fixed establishment;

(*c*) where a supply is made from more than one establishment, whether the place of business or fixed establishment, the location of the establishment most directly concerned with the provisions of the supply; and

(*d*) in absence of such places, the location of the usual place of residence of the supplier;

(72) "manufacture" means processing of raw material or inputs in any manner that results in emergence of a new product having a distinct name, character and use and the term "manufacturer" shall be construed accordingly;

(73) "market value" shall mean the full amount which a recipient of a supply is required to pay in order to obtain the goods or services or both of like kind and quality at or about the same time and at the same commercial level where the recipient and the supplier are not related;

(74) "mixed supply" means two or more individual supplies of goods or services, or any combination thereof, made in conjunction with each other by a taxable person for a single price where such supply does not constitute a composite supply:

Illustration : A supply of a package consisting of canned foods, sweets, chocolates, cakes, dry fruits, aerated drinks and fruit juices when supplied for a single price is a mixed supply. Each of these items can be supplied separately and is not dependent on any other. It shall not be a mixed supply if these items are supplied separately;

(*75*) "money" means the Indian legal tender or any foreign currency, cheque, promissory note, bill of exchange, letter of credit, draft, pay order, traveller cheque, money order, postal or electronic remittance or any other instrument recognised by the Reserve Bank of India when used as a consideration to settle an obligation or exchange with Indian legal tender of another denomination but shall not include any currency that is held for its numismatic value;

(*76*) "motor vehicle" shall have the same meaning as assigned to it in clause (*28*) of section 2 of the Motor Vehicles Act, 1988 (59 of 1988);

(*77*) "non-resident taxable person" means any person who occasionally undertakes transactions involving supply of goods or services or both, whether as principal or agent or in any other capacity, but who has no fixed place of business or residence in India;

(*78*) "non-taxable supply" means a supply of goods or services or both which is not leviable to tax under this Act or under the Integrated Goods and Services Tax Act;

(*79*) "non-taxable territory" means the territory which is outside the taxable territory;

(*80*) "notification" means a notification published in the Official Gazette and the expressions "notify" and "notified" shall be construed accordingly;

[11][(*80A*) "online gaming" means offering of a game on the internet or an electronic network and includes online money gaming;

(*80B*) "online money gaming" means online gaming in which players pay or deposit money or money's worth, including virtual digital

11. Inserted by the Central Goods and Services Tax (Amendment) Act, 2023, w.e.f. 1-10-2023.

assets, in the expectation of winning money or money's worth, including virtual digital assets, in any event including game, scheme, competition or any other activity or process, whether or not its outcome or performance is based on skill, chance or both and whether the same is permissible or otherwise under any other law for the time being in force;]

(*81*) "other territory" includes territories other than those comprising in a State and those referred to in sub-clauses (*a*) to (*e*) of clause (*114*);

(*82*) "output tax" in relation to a taxable person, means the tax chargeable under this Act on taxable supply of goods or services or both made by him or by his agent but excludes tax payable by him on reverse charge basis;

(*83*) "outward supply" in relation to a taxable person, means supply of goods or services or both, whether by sale, transfer, barter, exchange, licence, rental, lease or disposal or any other mode, made or agreed to be made by such person in the course or furtherance of business;

(*84*) "person" includes—

(*a*) an individual;

(*b*) a Hindu Undivided Family;

(*c*) a company;

(*d*) a firm;

(*e*) a Limited Liability Partnership;

(*f*) an association of persons or a body of individuals, whether incorporated or not, in India or outside India;

(*g*) any corporation established by or under any Central Act, State Act or Provincial Act or a Government company as defined in clause (*45*) of section 2 of the Companies Act, 2013 (18 of 2013);

(*h*) any body corporate incorporated by or under the laws of a country outside India;

(*i*) a co-operative society registered under any law relating to co-operative societies;

(*j*) a local authority;

(*k*) Central Government or a State Government;

(*l*) society as defined under the Societies Registration Act, 1860 (21 of 1860);

(*m*) trust; and

(*n*) every artificial juridical person, not falling within any of the above;

(*85*) "place of business" includes—

(*a*) a place from where the business is ordinarily carried on, and includes a warehouse, a godown or any other place where a taxable person stores his goods, supplies or receives goods or services or both; or

(*b*) a place where a taxable person maintains his books of account; or

(*c*) a place where a taxable person is engaged in business through an agent, by whatever name called;

(*86*) "place of supply" means the place of supply as referred to in Chapter V of the Integrated Goods and Services Tax Act;

(*87*) "prescribed" means prescribed by rules made under this Act on the recommendations of the Council;

(*88*) "principal" means a person on whose behalf an agent carries on the business of supply or receipt of goods or services or both;

(*89*) "principal place of business" means the place of business specified as the principal place of business in the certificate of registration;

(*90*) "principal supply" means the supply of goods or services which constitutes the predominant element of a composite supply and to which any other supply forming part of that composite supply is ancillary;

(*91*) "proper officer" in relation to any function to be performed under this Act, means the Commissioner or the officer of the central tax who is assigned that function by the Commissioner in the Board;

(*92*) "quarter" shall mean a period comprising three consecutive calendar months, ending on the last day of March, June, September and December of a calendar year;

(*93*) "recipient" of supply of goods or services or both, means—

(*a*) where a consideration is payable for the supply of goods or services or both, the person who is liable to pay that consideration;

(*b*) where no consideration is payable for the supply of goods, the person to whom the goods are delivered or made available, or to whom possession or use of the goods is given or made available; and

(*c*) where no consideration is payable for the supply of a service, the person to whom the service is rendered,

and any reference to a person to whom a supply is made shall be construed as a reference to the recipient of the supply and shall include an agent acting as such on behalf of the recipient in relation to the goods or services or both supplied;

(*94*) "registered person" means a person who is registered under section 25 but does not include a person having a Unique Identity Number;

(*95*) "regulations" means the regulations made by the Board under this Act on the recommendations of the Council;

(*96*) "removal" in relation to goods, means—

(*a*) despatch of the goods for delivery by the supplier thereof or by any other person acting on behalf of such supplier; or

(*b*) collection of the goods by the recipient thereof or by any other person acting on behalf of such recipient;

(*97*) "return" means any return prescribed or otherwise required to be furnished by or under this Act or the rules made thereunder;

(*98*) "reverse charge" means the liability to pay tax by the recipient of supply of goods or services or both instead of the supplier of such goods or services or both under sub-section (3) or sub-section (4) of section 9, or under sub-section (3) or sub-section (4) of section 5 of the Integrated Goods and Services Tax Act;

(*99*) "Revisional Authority" means an authority appointed or authorised for revision of decision or orders as referred to in section 108;

(*100*) "Schedule" means a Schedule appended to this Act;

(*101*) "securities" shall have the same meaning as assigned to it in clause (*h*) of section 2 of the Securities Contracts (Regulation) Act, 1956 (42 of 1956);

(*102*) "services" means anything other than goods, money and securities but includes activities relating to the use of money or its conversion by cash or by any other mode, from one form, currency or denomination, to another form, currency or denomination for which a separate consideration is charged.

[12][*Explanation*.—For the removal of doubts, it is hereby clarified that the expression "services" includes facilitating or arranging transactions in securities;]

[13-14][(*102A*) "specified actionable claim" means the actionable claim involved in or by way of—

(*i*) betting;

(*ii*) casinos;

(*iii*) gambling;

(*iv*) horse racing;

(*v*) lottery; or

(*vi*) online money gaming;]

(*103*) "State" includes a Union territory with Legislature;

(*104*) "State tax" means the tax levied under any State Goods and Services Tax Act;

(*105*) "supplier" in relation to any goods or services or both, shall mean the person supplying the said goods or services or both and shall include an agent acting as such on behalf of such supplier in relation to the goods or services or both supplied:

[13-14][**Provided** that a person who organises or arranges, directly or indirectly, supply of

12. Inserted by the Central Goods and Services Tax (Amendment) Act, 2018, w.e.f. 1-2-2019.

13-14. Inserted by the Central Goods and Services Tax (Amendment) Act, 2023, w.e.f. 1-10-2023.

specified actionable claims, including a person who owns, operates or manages digital or electronic platform for such supply, shall be deemed to be a supplier of such actionable claims, whether such actionable claims are supplied by him or through him and whether consideration in money or money's worth, including virtual digital assets, for supply of such actionable claims is paid or conveyed to him or through him or placed at his disposal in any manner, and all the provisions of this Act shall apply to such supplier of specified actionable claims, as if he is the supplier liable to pay the tax in relation to the supply of such actionable claims;]

(*106*) "tax period" means the period for which the return is required to be furnished;

(*107*) "taxable person" means a person who is registered or liable to be registered under section 22 or section 24;

(*108*) "taxable supply" means a supply of goods or services or both which is leviable to tax under this Act;

(*109*) "taxable territory" means the territory to which the provisions of this Act apply;

(*110*) "telecommunication service" means service of any description (including electronic mail, voice mail, data services, audio text services, video text services, radio paging and cellular mobile telephone services) which is made available to users by means of any transmission or reception of signs, signals, writing, images and sounds or intelligence of any nature, by wire, radio, visual or other electromagnetic means;

(*111*) "the State Goods and Services Tax Act" means the respective State Goods and Services Tax Act, 2017;

(*112*) "turnover in State" or "turnover in Union territory" means the aggregate value of all taxable supplies (excluding the value of inward supplies on which tax is payable by a person on reverse charge basis) and exempt supplies made within a State or Union territory by a taxable person, exports of goods or services or both and inter-State supplies of goods or services or both made from the State or Union territory by the said taxable person but excludes central tax, State tax, Union territory tax, integrated tax and cess;

(*113*) "usual place of residence" means—

(*a*) in case of an individual, the place where he ordinarily resides;

(*b*) in other cases, the place where the person is incorporated or otherwise legally constituted;

(*114*) "Union territory" means the territory of—

(*a*) the Andaman and Nicobar Islands;

(*b*) Lakshadweep;

[15][(*c*) Dadra and Nagar Haveli and Daman and Diu;]

[16][(*d*) Ladakh;]

(*e*) Chandigarh; and

(*f*) other territory.

Explanation.—For the purposes of this Act, each of the territories specified in sub-clauses (*a*) to (*f*) shall be considered to be a separate Union territory;

(*115*) "Union territory tax" means the Union territory goods and services tax levied under the Union Territory Goods and Services Tax Act;

---

15. Substituted by the Finance Act, 2020, w.e.f. 30-6-2020.

16. Inserted, *ibid*.

(*116*) "Union Territory Goods and Services Tax Act" means the Union Territory Goods and Services Tax Act, 2017;

(*117*) "valid return" means a return furnished under sub-section (1) of section 39 on which self-assessed tax has been paid in full;

[17][(*117A*) "virtual digital asset" shall have the same meaning as assigned to it in clause (*47A*) of section 2 of the Income-tax Act, 1961 (43 of 1961);]

(*118*) "voucher" means an instrument where there is an obligation to accept it as consideration or part consideration for a supply of goods or services or both and where the goods or services or both to be supplied or the identities of their potential suppliers are either indicated on the instrument itself or in related documentation, including the terms and conditions of use of such instrument;

(*119*) "works contract" means a contract for building, construction, fabrication, completion, erection, installation, fitting out, improvement, modification, repair, maintenance, renovation, alteration or commissioning of any immovable property wherein transfer of property in goods (whether as goods or in some other form) is involved in the execution of such contract;

(*120*) words and expressions used and not defined in this Act but defined in the Integrated Goods and Services Tax Act, the Union Territory Goods and Services Tax Act and the Goods and Services Tax (Compensation to States) Act shall have the same meaning as assigned to them in those Acts;

17. Inserted by the Central Goods and Services Tax (Amendment) Act, 2023, w.e.f. 1-10-2023.

(*121*) [18][***]

CHAPTER II

ADMINISTRATION

Officers under this Act.

3. The Government shall, by notification, appoint the following classes of officers for the purposes of this Act, namely:—

(*a*) Principal Chief Commissioners of Central Tax or Principal Directors General of Central Tax,

(*b*) Chief Commissioners of Central Tax or Directors General of Central Tax,

(*c*) Principal Commissioners of Central Tax or Principal Additional Directors General of Central Tax,

(*d*) Commissioners of Central Tax or Additional Directors General of Central Tax,

(*e*) Additional Commissioners of Central Tax or Additional Directors of Central Tax,

(*f*) Joint Commissioners of Central Tax or Joint Directors of Central Tax,

(*g*) Deputy Commissioners of Central Tax or Deputy Directors of Central Tax,

(*h*) Assistant Commissioners of Central Tax or Assistant Directors of Central Tax, and

(*i*) any other class of officers as it may deem fit:

Provided that the officers appointed under the Central Excise Act, 1944 (1 of 1944) shall be deemed to be the officers appointed under the provisions of this Act.

Appointment of officers.

4. (1) The Board may, in addition to the officers as may be notified by the Government under section 3,

---

18. Omitted by the Jammu and Kashmir Reorganisation (Adaptation of Central Laws) Order, 2020, w.e.f. 18-3-2020.

appoint such persons as it may think fit to be the officers under this Act.

(2) Without prejudice to the provisions of sub-section (1), the Board may, by order, authorise any officer referred to in clauses (*a*) to (*h*) of section 3 to appoint officers of central tax below the rank of Assistant Commissioner of central tax for the administration of this Act.

Powers of officers.

5. (1) Subject to such conditions and limitations as the Board may impose, an officer of central tax may exercise the powers and discharge the duties conferred or imposed on him under this Act.

(2) An officer of central tax may exercise the powers and discharge the duties conferred or imposed under this Act on any other officer of central tax who is subordinate to him.

(3) The Commissioner may, subject to such conditions and limitations as may be specified in this behalf by him, delegate his powers to any other officer who is subordinate to him.

(4) Notwithstanding anything contained in this section, an Appellate Authority shall not exercise the powers and discharge the duties conferred or imposed on any other officer of central tax.

Authorisation of officers of State tax or Union territory tax as proper officer in certain circumstances.

6. (1) Without prejudice to the provisions of this Act, the officers appointed under the State Goods and Services Tax Act or the Union Territory Goods and Services Tax Act are authorised to be the proper officers for the purposes of this Act, subject to such conditions as the Government shall, on the recommendations of the Council, by notification, specify.

(2) Subject to the conditions specified in the notification issued under sub-section (1),—

(*a*) where any proper officer issues an order under this Act, he shall also issue an order under the State Goods and Services Tax Act or the Union Territory Goods and Services Tax Act, as authorised by the State Goods and Services Tax Act or the Union Territory Goods and Services Tax Act, as the case may be, under intimation to the jurisdictional officer of State tax or Union territory tax;

(*b*) where a proper officer under the State Goods and Services Tax Act or the Union Territory Goods and Services Tax Act has initiated any proceedings on a subject matter, no proceedings shall be initiated by the proper officer under this Act on the same subject matter.

(3) Any proceedings for rectification, appeal and revision, wherever applicable, of any order passed by an officer appointed under this Act shall not lie before an officer appointed under the State Goods and Services Tax Act or the Union Territory Goods and Services Tax Act.

CHAPTER III

LEVY AND COLLECTION OF TAX

Scope of supply.

7. (1) For the purposes of this Act, the expression "supply" includes—

(*a*) all forms of supply of goods or services or both such as sale, transfer, barter, exchange, licence, rental, lease or disposal made or agreed to be made for a consideration by a person in the course or furtherance of business;

[19][(*aa*) the activities or transactions, by a person, other than an individual, to its members or

19. Inserted by the Finance Act, 2021, w.r.e.f. 1-7-2017. [However, Notification No. 39/2021-Central Tax, dated 21-12-2021 appoints 1-1-2022 as the date of enforcement]

constituents or *vice versa*, for cash, deferred payment or other valuable consideration.

Explanation.—For the purposes of this clause, it is hereby clarified that, notwithstanding anything contained in any other law for the time being in force or any judgment, decree or order of any Court, tribunal or authority, the person and its members or constituents shall be deemed to be two separate persons and the supply of activities or transactions *inter se* shall be deemed to take place from one such person to another;]

(*b*) import of services for a consideration whether or not in the course or furtherance of business; [20][and]

(*c*) the activities specified in Schedule I, made or agreed to be made without a consideration [21][***]

(*d*) [22][***]

[23][(1A) Where certain activities or transactions constitute a supply in accordance with the provisions of sub-section (1), they shall be treated either as supply of goods or supply of services as referred to in Schedule II.]

(2) Notwithstanding anything contained in sub-section (1),—

(*a*) activities or transactions specified in Schedule III; or

(*b*) such activities or transactions undertaken by the Central Government, a State Government or any local authority in which they are en-

---

20. Inserted by the Central Goods and Services Tax (Amendment) Act, 2018, w.r.e.f. 1-7-2017.
21. Word "; and" omitted, *ibid*.
22. Omitted, *ibid*.
23. Inserted, *ibid*.

gaged as public authorities, as may be notified by the Government on the recommendations of the Council,

shall be treated neither as a supply of goods nor a supply of services.

(3) Subject to the provisions of [24][sub-sections (1), (1A) and (2)], the Government may, on the recommendations of the Council, specify, by notification, the transactions that are to be treated as—

(*a*) a supply of goods and not as a supply of services; or

(*b*) a supply of services and not as a supply of goods.

Tax liability on composite and mixed supplies.

8. The tax liability on a composite or a mixed supply shall be determined in the following manner, namely:—

(*a*) a composite supply comprising two or more supplies, one of which is a principal supply, shall be treated as a supply of such principal supply; and

(*b*) a mixed supply comprising two or more supplies shall be treated as a supply of that particular supply which attracts the highest rate of tax.

Levy and Collection.

9. (1) Subject to the provisions of sub-section (2), there shall be levied a tax called the central goods and services tax on all intra-State supplies of goods or services or both, except on the supply of alcoholic liquor for human consumption [25]**[***and undenatured extra neutral alcohol or rectified spirit used for manufacture of alcoholic liquor, for human consumption***]**,

24. Substituted for "sub-sections (1) and (2)" by the Central Goods and Services Tax (Amendment) Act, 2018, w.r.e.f. 1-7-2017.

25. Inserted by the Finance (No. 2) Act, 2024, w.e.f. **1-11-2024**.

on the value determined under section 15 and at such rates, not exceeding twenty per cent, as may be notified by the Government on the recommendations of the Council and collected in such manner as may be prescribed and shall be paid by the taxable person.

(2) The central tax on the supply of petroleum crude, high speed diesel, motor spirit (commonly known as petrol), natural gas and aviation turbine fuel shall be levied with effect from such date as may be notified by the Government on the recommendations of the Council.

(3) The Government may, on the recommendations of the Council, by notification, specify categories of supply of goods or services or both, the tax on which shall be paid on reverse charge basis by the recipient of such goods or services or both and all the provisions of this Act shall apply to such recipient as if he is the person liable for paying the tax in relation to the supply of such goods or services or both.

[26][(4) The Government may, on the recommendations of the Council, by notification, specify a class of registered persons who shall, in respect of supply of specified categories of goods or services or both received from an unregistered supplier, pay the tax on reverse charge basis as the recipient of such supply of goods or services or both, and all the provisions of this Act shall apply to such recipient as if he is the person liable for paying the tax in relation to such supply of goods or services or both.]

(5) The Government may, on the recommendations of the Council, by notification, specify categories of services the tax on intra-State supplies of which shall be paid by the electronic commerce operator if such services are supplied through it, and all the provisions of this Act shall apply to such electronic commerce

26. Substituted by the Central Goods and Services Tax (Amendment) Act, 2018, w.e.f. 1-2-2019.

operator as if he is the supplier liable for paying the tax in relation to the supply of such services:

Provided that where an electronic commerce operator does not have a physical presence in the taxable territory, any person representing such electronic commerce operator for any purpose in the taxable territory shall be liable to pay tax:

Provided further that where an electronic commerce operator does not have a physical presence in the taxable territory and also he does not have a representative in the said territory, such electronic commerce operator shall appoint a person in the taxable territory for the purpose of paying tax and such person shall be liable to pay tax.

Composition levy.

10. (1) Notwithstanding anything to the contrary contained in this Act but subject to the provisions of sub-sections (3) and (4) of section 9, a registered person, whose aggregate turnover in the preceding financial year did not exceed fifty lakh rupees, may opt to pay, [27][in lieu of the tax payable by him under sub-section (1) of section 9, an amount of tax calculated at such rate] as may be prescribed, but not exceeding,—

(*a*) one per cent of the turnover in State or turnover in Union territory in case of a manufacturer,

(*b*) two and a half per cent of the turnover in State or turnover in Union territory in case of persons engaged in making supplies referred to in clause (*b*) of paragraph 6 of Schedule II, and

(*c*) half per cent of the turnover in State or turnover in Union territory in case of other suppliers,

27. Substituted for "in lieu of the tax payable by him, an amount calculated at such rate" by the Central Goods and Services Tax (Amendment) Act, 2018, w.e.f. 1-2-2019.

subject to such conditions and restrictions as may be prescribed:

Provided that the Government may, by notification, increase the said limit of fifty lakh rupees to such higher amount, not exceeding [28][one crore and fifty lakh rupees], as may be recommended by the Council:

[29][**Provided further** that a person who opts to pay tax under clause (*a*) or clause (*b*) or clause (*c*) may supply services (other than those referred to in clause (*b*) of paragraph 6 of Schedule II), of value not exceeding ten per cent of turnover in a State or Union territory in the preceding financial year or five lakh rupees, whichever is higher.]

[30][*Explanation.*—For the purposes of second proviso, the value of exempt supply of services provided by way of extending deposits, loans or advances in so far as the consideration is represented by way of interest or discount shall not be taken into account for determining the value of turnover in a State or Union territory.]

(2) The registered person shall be eligible to opt under sub-section (1), if—

[31][(*a*) save as provided in sub-section (1), he is not engaged in the supply of services;]

(*b*) he is not engaged in making any supply of goods [32][or services] which are not leviable to tax under this Act;

(*c*) he is not engaged in making any inter-State outward supplies of goods [32][or services];

---

28. Substituted for "one crore rupees" by the Central Goods and Services Tax (Amendment) Act, 2018, w.e.f. 1-2-2019.
29. Inserted, *ibid.*
30. Inserted by the Finance (No. 2) Act, 2019, w.e.f. 1-1-2020.
31. Substituted by the Central Goods and Services Tax (Amendment) Act, 2018, w.e.f. 1-2-2019.
32. Inserted by the Finance Act, 2020, w.e.f. 1-1-2021.

(*d*) he is not engaged in making any supply of [33][***] [34][services] through an electronic commerce operator who is required to collect tax at source under section 52; [35][***]

(*e*) he is not a manufacturer of such goods as may be notified by the Government on the recommendations of the [36][Council; and]

[37][(*f*) he is neither a casual taxable person nor a non-resident taxable person:]

Provided that where more than one registered persons are having the same Permanent Account Number [issued under the Income-tax Act, 1961 (43 of 1961)], the registered person shall not be eligible to opt for the scheme under sub-section (1) unless all such registered persons opt to pay tax under that sub-section.

[37][(2A) Notwithstanding anything to the contrary contained in this Act, but subject to the provisions of sub-sections (3) and (4) of section 9, a registered person, not eligible to opt to pay tax under sub-section (1) and sub-section (2), whose aggregate turnover in the preceding financial year did not exceed fifty lakh rupees, may opt to pay, in lieu of the tax payable by him under sub-section (1) of section 9, an amount of tax calculated at such rate as may be prescribed, but not exceeding three per cent of the turnover in State or turnover in Union territory, if he is not—

(*a*) engaged in making any supply of goods or services which are not leviable to tax under this Act;

---

33. Words "goods *or*" omitted by the Finance Act, 2023, w.e.f. 1-10-2023.
34. Inserted by the Finance Act, 2020, w.e.f. 1-1-2021.
35. Word "and" omitted by the Finance (No. 2) Act, 2019, w.e.f. 1-1-2020.
36. Substituted for "Council:", *ibid.*
37. Inserted, *ibid.*

(*b*) engaged in making any inter-State outward supplies of goods or services;

(*c*) engaged in making any supply of [38][***] services through an electronic commerce operator who is required to collect tax at source under section 52;

(*d*) a manufacturer of such goods or supplier of such services as may be notified by the Government on the recommendations of the Council; and

(*e*) a casual taxable person or a non-resident taxable person:

Provided that where more than one registered person are having the same Permanent Account Number issued under the Income-tax Act, 1961 (43 of 1961), the registered person shall not be eligible to opt for the scheme under this sub-section unless all such registered persons opt to pay tax under this sub-section.]

(3) The option availed of by a registered person under sub-section (1) [39][or sub-section (2A), as the case may be,] shall lapse with effect from the day on which his aggregate turnover during a financial year exceeds the limit specified under sub-section (1) [39][or sub-section (2A), as the case may be].

(4) A taxable person to whom the provisions of sub-section (1) [39][or, as the case may be, sub-section (2A)] apply shall not collect any tax from the recipient on supplies made by him nor shall he be entitled to any credit of input tax.

(5) If the proper officer has reasons to believe that a taxable person has paid tax under sub-section (1) [39][or sub-section (2A), as the case may be,] despite not being eligible, such person shall, in addition to any tax that may be payable by him under any other

38. Words "goods or" omitted by the Finance Act, 2023, w.e.f. 1-10-2023.

39. Inserted by the Finance (No. 2) Act, 2019, w.e.f. 1-1-2020.

provisions of this Act, be liable to a penalty and the provisions of section 73 or section 74 [40]**[***or section 74A***]** shall, *mutatis mutandis,* apply for determination of tax and penalty.

[40a][*Explanation 1.*—For the purposes of computing aggregate turnover of a person for determining his eligibility to pay tax under this section, the expression "aggregate turnover" shall include the value of supplies made by such person from the 1st day of April of a financial year upto the date when he becomes liable for registration under this Act, but shall not include the value of exempt supply of services provided by way of extending deposits, loans or advances in so far as the consideration is represented by way of interest or discount.

Explanation 2.—For the purposes of determining the tax payable by a person under this section, the expression "turnover in State or turnover in Union territory" shall not include the value of following supplies, namely:—

(*i*) supplies from the first day of April of a financial year upto the date when such person becomes liable for registration under this Act; and

(*ii*) exempt supply of services provided by way of extending deposits, loans or advances in so far as the consideration is represented by way of interest or discount.]

Power to grant exemption from tax.

11. (1) Where the Government is satisfied that it is necessary in the public interest so to do, it may, on the recommendations of the Council, by notification, exempt generally, either absolutely or subject to such conditions as may be specified therein, goods or services or both of any specified description from the whole or any part of the tax leviable thereon

40. Inserted by the Finance (No. 2) Act, 2024, w.e.f. **1-11-2024**.

40a. Inserted by the Finance (No. 2) Act, 2019, w.e.f. 1-1-2020.

with effect from such date as may be specified in such notification.

(2) Where the Government is satisfied that it is necessary in the public interest so to do, it may, on the recommendations of the Council, by special order in each case, under circumstances of an exceptional nature to be stated in such order, exempt from payment of tax any goods or services or both on which tax is leviable.

(3) The Government may, if it considers necessary or expedient so to do for the purpose of clarifying the scope or applicability of any notification issued under sub-section (1) or order issued under sub-section (2), insert an explanation in such notification or order, as the case may be, by notification at any time within one year of issue of the notification under sub-section (1) or order under sub-section (2), and every such explanation shall have effect as if it had always been the part of the first such notification or order, as the case may be.

Explanation.—For the purposes of this section, where an exemption in respect of any goods or services or both from the whole or part of the tax leviable thereon has been granted absolutely, the registered person supplying such goods or services or both shall not collect the tax, in excess of the effective rate, on such supply of goods or services or both.

[41]**[Power not to recover Goods and Services Tax not levied or short-levied as a result of general practice.**

11A. *Notwithstanding anything contained in this Act, if the Government is satisfied that —*

(a) *a practice was, or is, generally prevalent regarding levy of central tax (including non-levy thereof) on any supply of goods or services or both; and*

41. Inserted by the Finance (No. 2) Act, 2024, w.e.f. **1-11-2024**.

(b) *such supplies were, or are, liable to,—*

(i) *central tax, in cases where according to the said practice, central tax was not, or is not being, levied, or*

(ii) *a higher amount of central tax than what was, or is being, levied, in accordance with the said practice,*

the Government may, on the recommendation of the Council, by notification in the Official Gazette, direct that the whole of the central tax payable on such supplies, or, as the case may be, the central tax in excess of that payable on such supplies, but for the said practice, shall not be required to be paid in respect of the supplies on which the central tax was not, or is not being levied, or was, or is being, short-levied, in accordance with the said practice.]

CHAPTER IV

TIME AND VALUE OF SUPPLY

Time of supply of goods.

12. (1) The liability to pay tax on goods shall arise at the time of supply, as determined in accordance with the provisions of this section.

(2) The time of supply of goods shall be the earlier of the following dates, namely:—

(*a*) the date of issue of invoice by the supplier or the last date on which he is required, under [42][***] section 31, to issue the invoice with respect to the supply; or

(*b*) the date on which the supplier receives the payment with respect to the supply:

Provided that where the supplier of taxable goods receives an amount upto one thousand rupees in excess of the amount indicated in the tax invoice, the

42. Words "sub-section (1) of" omitted by the Central Goods and Services Tax (Amendment) Act, 2018, w.e.f. 1-2-2019.

time of supply to the extent of such excess amount shall, at the option of the said supplier, be the date of issue of invoice in respect of such excess amount.

Explanation 1.—For the purposes of clauses (*a*) and (*b*), "supply" shall be deemed to have been made to the extent it is covered by the invoice or, as the case may be, the payment.

Explanation 2.—For the purposes of clause (*b*), "the date on which the supplier receives the payment" shall be the date on which the payment is entered in his books of account or the date on which the payment is credited to his bank account, whichever is earlier.

(3) In case of supplies in respect of which tax is paid or liable to be paid on reverse charge basis, the time of supply shall be the earliest of the following dates, namely:—

(*a*) the date of the receipt of goods; or

(*b*) the date of payment as entered in the books of account of the recipient or the date on which the payment is debited in his bank account, whichever is earlier; or

(*c*) the date immediately following thirty days from the date of issue of invoice or any other document, by whatever name called, in lieu thereof by the supplier:

Provided that where it is not possible to determine the time of supply under clause (*a*) or clause (*b*) or clause (*c*), the time of supply shall be the date of entry in the books of account of the recipient of supply.

(4) In case of supply of vouchers by a supplier, the time of supply shall be—

(*a*) the date of issue of voucher, if the supply is identifiable at that point; or

(*b*) the date of redemption of voucher, in all other cases.

(5) Where it is not possible to determine the time of supply under the provisions of sub-section (2) or sub-section (3) or sub-section (4), the time of supply shall—

(*a*) in a case where a periodical return has to be filed, be the date on which such return is to be filed; or

(*b*) in any other case, be the date on which the tax is paid.

(6) The time of supply to the extent it relates to an addition in the value of supply by way of interest, late fee or penalty for delayed payment of any consideration shall be the date on which the supplier receives such addition in value.

Time of supply of services.

13. (1) The liability to pay tax on services shall arise at the time of supply, as determined in accordance with the provisions of this section.

(2) The time of supply of services shall be the earliest of the following dates, namely:—

(*a*) the date of issue of invoice by the supplier, if the invoice is issued within the period prescribed under [43][***] section 31 or the date of receipt of payment, whichever is earlier; or

(*b*) the date of provision of service, if the invoice is not issued within the period prescribed under [43][***] section 31 or the date of receipt of payment, whichever is earlier; or

(*c*) the date on which the recipient shows the receipt of services in his books of account, in a case where the provisions of clause (*a*) or clause (*b*) do not apply:

---

43. Words "sub-section (2) of" omitted by the Central Goods and Services Tax (Amendment) Act, 2018, w.e.f. 1-2-2019.

Provided that where the supplier of taxable service receives an amount upto one thousand rupees in excess of the amount indicated in the tax invoice, the time of supply to the extent of such excess amount shall, at the option of the said supplier, be the date of issue of invoice relating to such excess amount.

Explanation.—For the purposes of clauses (*a*) and (*b*)—

(*i*) the supply shall be deemed to have been made to the extent it is covered by the invoice or, as the case may be, the payment;

(*ii*) "the date of receipt of payment" shall be the date on which the payment is entered in the books of account of the supplier or the date on which the payment is credited to his bank account, whichever is earlier.

(3) In case of supplies in respect of which tax is paid or liable to be paid on reverse charge basis, the time of supply shall be the earlier of the following dates, namely:—

(*a*) the date of payment as entered in the books of account of the recipient or the date on which the payment is debited in his bank account, whichever is earlier; or

(*b*) the date immediately following sixty days from the date of issue of invoice or any other document, by whatever name called, in lieu thereof [44]**[***by the supplier, in cases where invoice is required to be issued by the supplier; or***]**;

[45]**[***(c) the date of issue of invoice by the recipient, in cases where invoice is to be issued by the recipient:***]**

Provided that where it is not possible to determine the time of supply under clause (*a*) or clause (*b*) [45]**[***or*

44. Substituted for "by the supplier" by the Finance (No. 2) Act, 2024, w.e.f. **1-11-2024**.

45. Inserted, *ibid.*

clause (c)], the time of supply shall be the date of entry in the books of account of the recipient of supply:

Provided further that in case of supply by associated enterprises, where the supplier of service is located outside India, the time of supply shall be the date of entry in the books of account of the recipient of supply or the date of payment, whichever is earlier.

(4) In case of supply of vouchers by a supplier, the time of supply shall be—

(*a*) the date of issue of voucher, if the supply is identifiable at that point; or

(*b*) the date of redemption of voucher, in all other cases.

(5) Where it is not possible to determine the time of supply under the provisions of sub-section (2) or sub-section (3) or sub-section (4), the time of supply shall—

(*a*) in a case where a periodical return has to be filed, be the date on which such return is to be filed; or

(*b*) in any other case, be the date on which the tax is paid.

(6) The time of supply to the extent it relates to an addition in the value of supply by way of interest, late fee or penalty for delayed payment of any consideration shall be the date on which the supplier receives such addition in value.

Change in rate of tax in respect of supply of goods or services.

14. Notwithstanding anything contained in section 12 or section 13, the time of supply, where there is a change in the rate of tax in respect of goods or services or both, shall be determined in the following manner, namely:—

(*a*) in case the goods or services or both have been supplied before the change in rate of tax,—

(*i*) where the invoice for the same has been issued and the payment is also received after the change in rate of tax, the time of supply shall be the date of receipt of payment or the date of issue of invoice, whichever is earlier; or

(*ii*) where the invoice has been issued prior to the change in rate of tax but payment is received after the change in rate of tax, the time of supply shall be the date of issue of invoice; or

(*iii*) where the payment has been received before the change in rate of tax, but the invoice for the same is issued after the change in rate of tax, the time of supply shall be the date of receipt of payment;

(*b*) in case the goods or services or both have been supplied after the change in rate of tax,—

(*i*) where the payment is received after the change in rate of tax but the invoice has been issued prior to the change in rate of tax, the time of supply shall be the date of receipt of payment; or

(*ii*) where the invoice has been issued and payment is received before the change in rate of tax, the time of supply shall be the date of receipt of payment or date of issue of invoice, whichever is earlier; or

(*iii*) where the invoice has been issued after the change in rate of tax but the payment is received before the change in rate of tax, the time of supply shall be the date of issue of invoice:

Provided that the date of receipt of payment shall be the date of credit in the bank account if such credit in the bank account is after four working days from the date of change in the rate of tax.

Explanation.—For the purposes of this section, "the date of receipt of payment" shall be the date on which the payment is entered in the books of account of the supplier or the date on which the payment is credited to his bank account, whichever is earlier.

Value of taxable supply.

15. (1) The value of a supply of goods or services or both shall be the transaction value, which is the price actually paid or payable for the said supply of goods or services or both where the supplier and the recipient of the supply are not related and the price is the sole consideration for the supply.

(2) The value of supply shall include—

(*a*) any taxes, duties, cesses, fees and charges levied under any law for the time being in force other than this Act, the State Goods and Services Tax Act, the Union Territory Goods and Services Tax Act and the Goods and Services Tax (Compensation to States) Act, if charged separately by the supplier;

(*b*) any amount that the supplier is liable to pay in relation to such supply but which has been incurred by the recipient of the supply and not included in the price actually paid or payable for the goods or services or both;

(*c*) incidental expenses, including commission and packing, charged by the supplier to the recipient of a supply and any amount charged for anything done by the supplier in respect of the supply of goods or services or both at the time of, or before delivery of goods or supply of services;

(*d*) interest or late fee or penalty for delayed payment of any consideration for any supply; and

(*e*) subsidies directly linked to the price excluding subsidies provided by the Central Government and the State Governments.

Explanation.— For the purposes of this sub-section, the amount of subsidy shall be included in the value of supply of the supplier who receives the subsidy.

(3) The value of the supply shall not include any discount which is given—

(*a*) before or at the time of the supply if such discount has been duly recorded in the invoice issued in respect of such supply; and

(*b*) after the supply has been effected, if—

(*i*) such discount is established in terms of an agreement entered into at or before the time of such supply and specifically linked to relevant invoices; and

(*ii*) input tax credit as is attributable to the discount on the basis of document issued by the supplier has been reversed by the recipient of the supply.

(4) Where the value of the supply of goods or services or both cannot be determined under sub-section (1), the same shall be determined in such manner as may be prescribed.

(5) Notwithstanding anything contained in sub-section (1) or sub-section (4), the value of such supplies as may be notified by the Government on the recommendations of the Council shall be determined in such manner as may be prescribed.

Explanation.—For the purposes of this Act,—

(*a*) persons shall be deemed to be "related persons" if—

(*i*) such persons are officers or directors of one another's businesses;

(*ii*) such persons are legally recognised partners in business;

(*iii*) such persons are employer and employee;

(*iv*) any person directly or indirectly owns, controls or holds twenty-five per cent or more of the outstanding voting stock or shares of both of them;

(*v*) one of them directly or indirectly controls the other;

(*vi*) both of them are directly or indirectly controlled by a third person;

(*vii*) together they directly or indirectly control a third person; or

(*viii*) they are members of the same family;

(*b*) the term "person" also includes legal persons;

(*c*) persons who are associated in the business of one another in that one is the sole agent or sole distributor or sole concessionaire, howsoever described, of the other, shall be deemed to be related.

CHAPTER V

INPUT TAX CREDIT

Eligibility and condition for taking input tax credit.

16. (1) Every registered person shall, subject to such conditions and restrictions as may be prescribed and in the manner specified in section 49, be entitled to take credit of input tax charged on any supply of goods or services or both to him which are used or intended to be used in the course or furtherance of his business and the said amount shall be credited to the electronic credit ledger of such person.

(2) Notwithstanding anything contained in this section, no registered person shall be entitled to the credit of any input tax in respect of any supply of goods or services or both to him unless,—

(*a*) he is in possession of a tax invoice or debit note issued by a supplier registered under this Act, or such other tax paying documents as may be prescribed;

[46][(*aa*) the details of the invoice or debit note referred to in clause (*a*) has been furnished by the supplier in the statement of outward supplies and such details have been communicated to the recipient of such invoice or debit note in the manner specified under section 37;]

(*b*) he has received the goods or services or both.

[47][*Explanation*.—For the purposes of this clause, it shall be deemed that the registered person has received the goods or, as the case may be, services—

(*i*) where the goods are delivered by the supplier to a recipient or any other person on the direction of such registered person, whether acting as an agent or otherwise, before or during movement of goods, either by way of transfer of documents of title to goods or otherwise;

(*ii*) where the services are provided by the supplier to any person on the direction of and on account of such registered person.]

---

46. Inserted by the Finance Act, 2021, w.e.f. 1-1-2022.

47. Substituted by the Central Goods and Services Tax (Amendment) Act, 2018, w.e.f. 1-2-2019.

[48][(*ba*) the details of input tax credit in respect of the said supply communicated to such registered person under section 38 has not been restricted;]

(*c*) subject to the provisions of [49]**[***section 41*** [50][***]]**, the tax charged in respect of such supply has been actually paid to the Government, either in cash or through utilisation of input tax credit admissible in respect of the said supply; and

(*d*) he has furnished the return under section 39:

Provided that where the goods against an invoice are received in lots or instalments, the registered person shall be entitled to take credit upon receipt of the last lot or instalment:

Provided further that where a recipient fails to pay to the supplier of goods or services or both, other than the supplies on which tax is payable on reverse charge basis, the amount towards the value of supply along with tax payable thereon within a period of one hundred and eighty days from the date of issue of invoice by the supplier, an amount equal to the input tax credit availed by the recipient shall be [51][paid by him along with interest payable under section 50], in such manner as may be prescribed:

Provided also that the recipient shall be entitled to avail of the credit of input tax on payment made by him [52][to the supplier] of the amount towards the value of supply of goods or services or both along with tax payable thereon.

---

48. Inserted by the Finance Act, 2022, w.e.f. 1-10-2022.
49. Substituted for "section 41" by the Central Goods and Services Tax (Amendment) Act, 2018, with effect from a date yet to be notified.
50. Words "or section 43A" omitted by the Finance Act, 2022, w.e.f. 1-10-2022.
51. Substituted for "added to his output tax liability, along with interest thereon" by the Finance Act, 2023, w.e.f. 1-10-2023.
52. Inserted, *ibid*.

(3) Where the registered person has claimed depreciation on the tax component of the cost of capital goods and plant and machinery under the provisions of the Income-tax Act, 1961 (43 of 1961), the input tax credit on the said tax component shall not be allowed.

(4) A registered person shall not be entitled to take input tax credit in respect of any invoice or debit note for supply of goods or services or both after the [53][thirtieth day of November] following the end of financial year to which such invoice or [54][***] debit note pertains or furnishing of the relevant annual return, whichever is earlier:

[55][**Provided** that the registered person shall be entitled to take input tax credit after the due date of furnishing of the return under section 39 for the month of September, 2018 till the due date of furnishing of the return under the said section for the month of March, 2019 in respect of any invoice or invoice relating to such debit note for supply of goods or services or both made during the financial year 2017-18, the details of which have been uploaded by the supplier under sub-section (1) of section 37 till the due date for furnishing the details under sub-section (1) of said section for the month of March, 2019.]

[56]**[***(5) Notwithstanding anything contained in sub-section (4), in respect of an invoice or debit note for supply of goods or services or both pertaining to the Financial Years 2017-18, 2018-19, 2019-20 and 2020-21, the registered person shall be entitled to take input tax credit*

53. Substituted for "due date of furnishing of the return under section 39 for the month of September" by the Finance Act, 2022, w.e.f. 1-10-2022.

54. Words "invoice relating to such" omitted by the Finance Act, 2020, w.e.f. 1-1-2021.

55. Inserted by the Central Goods and Services Tax (Second Removal of Difficulties) Order, 2018, w.e.f. 31-12-2018.

56. Sub-sections (5) and (6) inserted by the Finance (No. 2) Act, 2024, w.r.e.f. **1-7-2017**. [However, Notification No. 17/2024-Central Tax, dated 27-9-2024 appoints 27-9-2024 as the date of enforcement].

in any return under section 39 which is filed upto the thirtieth day of November, 2021.

(6) Where registration of a registered person is cancelled under section 29 and subsequently the cancellation of registration is revoked by any order, either under section 30 or pursuant to any order made by the Appellate Authority or the Appellate Tribunal or court and where availment of input tax credit in respect of an invoice or debit note was not restricted under sub-section (4) on the date of order of cancellation of registration, the said person shall be entitled to take the input tax credit in respect of such invoice or debit note for supply of goods or services or both, in a return under section 39,—

(i) *filed upto thirtieth day of November following the financial year to which such invoice or debit note pertains or furnishing of the relevant annual return, whichever is earlier; or*

(ii) *for the period from the date of cancellation of registration or the effective date of cancellation of registration, as the case may be, till the date of order of revocation of cancellation of registration, where such return is filed within thirty days from the date of order of revocation of cancellation of registration,*

whichever is later.]

Apportionment of credit and blocked credits.

17. (1) Where the goods or services or both are used by the registered person partly for the purpose of any business and partly for other purposes, the amount of credit shall be restricted to so much of the input tax as is attributable to the purposes of his business.

(2) Where the goods or services or both are used by the registered person partly for effecting taxable supplies including zero-rated supplies under this Act or under the Integrated Goods and Services Tax Act and partly for effecting exempt supplies under the said Acts, the amount of credit shall be restricted

to so much of the input tax as is attributable to the said taxable supplies including zero-rated supplies.

(3) The value of exempt supply under sub-section (2) shall be such as may be prescribed, and shall include supplies on which the recipient is liable to pay tax on reverse charge basis, transactions in securities, sale of land and, subject to clause (*b*) of paragraph 5 of Schedule II, sale of building.

[57][*Explanation*.—For the purposes of this sub-section, the expression "value of exempt supply" shall not include the value of activities or transactions specified in Schedule III, [58][except,—

(*i*) the value of activities or transactions specified in paragraph 5 of the said Schedule; and

(*ii*) the value of such activities or transactions as may be prescribed in respect of clause (*a*) of paragraph 8 of the said Schedule.]]

(4) A banking company or a financial institution including a non-banking financial company, engaged in supplying services by way of accepting deposits, extending loans or advances shall have the option to either comply with the provisions of sub-section (2), or avail of, every month, an amount equal to fifty per cent of the eligible input tax credit on inputs, capital goods and input services in that month and the rest shall lapse:

Provided that the option once exercised shall not be withdrawn during the remaining part of the financial year:

Provided further that the restriction of fifty per cent shall not apply to the tax paid on supplies made by one registered person to another registered person having the same Permanent Account Number.

---

57. Inserted by the Central Goods and Services Tax (Amendment) Act, 2018, w.e.f. 1-2-2019.

58. Substituted for "except those specified in paragraph 5 of the said Schedule" by the Finance Act, 2023, w.e.f. 1-10-2023.

(5) Notwithstanding anything contained in sub-section (1) of section 16 and sub-section (1) of section 18, input tax credit shall not be available in respect of the following, namely:—

[59][(*a*) motor vehicles for transportation of persons having approved seating capacity of not more than thirteen persons (including the driver), except when they are used for making the following taxable supplies, namely:—

(*A*) further supply of such motor vehicles; or

(*B*) transportation of passengers; or

(*C*) imparting training on driving such motor vehicles;

(*aa*) vessels and aircraft except when they are used—

(*i*) for making the following taxable supplies, namely:—

(*A*) further supply of such vessels or aircraft; or

(*B*) transportation of passengers; or

(*C*) imparting training on navigating such vessels; or

(*D*) imparting training on flying such aircraft;

(*ii*) for transportation of goods;

(*ab*) services of general insurance, servicing, repair and maintenance in so far as they relate to motor vehicles, vessels or aircraft referred to in clause (*a*) or clause (*aa*):

Provided that the input tax credit in respect of such services shall be available—

59. Clauses (*a*), (*aa*), (*ab*) and (*b*) substituted for clauses (*a*) and (*b*) by the Central Goods and Services Tax (Amendment) Act, 2018, w.e.f. 1-2-2019.

(*i*) where the motor vehicles, vessels or aircraft referred to in clause (*a*) or clause (*aa*) are used for the purposes specified therein;

(*ii*) where received by a taxable person engaged—

(*I*) in the manufacture of such motor vehicles, vessels or aircraft; or

(*II*) in the supply of general insurance services in respect of such motor vehicles, vessels or aircraft insured by him;

(*b*) the following supply of goods or services or both—

(*i*) food and beverages, outdoor catering, beauty treatment, health services, cosmetic and plastic surgery, leasing, renting or hiring of motor vehicles, vessels or aircraft referred to in clause (*a*) or clause (*aa*) except when used for the purposes specified therein, life insurance and health insurance:

Provided that the input tax credit in respect of such goods or services or both shall be available where an inward supply of such goods or services or both is used by a registered person for making an outward taxable supply of the same category of goods or services or both or as an element of a taxable composite or mixed supply;

(*ii*) membership of a club, health and fitness centre; and

(*iii*) travel benefits extended to employees on vacation such as leave or home travel concession:

Provided that the input tax credit in respect of such goods or services or both shall be available, where it is obligatory for an employer to provide the same to its employees under any law for the time being in force;]

(*c*) works contract services when supplied for construction of an immovable property (other than plant and machinery) except where it is an input service for further supply of works contract service;

(*d*) goods or services or both received by a taxable person for construction of an immovable property (other than plant or machinery) on his own account including when such goods or services or both are used in the course or furtherance of business.

Explanation.—For the purposes of clauses (*c*) and (*d*), the expression "construction" includes re-construction, renovation, additions or alterations or repairs, to the extent of capitalisation, to the said immovable property;

(*e*) goods or services or both on which tax has been paid under section 10;

(*f*) goods or services or both received by a non-resident taxable person except on goods imported by him;

[60][(*fa*) goods or services or both received by a taxable person, which are used or intended to be used for activities relating to his obligations under corporate social responsibility referred to in section 135 of the Companies Act, 2013 (18 of 2013);]

(*g*) goods or services or both used for personal consumption;

60. Inserted by the Finance Act, 2023, w.e.f. 1-10-2023.

(*h*) goods lost, stolen, destroyed, written off or disposed of by way of gift or free samples; and

(*i*) any tax paid in accordance with the provisions of [61][*section 74 in respect of any period upto Financial Year 2023-24*].

(6) The Government may prescribe the manner in which the credit referred to in sub-sections (1) and (2) may be attributed.

Explanation.— For the purposes of this Chapter and Chapter VI, the expression "plant and machinery" means apparatus, equipment, and machinery fixed to earth by foundation or structural support that are used for making outward supply of goods or services or both and includes such foundation and structural supports but excludes—

(*i*) land, building or any other civil structures;

(*ii*) telecommunication towers; and

(*iii*) pipelines laid outside the factory premises.

Availability of credit in special circumstances.

18. (1) Subject to such conditions and restrictions as may be prescribed—

(*a*) a person who has applied for registration under this Act within thirty days from the date on which he becomes liable to registration and has been granted such registration shall be entitled to take credit of input tax in respect of inputs held in stock and inputs contained in semi-finished or finished goods held in stock on the day immediately preceding the date from which he becomes liable to pay tax under the provisions of this Act;

(*b*) a person who takes registration under sub-section (3) of section 25 shall be entitled to take

61. Substituted for "sections 74, 129 and 130" by the Finance (No. 2) Act, 2024, w.e.f. **1-11-2024**.

credit of input tax in respect of inputs held in stock and inputs contained in semi-finished or finished goods held in stock on the day immediately preceding the date of grant of registration;

(*c*) where any registered person ceases to pay tax under section 10, he shall be entitled to take credit of input tax in respect of inputs held in stock, inputs contained in semi-finished or finished goods held in stock and on capital goods on the day immediately preceding the date from which he becomes liable to pay tax under section 9:

Provided that the credit on capital goods shall be reduced by such percentage points as may be prescribed;

(*d*) where an exempt supply of goods or services or both by a registered person becomes a taxable supply, such person shall be entitled to take credit of input tax in respect of inputs held in stock and inputs contained in semi-finished or finished goods held in stock relatable to such exempt supply and on capital goods exclusively used for such exempt supply on the day immediately preceding the date from which such supply becomes taxable:

Provided that the credit on capital goods shall be reduced by such percentage points as may be prescribed.

(2) A registered person shall not be entitled to take input tax credit under sub-section (1) in respect of any supply of goods or services or both to him after the expiry of one year from the date of issue of tax invoice relating to such supply.

(3) Where there is a change in the constitution of a registered person on account of sale, merger, demerger, amalgamation, lease or transfer of the business with

the specific provisions for transfer of liabilities, the said registered person shall be allowed to transfer the input tax credit which remains unutilised in his electronic credit ledger to such sold, merged, demerged, amalgamated, leased or transferred business in such manner as may be prescribed.

(4) Where any registered person who has availed of input tax credit opts to pay tax under section 10 or, where the goods or services or both supplied by him become wholly exempt, he shall pay an amount, by way of debit in the electronic credit ledger or electronic cash ledger, equivalent to the credit of input tax in respect of inputs held in stock and inputs contained in semi-finished or finished goods held in stock and on capital goods, reduced by such percentage points as may be prescribed, on the day immediately preceding the date of exercising of such option or, as the case may be, the date of such exemption:

Provided that after payment of such amount, the balance of input tax credit, if any, lying in his electronic credit ledger shall lapse.

(5) The amount of credit under sub-section (1) and the amount payable under sub-section (4) shall be calculated in such manner as may be prescribed.

(6) In case of supply of capital goods or plant and machinery, on which input tax credit has been taken, the registered person shall pay an amount equal to the input tax credit taken on the said capital goods or plant and machinery reduced by such percentage points as may be prescribed or the tax on the transaction value of such capital goods or plant and machinery determined under section 15, whichever is higher:

Provided that where refractory bricks, moulds and dies, jigs and fixtures are supplied as scrap, the taxable person may pay tax on the transaction value of such goods determined under section 15.

Taking input tax credit in respect of inputs and capital goods sent for job work.

19. (1) The principal shall, subject to such conditions and restrictions as may be prescribed, be allowed input tax credit on inputs sent to a job worker for job work.

(2) Notwithstanding anything contained in clause (*b*) of sub-section (2) of section 16, the principal shall be entitled to take credit of input tax on inputs even if the inputs are directly sent to a job worker for job work without being first brought to his place of business.

(3) Where the inputs sent for job work are not received back by the principal after completion of job work or otherwise or are not supplied from the place of business of the job worker in accordance with clause (*a*) or clause (*b*) of sub-section (1) of section 143 within one year of being sent out, it shall be deemed that such inputs had been supplied by the principal to the job worker on the day when the said inputs were sent out:

Provided that where the inputs are sent directly to a job worker, the period of one year shall be counted from the date of receipt of inputs by the job worker.

(4) The principal shall, subject to such conditions and restrictions as may be prescribed, be allowed input tax credit on capital goods sent to a job worker for job work.

(5) Notwithstanding anything contained in clause (*b*) of sub-section (2) of section 16, the principal shall be entitled to take credit of input tax on capital goods even if the capital goods are directly sent to a job worker for job work without being first brought to his place of business.

(6) Where the capital goods sent for job work are not received back by the principal within a period of three years of being sent out, it shall be deemed that such capital goods had been supplied by the principal

to the job worker on the day when the said capital goods were sent out:

Provided that where the capital goods are sent directly to a job worker, the period of three years shall be counted from the date of receipt of capital goods by the job worker.

(7) Nothing contained in sub-section (3) or sub-section (6) shall apply to moulds and dies, jigs and fixtures, or tools sent out to a job worker for job work.

Explanation.—For the purpose of this section, "principal" means the person referred to in section 143.

[62][**Manner of distribution of credit by Input Service Distributor.**

20. *(1) Any office of the supplier of goods or services or both which receives tax invoices towards the receipt of input services, including invoices in respect of services liable to tax under sub-section (3) or sub-section (4) of section 9, for or on behalf of distinct persons referred to in section 25, shall be required to be registered as Input Service Distributor under clause (*viii*) of section 24 and shall distribute the input tax credit in respect of such invoices.*

(2) The Input Service Distributor shall distribute the credit of central tax or integrated tax charged on invoices received by him, including the credit of central or integrated tax in respect of services subject to levy of tax under sub-section (3) or sub-section (4) of section 9 paid by a distinct person registered in the same State as the said Input Service Distributor, in such manner, within such time and subject to such restrictions and conditions as may be prescribed.

(3) The credit of central tax shall be distributed as central tax or integrated tax and integrated tax as integrated tax or central tax, by way of issue of a document containing the amount of input tax credit, in such manner as may be prescribed.]

62. Substituted by the Finance Act, 2024, w.e.f. **1-4-2025**.

Manner of recovery of credit distributed in excess.

21. Where the Input Service Distributor distributes the credit in contravention of the provisions contained in section 20 resulting in excess distribution of credit to one or more recipients of credit, the excess credit so distributed shall be recovered from such recipients along with interest, and the provisions of section 73 or section 74 [63][*or section 74A*], as the case may be, shall, *mutatis mutandis,* apply for determination of amount to be recovered.

CHAPTER VI

REGISTRATION

Persons liable for registration.

22. (1) Every supplier shall be liable to be registered under this Act in the State or Union territory, other than special category States, from where he makes a taxable supply of goods or services or both, if his aggregate turnover in a financial year exceeds twenty lakh rupees:

Provided that where such person makes taxable supplies of goods or services or both from any of the special category States, he shall be liable to be registered if his aggregate turnover in a financial year exceeds ten lakh rupees:

[64][**Provided further** that the Government may, at the request of a special category State and on the recommendations of the Council, enhance the aggregate turnover referred to in the first proviso from ten lakh rupees to such amount, not exceeding twenty lakh rupees and subject to such conditions and limitations, as may be so notified:]

---

63. Inserted by the Finance (No. 2) Act, 2024, w.e.f. **1-11-2024**.

64. Inserted by the Central Goods and Services Tax (Amendment) Act, 2018, w.e.f. 1-2-2019.

[65][**Provided also** that the Government may, at the request of a State and on the recommendations of the Council, enhance the aggregate turnover from twenty lakh rupees to such amount not exceeding forty lakh rupees in case of supplier who is engaged exclusively in the supply of goods, subject to such conditions and limitations, as may be notified.

Explanation.—For the purposes of this sub-section, a person shall be considered to be engaged exclusively in the supply of goods even if he is engaged in exempt supply of services provided by way of extending deposits, loans or advances in so far as the consideration is represented by way of interest or discount.]

(2) Every person who, on the day immediately preceding the appointed day, is registered or holds a license under an existing law, shall be liable to be registered under this Act with effect from the appointed day.

(3) Where a business carried on by a taxable person registered under this Act is transferred, whether on account of succession or otherwise, to another person as a going concern, the transferee or the successor, as the case may be, shall be liable to be registered with effect from the date of such transfer or succession.

(4) Notwithstanding anything contained in sub-sections (1) and (3), in a case of transfer pursuant to sanction of a scheme or an arrangement for amalgamation or, as the case may be, demerger of two or more companies pursuant to an order of a High Court, Tribunal or otherwise, the transferee shall be liable to be registered, with effect from the date on which the Registrar of Companies issues a certificate of incorporation giving effect to such order of the High Court or Tribunal.

Explanation.— For the purposes of this section,—

(*i*) the expression "aggregate turnover" shall include all supplies made by the taxable

65. Inserted by the Finance (No. 2) Act, 2019, w.e.f. 1-1-2020.

person, whether on his own account or made on behalf of all his principals;

(*ii*) the supply of goods, after completion of job work, by a registered job worker shall be treated as the supply of goods by the principal referred to in section 143, and the value of such goods shall not be included in the aggregate turnover of the registered job worker;

(*iii*) the expression "special category States" shall mean the States as specified in sub-clause (*g*) of clause (*4*) of article 279A of the Constitution [66][except the State of Jammu and Kashmir] [67][and States of Arunachal Pradesh, Assam, Himachal Pradesh, Meghalaya, Sikkim and Uttarakhand].

Persons not liable for registration.

23. (1) The following persons shall not be liable to registration, namely:—

(*a*) any person engaged exclusively in the business of supplying goods or services or both that are not liable to tax or wholly exempt from tax under this Act or under the Integrated Goods and Services Tax Act;

(*b*) an agriculturist, to the extent of supply of produce out of cultivation of land.

[68][(2) Notwithstanding anything to the contrary contained in sub-section (1) of section 22 or section 24, the Government may, on the recommendations of the Council, by notification, subject to such conditions and restrictions as may be specified therein, specify the category of persons who may be exempted from obtaining registration under this Act.]

---

66. Inserted by the Central Goods and Services Tax (Extension to Jammu and Kashmir) Act, 2017, w.r.e.f. 8-7-2017.

67. Inserted by the Central Goods and Services Tax (Amendment) Act, 2018, w.e.f. 1-2-2019.

68. Substituted by the Finance Act, 2023, w.r.e.f. 1-7-2017.

Compulsory registration in certain cases.

24. Notwithstanding anything contained in sub-section (1) of section 22, the following categories of persons shall be required to be registered under this Act,—

(*i*) persons making any inter-State taxable supply;

(*ii*) casual taxable persons making taxable supply;

(*iii*) persons who are required to pay tax under reverse charge;

(*iv*) persons who are required to pay tax under sub-section (5) of section 9;

(*v*) non-resident taxable persons making taxable supply;

(*vi*) persons who are required to deduct tax under section 51, whether or not separately registered under this Act;

(*vii*) persons who make taxable supply of goods or services or both on behalf of other taxable persons whether as an agent or otherwise;

(*viii*) Input Service Distributor, whether or not separately registered under this Act;

(*ix*) persons who supply goods or services or both, other than supplies specified under sub-section (5) of section 9, through such electronic commerce operator who is required to collect tax at source under section 52;

(*x*) every electronic commerce operator [69][who is required to collect tax at source under section 52];

(*xi*) every person supplying online information and data base access or retrieval services from

69. Inserted by the Central Goods and Services Tax (Amendment) Act, 2018, w.e.f. 1-2-2019.

a place outside India to a person in India, other than a registered person; [70][***]

[71][(*xia*) every person supplying online money gaming from a place outside India to a person in India; and]

(*xii*) such other person or class of persons as may be notified by the Government on the recommendations of the Council.

Procedure for registration.

25. (1) Every person who is liable to be registered under section 22 or section 24 shall apply for registration in every such State or Union territory in which he is so liable within thirty days from the date on which he becomes liable to registration, in such manner and subject to such conditions as may be prescribed:

Provided that a casual taxable person or a non-resident taxable person shall apply for registration at least five days prior to the commencement of business:

[72][**Provided further** that a person having a unit, as defined in the Special Economic Zones Act, 2005 (28 of 2005), in a Special Economic Zone or being a Special Economic Zone developer shall have to apply for a separate registration, as distinct from his place of business located outside the Special Economic Zone in the same State or Union territory.]

Explanation.—Every person who makes a supply from the territorial waters of India shall obtain registration in the coastal State or Union territory where the nearest point of the appropriate base line is located.

(2) A person seeking registration under this Act shall be granted a single registration in a State or Union territory:

70. Word "and" omitted by the Central Goods and Services Tax (Amendment) Act, 2023, w.e.f. 1-10-2023.

71. Inserted, *ibid*.

72. Inserted by the Central Goods and Services Tax (Amendment) Act, 2018, w.e.f. 1-2-2019.

[73][**Provided** that a person having multiple places of business in a State or Union territory may be granted a separate registration for each such place of business, subject to such conditions as may be prescribed.]

(3) A person, though not liable to be registered under section 22 or section 24 may get himself registered voluntarily, and all provisions of this Act, as are applicable to a registered person, shall apply to such person.

(4) A person who has obtained or is required to obtain more than one registration, whether in one State or Union territory or more than one State or Union territory shall, in respect of each such registration, be treated as distinct persons for the purposes of this Act.

(5) Where a person who has obtained or is required to obtain registration in a State or Union territory in respect of an establishment, has an establishment in another State or Union territory, then such establishments shall be treated as establishments of distinct persons for the purposes of this Act.

(6) Every person shall have a Permanent Account Number issued under the Income-tax Act, 1961 (43 of 1961) in order to be eligible for grant of registration:

Provided that a person required to deduct tax under section 51 may have, in lieu of a Permanent Account Number, a Tax Deduction and Collection Account Number issued under the said Act in order to be eligible for grant of registration.

[74][(6A) Every registered person shall undergo authentication, or furnish proof of possession of Aadhaar number, in such form and manner and within such time as may be prescribed:

Provided that if an Aadhaar number is not assigned to the registered person, such person shall be offered alternate and viable means of identification in such

73. Substituted by the Central Goods and Services Tax (Amendment) Act, 2018, w.e.f. 1-2-2019.

74. Inserted by the Finance (No. 2) Act, 2019, w.e.f. 1-1-2020.

manner as Government may, on the recommendations of the Council, prescribe:

Provided further that in case of failure to undergo authentication or furnish proof of possession of Aadhaar number or furnish alternate and viable means of identification, registration allotted to such person shall be deemed to be invalid and the other provisions of this Act shall apply as if such person does not have a registration.

(6B) On and from the date of notification, every individual shall, in order to be eligible for grant of registration, undergo authentication, or furnish proof of possession of Aadhaar number, in such manner as the Government may, on the recommendations of the Council, specify in the said notification:

Provided that if an Aadhaar number is not assigned to an individual, such individual shall be offered alternate and viable means of identification in such manner as the Government may, on the recommendations of the Council, specify in the said notification.

(6C) On and from the date of notification, every person, other than an individual, shall, in order to be eligible for grant of registration, undergo authentication, or furnish proof of possession of Aadhaar number of the Karta, Managing Director, whole time Director, such number of partners, Members of Managing Committee of Association, Board of Trustees, authorised representative, authorised signatory and such other class of persons, in such manner, as the Government may, on the recommendation of the Council, specify in the said notification:

Provided that where such person or class of persons have not been assigned the Aadhaar Number, such person or class of persons shall be offered alternate and viable means of identification in such manner as the Government may, on the recommendations of the Council, specify in the said notification.

(6D) The provisions of sub-section (6A) or sub-section (6B) or sub-section (6C) shall not apply to such person or class of persons or any State or Union territory or part thereof, as the Government may, on the recommendations of the Council, specify by notification.

Explanation.—For the purposes of this section, the expression "Aadhaar Number" shall have the same meaning as assigned to it in clause (*a*) of section 2 of the Aadhaar (Targeted Delivery of Financial and Other Subsidies, Benefits and Services) Act, 2016 (18 of 2016).]

(7) Notwithstanding anything contained in sub-section (6), a non-resident taxable person may be granted registration under sub-section (1) on the basis of such other documents as may be prescribed.

(8) Where a person who is liable to be registered under this Act fails to obtain registration, the proper officer may, without prejudice to any action which may be taken under this Act or under any other law for the time being in force, proceed to register such person in such manner as may be prescribed.

(9) Notwithstanding anything contained in sub-section (1),—

(*a*) any specialised agency of the United Nations Organisation or any Multilateral Financial Institution and Organisation notified under the United Nations (Privileges and Immunities) Act, 1947 (46 of 1947), Consulate or Embassy of foreign countries ; and

(*b*) any other person or class of persons, as may be notified by the Commissioner,

shall be granted a Unique Identity Number in such manner and for such purposes, including refund of taxes on the notified supplies of goods or services or both received by them, as may be prescribed.

(10) The registration or the Unique Identity Number shall be granted or rejected after due verification

in such manner and within such period as may be prescribed.

(11) A certificate of registration shall be issued in such form and with effect from such date as may be prescribed.

(12) A registration or a Unique Identity Number shall be deemed to have been granted after the expiry of the period prescribed under sub-section (10), if no deficiency has been communicated to the applicant within that period.

Deemed registration.

26. (1) The grant of registration or the Unique Identity Number under the State Goods and Services Tax Act or the Union Territory Goods and Services Tax Act shall be deemed to be a grant of registration or the Unique Identity Number under this Act subject to the condition that the application for registration or the Unique Identity Number has not been rejected under this Act within the time specified in sub-section (10) of section 25.

(2) Notwithstanding anything contained in sub-section (10) of section 25, any rejection of application for registration or the Unique Identity Number under the State Goods and Services Tax Act or the Union Territory Goods and Services Tax Act shall be deemed to be a rejection of application for registration under this Act.

Special provisions relating to casual taxable person and non-resident taxable person.

27. (1) The certificate of registration issued to a casual taxable person or a non-resident taxable person shall be valid for the period specified in the application for registration or ninety days from the effective date of registration, whichever is earlier and such person shall make taxable supplies only after the issuance of the certificate of registration:

Provided that the proper officer may, on sufficient cause being shown by the said taxable person, extend the said period of ninety days by a further period not exceeding ninety days.

(2) A casual taxable person or a non-resident taxable person shall, at the time of submission of application for registration under sub-section (1) of section 25, make an advance deposit of tax in an amount equivalent to the estimated tax liability of such person for the period for which the registration is sought:

Provided that where any extension of time is sought under sub-section (1), such taxable person shall deposit an additional amount of tax equivalent to the estimated tax liability of such person for the period for which the extension is sought.

(3) The amount deposited under sub-section (2) shall be credited to the electronic cash ledger of such person and shall be utilised in the manner provided under section 49.

Amendment of registration.

28. (1) Every registered person and a person to whom a Unique Identity Number has been assigned shall inform the proper officer of any changes in the information furnished at the time of registration or subsequent thereto, in such form and manner and within such period as may be prescribed.

(2) The proper officer may, on the basis of information furnished under sub-section (1) or as ascertained by him, approve or reject amendments in the registration particulars in such manner and within such period as may be prescribed:

Provided that approval of the proper officer shall not be required in respect of amendment of such particulars as may be prescribed:

Provided further that the proper officer shall not reject the application for amendment in the registration particulars without giving the person an opportunity of being heard.

(3) Any rejection or approval of amendments under the State Goods and Services Tax Act or the Union Territory Goods and Services Tax Act, as the case may be, shall be deemed to be a rejection or approval under this Act.

Cancellation [75][or suspension] of registration.

29. (1) The proper officer may, either on his own motion or on an application filed by the registered person or by his legal heirs, in case of death of such person, cancel the registration, in such manner and within such period as may be prescribed, having regard to the circumstances where,—

(*a*) the business has been discontinued, transferred fully for any reason including death of the proprietor, amalgamated with other legal entity, demerged or otherwise disposed of; or

(*b*) there is any change in the constitution of the business; or

[76][(*c*) the taxable person is no longer liable to be registered under section 22 or section 24 or intends to opt out of the registration voluntarily made under sub-section (3) of section 25:]

[77][**Provided** that during pendency of the proceedings relating to cancellation of registration filed by the registered person, the registration may be suspended for such period and in such manner as may be prescribed.]

---

75. Inserted by the Central Goods and Services Tax (Amendment) Act, 2018, w.e.f. 1-2-2019.

76. Substituted by the Finance Act, 2020, w.e.f. 1-1-2021.

77. Inserted by the Central Goods and Services Tax (Amendment) Act, 2018, w.e.f. 1-2-2019.

(2) The proper officer may cancel the registration of a person from such date, including any retrospective date, as he may deem fit, where,—

(*a*) a registered person has contravened such provisions of the Act or the rules made thereunder as may be prescribed; or

(*b*) a person paying tax under section 10 has not furnished [78][the return for a financial year beyond three months from the due date of furnishing the said return]; or

(*c*) any registered person, other than a person specified in clause (*b*), has not furnished returns for [79][such continuous tax period as may be prescribed]; or

(*d*) any person who has taken voluntary registration under sub-section (3) of section 25 has not commenced business within six months from the date of registration; or

(*e*) registration has been obtained by means of fraud, wilful misstatement or suppression of facts:

Provided that the proper officer shall not cancel the registration without giving the person an opportunity of being heard:

[80][**Provided further** that during pendency of the proceedings relating to cancellation of registration, the proper officer may suspend the registration for such period and in such manner as may be prescribed.]

(3) The cancellation of registration under this section shall not affect the liability of the person to pay tax and other dues under this Act or to discharge any obligation under this Act or the rules made thereunder for

---

78. Substituted for "returns for three consecutive tax periods" by the Finance Act, 2022, w.e.f. 1-10-2022.

79. Substituted for "a continuous period of six months", *ibid.*

80. Inserted by the Central Goods and Services Tax (Amendment) Act, 2018, w.e.f. 1-2-2019.

any period prior to the date of cancellation whether or not such tax and other dues are determined before or after the date of cancellation.

(4) The cancellation of registration under the State Goods and Services Tax Act or the Union Territory Goods and Services Tax Act, as the case may be, shall be deemed to be a cancellation of registration under this Act.

(5) Every registered person whose registration is cancelled shall pay an amount, by way of debit in the electronic credit ledger or electronic cash ledger, equivalent to the credit of input tax in respect of inputs held in stock and inputs contained in semi-finished or finished goods held in stock or capital goods or plant and machinery on the day immediately preceding the date of such cancellation or the output tax payable on such goods, whichever is higher, calculated in such manner as may be prescribed:

Provided that in case of capital goods or plant and machinery, the taxable person shall pay an amount equal to the input tax credit taken on the said capital goods or plant and machinery, reduced by such percentage points as may be prescribed or the tax on the transaction value of such capital goods or plant and machinery under section 15, whichever is higher.

(6) The amount payable under sub-section (5) shall be calculated in such manner as may be prescribed.

Revocation of cancellation of registration.

30. (1) Subject to such conditions as may be prescribed, any registered person, whose registration is cancelled by the proper officer on his own motion, may apply to such officer for revocation of cancellation of the registration in [81][such manner, within such time and subject to such conditions and restrictions, as may be prescribed.]

81. Substituted for "the prescribed manner within thirty days from the date of service of the cancellation order:" by the Finance Act, 2023, w.e.f. 1-10-2023.

[82][***]

(2) The proper officer may, in such manner and within such period as may be prescribed, by order, either revoke cancellation of the registration or reject the application:

Provided that the application for revocation of cancellation of registration shall not be rejected unless the applicant has been given an opportunity of being heard:

[83]**[Provided further** *that such revocation of cancellation of registration shall be subject to such conditions and restrictions, as may be prescribed.***]**

(3) The revocation of cancellation of registration under the State Goods and Services Tax Act or the Union Territory Goods and Services Tax Act, as the case may be, shall be deemed to be a revocation of cancellation of registration under this Act.

CHAPTER VII

TAX INVOICE, CREDIT AND DEBIT NOTES

Tax invoice.

31. (1) A registered person supplying taxable goods shall, before or at the time of,—

(*a*) removal of goods for supply to the recipient, where the supply involves movement of goods; or

(*b*) delivery of goods or making available thereof to the recipient, in any other case,

issue a tax invoice showing the description, quantity and value of goods, the tax charged thereon and such other particulars as may be prescribed:

82. Omitted by the Finance Act, 2023, w.e.f. 1-10-2023.

83. Inserted by the Finance (No. 2) Act, 2024, w.e.f. **1-11-2024**.

Provided that the Government may, on the recommendations of the Council, by notification, specify the categories of goods or supplies in respect of which a tax invoice shall be issued, within such time and in such manner as may be prescribed.

(2) A registered person supplying taxable services shall, before or after the provision of service but within a prescribed period, issue a tax invoice, showing the description, value, tax charged thereon and such other particulars as may be prescribed:

[84][**Provided** that the Government may, on the recommendations of the Council, by notification,—

(*a*) specify the categories of services or supplies in respect of which a tax invoice shall be issued, within such time and in such manner as may be prescribed;

(*b*) subject to the condition mentioned therein, specify the categories of services in respect of which—

(*i*) any other document issued in relation to the supply shall be deemed to be a tax invoice; or

(*ii*) tax invoice may not be issued.]

(3) Notwithstanding anything contained in sub-sections (1) and (2)—

(*a*) a registered person may, within one month from the date of issuance of certificate of registration and in such manner as may be prescribed, issue a revised invoice against the invoice already issued during the period beginning with the effective date of registration till the date of issuance of certificate of registration to him;

(*b*) a registered person may not issue a tax invoice if the value of the goods or services or both

84. Substituted by the Finance Act, 2020, w.e.f. 1-1-2021.

supplied is less than two hundred rupees subject to such conditions and in such manner as may be prescribed;

(*c*) a registered person supplying exempted goods or services or both or paying tax under the provisions of section 10 shall issue, instead of a tax invoice, a bill of supply containing such particulars and in such manner as may be prescribed:

Provided that the registered person may not issue a bill of supply if the value of the goods or services or both supplied is less than two hundred rupees subject to such conditions and in such manner as may be prescribed;

(*d*) a registered person shall, on receipt of advance payment with respect to any supply of goods or services or both, issue a receipt voucher or any other document, containing such particulars as may be prescribed, evidencing receipt of such payment;

(*e*) where, on receipt of advance payment with respect to any supply of goods or services or both the registered person issues a receipt voucher, but subsequently no supply is made and no tax invoice is issued in pursuance thereof, the said registered person may issue to the person who had made the payment, a refund voucher against such payment;

(*f*) a registered person who is liable to pay tax under sub-section (3) or sub-section (4) of section 9 shall [85]**[** *within the period as may be prescribed,* **]** issue an invoice in respect of goods or services or both received by him from the supplier who is not registered on the date of receipt of goods or services or both;

85. Inserted by the Finance (No. 2) Act, 2024, w.e.f. **1-11-2024**.

(*g*) a registered person who is liable to pay tax under sub-section (3) or sub-section (4) of section 9 shall issue a payment voucher at the time of making payment to the supplier.

[85a]**[**Explanation.—*For the purposes of clause (f), the expression "supplier who is not registered" shall include the supplier who is registered solely for the purpose of deduction of tax under section 51.***]**

(4) In case of continuous supply of goods, where successive statements of accounts or successive payments are involved, the invoice shall be issued before or at the time each such statement is issued or, as the case may be, each such payment is received.

(5) Subject to the provisions of clause (*d*) of sub-section (3), in case of continuous supply of services,—

(*a*) where the due date of payment is ascertainable from the contract, the invoice shall be issued on or before the due date of payment;

(*b*) where the due date of payment is not ascertainable from the contract, the invoice shall be issued before or at the time when the supplier of service receives the payment;

(*c*) where the payment is linked to the completion of an event, the invoice shall be issued on or before the date of completion of that event.

(6) In a case where the supply of services ceases under a contract before the completion of the supply, the invoice shall be issued at the time when the supply ceases and such invoice shall be issued to the extent of the supply made before such cessation.

(7) Notwithstanding anything contained in sub-section (1), where the goods being sent or taken on approval for sale or return are removed before the supply takes place, the invoice shall be issued before or at the time of supply or six months from the date of removal, whichever is earlier.

85a. Inserted by the Finance (No. 2) Act, 2024, w.e.f. **1-11-2024**.

Explanation.—For the purposes of this section, the expression "tax invoice" shall include any revised invoice issued by the supplier in respect of a supply made earlier.

[86][Facility of digital payment to recipient.

31A. The Government may, on the recommendations of the Council, prescribe a class of registered persons who shall provide prescribed modes of electronic payment to the recipient of supply of goods or services or both made by him and give option to such recipient to make payment accordingly, in such manner and subject to such conditions and restrictions, as may be prescribed.]

Prohibition of unauthorized collection of tax.

32. (1) A person who is not a registered person shall not collect in respect of any supply of goods or services or both any amount by way of tax under this Act.

(2) No registered person shall collect tax except in accordance with the provisions of this Act or the rules made thereunder.

Amount of tax to be indicated in tax invoice and other documents.

33. Notwithstanding anything contained in this Act or any other law for the time being in force, where any supply is made for a consideration, every person who is liable to pay tax for such supply shall prominently indicate in all documents relating to assessment, tax invoice and other like documents, the amount of tax which shall form part of the price at which such supply is made.

Credit and debit notes.

34. (1) [87][Where one or more tax invoices have] been issued for supply of any goods or services or both and

---

86. Inserted by the Finance (No. 2) Act, 2019, w.e.f. 1-1-2020.

87. Substituted for "Where a tax invoice has" by the Central Goods and Services Tax (Amendment) Act, 2018, w.e.f. 1-2-2019.

the taxable value or tax charged in that tax invoice is found to exceed the taxable value or tax payable in respect of such supply, or where the goods supplied are returned by the recipient, or where goods or services or both supplied are found to be deficient, the registered person, who has supplied such goods or services or both, may issue to the recipient [88][one or more credit notes for supplies made in a financial year] containing such particulars as may be prescribed.

(2) Any registered person who issues a credit note in relation to a supply of goods or services or both shall declare the details of such credit note in the return for the month during which such credit note has been issued but not later than [89][the thirtieth day of November] following the end of the financial year in which such supply was made, or the date of furnishing of the relevant annual return, whichever is earlier, and the tax liability shall be adjusted in such manner as may be prescribed:

Provided that no reduction in output tax liability of the supplier shall be permitted, if the incidence of tax and interest on such supply has been passed on to any other person.

(3) [90][Where one or more tax invoices have] been issued for supply of any goods or services or both and the taxable value or tax charged in that tax invoice is found to be less than the taxable value or tax payable in respect of such supply, the registered person, who has supplied such goods or services or both, shall issue to the recipient [91][one or more debit notes for supplies made in a financial year] containing such particulars as may be prescribed.

---

88. Substituted for "a credit note"by the Central Goods and Services Tax (Amendment) Act, 2018, w.e.f. 1-2-2019.
89. Substituted for "September" by the Finance Act, 2022, w.e.f. 1-10-2022.
90. Substituted for "Where a tax invoice has" by the Central Goods and Services Tax (Amendment) Act, 2018, w.e.f. 1-2-2019.
91. Substituted for "a debit note", *ibid.*

(4) Any registered person who issues a debit note in relation to a supply of goods or services or both shall declare the details of such debit note in the return for the month during which such debit note has been issued and the tax liability shall be adjusted in such manner as may be prescribed.

Explanation.—For the purposes of this Act, the expression "debit note" shall include a supplementary invoice.

CHAPTER VIII

ACCOUNTS AND RECORDS

Accounts and other records.

35. (1) Every registered person shall keep and maintain, at his principal place of business, as mentioned in the certificate of registration, a true and correct account of—

(*a*) production or manufacture of goods;

(*b*) inward and outward supply of goods or services or both;

(*c*) stock of goods;

(*d*) input tax credit availed;

(*e*) output tax payable and paid; and

(*f*) such other particulars as may be prescribed:

Provided that where more than one place of business is specified in the certificate of registration, the accounts relating to each place of business shall be kept at such places of business:

Provided further that the registered person may keep and maintain such accounts and other particulars in electronic form in such manner as may be prescribed.

(2) Every owner or operator of warehouse or godown or any other place used for storage of goods and every transporter, irrespective of whether he is a registered

person or not, shall maintain records of the consigner, consignee and other relevant details of the goods in such manner as may be prescribed.

(3) The Commissioner may notify a class of taxable persons to maintain additional accounts or documents for such purpose as may be specified therein.

(4) Where the Commissioner considers that any class of taxable persons is not in a position to keep and maintain accounts in accordance with the provisions of this section, he may, for reasons to be recorded in writing, permit such class of taxable persons to maintain accounts in such manner as may be prescribed.

(5) [92][***]

(6) Subject to the provisions of clause (*h*) of sub-section (5) of section 17, where the registered person fails to account for the goods or services or both in accordance with the provisions of sub-section (1), the proper officer shall determine the amount of tax payable on the goods or services or both that are not accounted for, as if such goods or services or both had been supplied by such person and the provisions of section 73 or section 74 [93]**[*or section 74A*]**, as the case may be, shall, *mutatis mutandis,* apply for determination of such tax.

Period of retention of accounts.

36. Every registered person required to keep and maintain books of account or other records in accordance with the provisions of sub-section (1) of section 35 shall retain them until the expiry of seventy two months from the due date of furnishing of annual return for the year pertaining to such accounts and records:

Provided that a registered person, who is a party to an appeal or revision or any other proceedings before

92. Omitted by the Finance Act, 2021, w.e.f. 1-8-2021.

93. Inserted by the Finance (No. 2) Act, 2024, w.e.f. **1-11-2024**.

any Appellate Authority or Revisional Authority or Appellate Tribunal or court, whether filed by him or by the Commissioner, or is under investigation for an offence under Chapter XIX, shall retain the books of account and other records pertaining to the subject matter of such appeal or revision or proceedings or investigation for a period of one year after final disposal of such appeal or revision or proceedings or investigation, or for the period specified above, whichever is later.

CHAPTER IX

RETURNS

Furnishing details of outward supplies.

37. (1) Every registered person, other than an Input Service Distributor, a non-resident taxable person and a person paying tax under the provisions of section 10 or section 51 or section 52, shall furnish, electronically, [94][subject to such conditions and restrictions and] in such form and manner as may be prescribed, the details of outward supplies of goods or services or both effected during a tax period on or before the tenth day of the month succeeding the said tax period and such details [95][shall, subject to such conditions and restrictions, within such time and in such manner as may be prescribed, be communicated to the recipient of the said supplies]:

[96][***]

[97][**Provided** that] the Commissioner may, for reasons to be recorded in writing, by notification, extend the

94. Inserted by the Finance Act, 2022, w.e.f. 1-10-2022.

95. Substituted for "shall be communicated to the recipient of the said supplies within such time and in such manner as may be prescribed", *ibid.*

96. Omitted, *ibid.*

97. Substituted for "**Provided further** that", *ibid.*

time limit for furnishing such details for such class of taxable persons as may be specified therein:

[98][**Provided further** that] any extension of time limit notified by the Commissioner of State tax or Commissioner of Union territory tax shall be deemed to be notified by the Commissioner.

(2) [99][***]

(3) Any registered person, who has furnished the details under sub-section (1) for any tax period [1][***], shall, upon discovery of any error or omission therein, rectify such error or omission in such manner as may be prescribed, and shall pay the tax and interest, if any, in case there is a short payment of tax on account of such error or omission, in the return to be furnished for such tax period:

Provided that no rectification of error or omission in respect of the details furnished under sub-section (1) shall be allowed after [2][the thirtieth day of November] following the end of the financial year to which such details pertain, or furnishing of the relevant annual return, whichever is earlier:

[3][**Provided further** that the rectification of error or omission in respect of the details furnished under sub-section (1) shall be allowed after furnishing of the return under section 39 for the month of September, 2018 till the due date for furnishing the details under sub-section (1) for the month of March, 2019 or for the quarter January, 2019 to March, 2019.]

---

98. Substituted for "**Provided also** that" by the Finance Act, 2022, w.e.f. 1-10-2022.

99. Omitted, *ibid.*

1. Words "and which have remained unmatched under section 42 or section 43" omitted, *ibid.*

2. Substituted for "furnishing of the return under section 39 for the month of September", *ibid.*

3. Inserted by the Central Goods and Services Tax (Second Removal of Difficulties) Order, 2018, w.e.f. 31-12-2018.

[4][(4) A registered person shall not be allowed to furnish the details of outward supplies under sub-section (1) for a tax period, if the details of outward supplies for any of the previous tax periods has not been furnished by him:

Provided that the Government may, on the recommendations of the Council, by notification, subject to such conditions and restrictions as may be specified therein, allow a registered person or a class of registered persons to furnish the details of outward supplies under sub-section (1), even if he has not furnished the details of outward supplies for one or more previous tax periods.]

[5][(5) A registered person shall not be allowed to furnish the details of outward supplies under sub-section (1) for a tax period after the expiry of a period of three years from the due date of furnishing the said details:

Provided that the Government may, on the recommendations of the Council, by notification, subject to such conditions and restrictions as may be specified therein, allow a registered person or a class of registered persons to furnish the details of outward supplies for a tax period under sub-section (1), even after the expiry of the said period of three years from the due date of furnishing the said details.]

Explanation.—For the purposes of this Chapter, the expression "details of outward supplies" shall include details of invoices, debit notes, credit notes and revised invoices issued in relation to outward supplies made during any tax period.

[6][**Communication of details of inward supplies and input tax credit.**

38. (1) The details of outward supplies furnished by the registered persons under sub-section (1) of section 37 and of such other supplies as may be prescribed, and

4. Inserted by the Finance Act, 2022, w.e.f. 1-10-2022.
5. Inserted by the Finance Act, 2023, w.e.f. 1-10-2023.
6. Substituted by the Finance Act, 2022, w.e.f. 1-10-2022.

an auto-generated statement containing the details of input tax credit shall be made available electronically to the recipients of such supplies in such form and manner, within such time, and subject to such conditions and restrictions as may be prescribed.

(2) The auto-generated statement under sub-section (1) shall consist of—

(*a*) details of inward supplies in respect of which credit of input tax may be available to the recipient; and

(*b*) details of supplies in respect of which such credit cannot be availed, whether wholly or partly, by the recipient, on account of the details of the said supplies being furnished under sub-section (1) of section 37,—

(*i*) by any registered person within such period of taking registration as may be prescribed; or

(*ii*) by any registered person, who has defaulted in payment of tax and where such default has continued for such period as may be prescribed; or

(*iii*) by any registered person, the output tax payable by whom in accordance with the statement of outward supplies furnished by him under the said sub-section during such period, as may be prescribed, exceeds the output tax paid by him during the said period by such limit as may be prescribed; or

(*iv*) by any registered person who, during such period as may be prescribed, has availed credit of input tax of an amount that exceeds the credit that can be availed by him in accordance with clause (*a*), by such limit as may be prescribed; or (*v*) by any registered person, who has defaulted in discharging his tax liability in accordance with the provisions of sub-section (12) of section 49 subject to such conditions and restrictions as may be prescribed; or

(*vi*) by such other class of persons as may be prescribed.]

Furnishing of returns.

39. [7][(1) Every registered person, other than an Input Service Distributor or a non-resident taxable person or a person paying tax under the provisions of section 10 or section 51 or section 52 shall, for every calendar month or part thereof, furnish, a return, electronically, of inward and outward supplies of goods or services or both, input tax credit availed, tax payable, tax paid and such other particulars, in such form and manner, and within such time, as may be prescribed :

Provided that the Government may, on the recommendations of the Council, notify certain class of registered persons who shall furnish a return for every quarter or part thereof, subject to such conditions and restrictions as may be specified therein.

(2) A registered person paying tax under the provisions of section 10, shall, for each financial year or part thereof, furnish a return, electronically, of turnover in the State or Union territory, inward supplies of goods or services or both, tax payable, tax paid and such other particulars in such form and manner, and within such time, as may be prescribed.]

[8]**[***(3) Every registered person required to deduct tax at source under section 51 shall electronically furnish a return for every calendar month of the deductions*

---

7. Substituted by the Finance (No. 2) Act, 2019, w.e.f. 10-11-2020.

8. Substituted by the Finance (No. 2) Act, 2024, w.e.f. **1-11-2024**.

made during the month in such form and manner and within such time as may be prescribed:

Provided *that the said registered person shall furnish a return for every calendar month whether or not any deductions have been made during the said month.*]

(4) Every taxable person registered as an Input Service Distributor shall, for every calendar month or part thereof, furnish, in such form and manner as may be prescribed, a return, electronically, within thirteen days after the end of such month.

(5) Every registered non-resident taxable person shall, for every calendar month or part thereof, furnish, in such form and manner as may be prescribed, a return, electronically, within [9][thirteen] days after the end of a calendar month or within seven days after the last day of the period of registration specified under sub-section (1) of section 27, whichever is earlier.

(6) The Commissioner may, for reasons to be recorded in writing, by notification, extend the time limit for furnishing the returns under this section for such class of registered persons as may be specified therein:

Provided that any extension of time limit notified by the Commissioner of State tax or Union territory tax shall be deemed to be notified by the Commissioner.

[10][(7) Every registered person who is required to furnish a return under sub-section (1), other than the person referred to in the proviso thereto, or sub-section (3) or sub-section (5), shall pay to the Government the tax due as per such return not later than the last date on which he is required to furnish such return:

[11][**Provided** that every registered person furnishing return under the proviso to sub-section (1) shall pay

9. Substituted for "twenty" by the Finance Act, 2022, w.e.f. 1-10-2022.

10. Substituted by the Finance (No. 2) Act, 2019, w.e.f. 10-11-2020.

11. Substituted by the Finance Act, 2022, w.e.f. 1-10-2022.

to the Government, in such form and manner, and within such time, as may be prescribed,—

(*a*) an amount equal to the tax due taking into account inward and outward supplies of goods or services or both, input tax credit availed, tax payable and such other particulars during a month; or

(*b*) in lieu of the amount referred to in clause (*a*), an amount determined in such manner and subject to such conditions and restrictions as may be prescribed:]

Provided further that every registered person furnishing return under sub-section (2) shall pay to the Government the tax due taking into account turnover in the State or Union territory, inward supplies of goods or services or both, tax payable, and such other particulars during a quarter, in such form and manner, and within such time, as may be prescribed.]

(8) Every registered person who is required to furnish a return under sub-section (1) or sub-section (2) shall furnish a return for every tax period whether or not any supplies of goods or services or both have been made during such tax period.

(9) [12][Where] any registered person after furnishing a return under sub-section (1) or sub-section (2) or sub-section (3) or sub-section (4) or sub-section (5) discovers any omission or incorrect particulars therein, other than as a result of scrutiny, audit, inspection or enforcement activity by the tax authorities, he shall rectify such omission or incorrect particulars [13]**[***in*

12. Substituted for "Subject to the provisions of sections 37 and 38, if" by the Finance Act, 2022, w.e.f. 1-10-2022.

13. Substituted for "in the return to be furnished for the month or quarter during which such omission or incorrect particulars are noticed" by the Central Goods and Services Tax (Amendment) Act, 2018, with effect from a date yet to be notified.

*such form and manner as may be prescribed***]**, subject to payment of interest under this Act:

Provided that no such rectification of any omission or incorrect particulars shall be allowed after [14][the thirtieth day of November] following [15]**[***the end of the financial year to which such details pertain***]**, or the actual date of furnishing of relevant annual return, whichever is earlier.

(10) A registered person shall not be allowed to furnish a return for a tax period if the return for any of the previous tax periods [16][or the details of outward supplies under sub-section (1) of section 37 for the said tax period has not been furnished by him:

Provided that the Government may, on the recommendations of the Council, by notification, subject to such conditions and restrictions as may be specified therein, allow a registered person or a class of registered persons to furnish the return, even if he has not furnished the returns for one or more previous tax periods or has not furnished the details of outward supplies under sub-section (1) of section 37 for the said tax period].

[17][(11) A registered person shall not be allowed to furnish a return for a tax period after the expiry of a period of three years from the due date of furnishing the said return:

Provided that the Government may, on the recommendations of the Council, by notification, subject to such conditions and restrictions as may be specified

---

14. Substituted for "the due date for furnishing of return for the month of September or second quarter" by the Finance Act, 2022, w.e.f. 1-10-2022.
15. Substituted for "the end of the financial year" by the Central Goods and Services Tax (Amendment) Act, 2018, with effect from a date yet to be notified.
16. Substituted for "has not been furnished by him" by the Finance Act, 2022, w.e.f. 1-10-2022.
17. Inserted by the Finance Act, 2023, w.e.f. 1-10-2023.

therein, allow a registered person or a class of registered persons to furnish the return for a tax period, even after the expiry of the said period of three years from the due date of furnishing the said return.]

First return.

40. Every registered person who has made outward supplies in the period between the date on which he became liable to registration till the date on which registration has been granted shall declare the same in the first return furnished by him after grant of registration.

[18][**Availment of input tax credit.**

41. (1) Every registered person shall, subject to such conditions and restrictions as may be prescribed, be entitled to avail the credit of eligible input tax, as self-assessed, in his return and such amount shall be credited to his electronic credit ledger.

(2) The credit of input tax availed by a registered person under sub-section (1) in respect of such supplies of goods or services or both, the tax payable whereon has not been paid by the supplier, shall be reversed along with applicable interest, by the said person in such manner as may be prescribed:

Provided that where the said supplier makes payment of the tax payable in respect of the aforesaid supplies, the said registered person may re-avail the amount of credit reversed by him in such manner as may be prescribed.]

Matching, reversal and reclaim of input tax credit.

42. [19][***]

Matching, reversal and reclaim of reduction in output tax liability.

43. [19][***]

18. Substituted by the Finance Act, 2022, w.e.f. 1-10-2022.

19. Omitted, *ibid*.

Procedure for furnishing return and availing input tax credit.

43A. [20][***]

[21][**Annual return.**

44. [22][(1)] Every registered person, other than an Input Service Distributor, a person paying tax under section 51 or section 52, a casual taxable person and a non-resident taxable person shall furnish an annual return which may include a self-certified reconciliation statement, reconciling the value of supplies declared in the return furnished for the financial year, with the audited annual financial statement for every financial year electronically, within such time and in such form and in such manner as may be prescribed:

Provided that the Commissioner may, on the recommendations of the Council, by notification, exempt any class of registered persons from filing annual return under this section:

Provided further that nothing contained in this section shall apply to any department of the Central Government or a State Government or a local authority, whose books of account are subject to audit by the Comptroller and Auditor-General of India or an auditor appointed for auditing the accounts of local authorities under any law for the time being in force.]

[22][(2) A registered person shall not be allowed to furnish an annual return under sub-section (1) for a financial year after the expiry of a period of three years from the due date of furnishing the said annual return:

Provided that the Government may, on the recommendations of the Council, by notification, and

---

20. Omitted by the Finance Act, 2022, w.e.f. 1-10-2022.
21. Substituted by the Finance Act, 2021, w.e.f. 1-8-2021.
22. Inserted by the Finance Act, 2023, w.e.f. 1-10-2023.

subject to such conditions and restrictions as may be specified therein, allow a registered person or a class of registered persons to furnish an annual return for a financial year under sub-section (1), even after the expiry of the said period of three years from the due date of furnishing the said annual return.]

Final return.

45. Every registered person who is required to furnish a return under sub-section (1) of section 39 and whose registration has been cancelled shall furnish a final return within three months of the date of cancellation or date of order of cancellation, whichever is later, in such form and manner as may be prescribed.

Notice to return defaulters.

46. Where a registered person fails to furnish a return under section 39 or section 44 or section 45, a notice shall be issued requiring him to furnish such return within fifteen days in such form and manner as may be prescribed.

Levy of late fee.

47. (1) Any registered person who fails to furnish the details of outward [23][***] supplies required under section 37 [24][***] or returns required under section 39 or section 45 [25][or section 52] by the due date shall pay a late fee of one hundred rupees for every day during which such failure continues subject to a maximum amount of five thousand rupees.

(2) Any registered person who fails to furnish the return required under section 44 by the due date shall be liable to pay a late fee of one hundred rupees for every day during which such failure continues subject to a maximum of an amount calculated at a quarter per cent of his turnover in the State or Union territory.

---

23. Words "or inward" omitted by the Finance Act, 2022, w.e.f. 1-10-2022.
24. Words "or section 38" omitted, *ibid.*
25. Inserted, *ibid.*

Goods and services tax practitioners.

48. (1) The manner of approval of goods and services tax practitioners, their eligibility conditions, duties and obligations, manner of removal and other conditions relevant for their functioning shall be such as may be prescribed.

(2) A registered person may authorise an approved goods and services tax practitioner to furnish the details of outward supplies under section 37 [25a][***] and the return under section 39 or section 44 or section 45 [26][and to perform such other functions] in such manner as may be prescribed.

(3) Notwithstanding anything contained in sub-section (2), the responsibility for correctness of any particulars furnished in the return or other details filed by the goods and services tax practitioners shall continue to rest with the registered person on whose behalf such return and details are furnished.

CHAPTER X

PAYMENT OF TAX

Payment of tax, interest, penalty and other amounts.

49. (1) Every deposit made towards tax, interest, penalty, fee or any other amount by a person by internet banking or by using credit or debit cards or National Electronic Fund Transfer or Real Time Gross Settlement or by such other mode and subject to such conditions and restrictions as may be prescribed, shall be credited to the electronic cash ledger of such person to be maintained in such manner as may be prescribed.

25a. Words ", the details of inward supplies under section 38" omitted by the Finance Act, 2022, w.e.f. 1-10-2022.

26. Inserted by the Central Goods and Services Tax (Amendment) Act, 2018, w.e.f. 1-2-2019.

(2) The input tax credit as self-assessed in the return of a registered person shall be credited to his electronic credit ledger, in accordance with [27][*section 41* [28][***]], to be maintained in such manner as may be prescribed.

(3) The amount available in the electronic cash ledger may be used for making any payment towards tax, interest, penalty, fees or any other amount payable under the provisions of this Act or the rules made thereunder in such manner and subject to such conditions and within such time as may be prescribed.

(4) The amount available in the electronic credit ledger may be used for making any payment towards output tax under this Act or under the Integrated Goods and Services Tax Act in such manner and subject to such conditions [29][and restrictions] and within such time as may be prescribed.

(5) The amount of input tax credit available in the electronic credit ledger of the registered person on account of—

(*a*) integrated tax shall first be utilised towards payment of integrated tax and the amount remaining, if any, may be utilised towards the payment of central tax and State tax, or as the case may be, Union territory tax, in that order;

(*b*) the central tax shall first be utilised towards payment of central tax and the amount remaining, if any, may be utilised towards the payment of integrated tax;

---

27. Substituted for "section 41" by the Central Goods and Services Tax (Amendment) Act, 2018, with effect from a date yet to be notified.

28. Words "or section 43A" omitted by the Finance Act, 2022, w.e.f. 1-10-2022.

29. Inserted, *ibid*.

(*c*) the State tax shall first be utilised towards payment of State tax and the amount remaining, if any, may be utilised towards payment of integrated tax:

[30][**Provided** that the input tax credit on account of State tax shall be utilised towards payment of integrated tax only where the balance of the input tax credit on account of central tax is not available for payment of integrated tax;]

(*d*) the Union territory tax shall first be utilised towards payment of Union territory tax and the amount remaining, if any, may be utilised towards payment of integrated tax:

[30][**Provided** that the input tax credit on account of Union territory tax shall be utilised towards payment of integrated tax only where the balance of the input tax credit on account of central tax is not available for payment of integrated tax;]

(*e*) the central tax shall not be utilised towards payment of State tax or Union territory tax; and

(*f*) the State tax or Union territory tax shall not be utilised towards payment of central tax.

(6) The balance in the electronic cash ledger or electronic credit ledger after payment of tax, interest, penalty, fee or any other amount payable under this Act or the rules made thereunder may be refunded in accordance with the provisions of section 54.

(7) All liabilities of a taxable person under this Act shall be recorded and maintained in an electronic liability register in such manner as may be prescribed.

---

30. Inserted by the Central Goods and Services Tax (Amendment) Act, 2018, w.e.f. 1-2-2019.

(8) Every taxable person shall discharge his tax and other dues under this Act or the rules made thereunder in the following order, namely:—

(*a*) self-assessed tax, and other dues related to returns of previous tax periods;

(*b*) self-assessed tax, and other dues related to the return of the current tax period;

(*c*) any other amount payable under this Act or the rules made thereunder including the demand determined under section 73 or section 74 [31]**[*or section 74A*]**;

(9) Every person who has paid the tax on goods or services or both under this Act shall, unless the contrary is proved by him, be deemed to have passed on the full incidence of such tax to the recipient of such goods or services or both.

[32][[33][(10) A registered person may, on the common portal, transfer any amount of tax, interest, penalty, fee or any other amount available in the electronic cash ledger under this Act, to the electronic cash ledger for,—

(*a*) integrated tax, central tax, State tax, Union territory tax or cess; or

(*b*) integrated tax or central tax of a distinct person as specified in sub-section (4) or, as the case may be, sub-section (5) of section 25,

in such form and manner and subject to such conditions and restrictions as may be prescribed and such transfer shall be deemed to be a refund from the electronic cash ledger under this Act:

---

31. Inserted by the Finance (No. 2) Act, 2024, w.e.f. **1-11-2024**.
32. Sub-sections (10) and (11) inserted by the Finance (No. 2) Act, 2019, w.e.f. 1-1-2020.
33. Substituted by the Finance Act, 2022, w.e.f. 5-7-2022.

Provided that no such transfer under clause (*b*) shall be allowed if the said registered person has any unpaid liability in his electronic liability register.]

(11) Where any amount has been transferred to the electronic cash ledger under this Act, the same shall be deemed to be deposited in the said ledger as provided in sub-section (1).]

[34][(12) Notwithstanding anything contained in this Act, the Government may, on the recommendations of the Council, subject to such conditions and restrictions, specify such maximum proportion of output tax liability under this Act or under the Integrated Goods and Services Tax Act, 2017 (13 of 2017) which may be discharged through the electronic credit ledger by a registered person or a class of registered persons, as may be prescribed.]

Explanation.—For the purposes of this section,—

(*a*) the date of credit to the account of the Government in the authorised bank shall be deemed to be the date of deposit in the electronic cash ledger;

(*b*) the expression,—

(*i*) "tax dues" means the tax payable under this Act and does not include interest, fee and penalty; and

(*ii*) "other dues" means interest, penalty, fee or any other amount payable under this Act or the rules made thereunder.

[35][**Utilisation of input tax credit subject to certain conditions.**

49A. Notwithstanding anything contained in section 49, the input tax credit on account of central tax, State tax or Union territory tax shall be utilised towards

34. Inserted by the Finance Act, 2022, w.e.f. 1-10-2022.

35. Inserted by the Central Goods and Services Tax (Amendment) Act, 2018, w.e.f. 1-2-2019.

payment of integrated tax, central tax, State tax or Union territory tax, as the case may be, only after the input tax credit available on account of integrated tax has first been utilised fully towards such payment.

Order of utilisation of input tax credit.

49B. Notwithstanding anything contained in this Chapter and subject to the provisions of clause (*e*) and clause (*f*) of sub-section (5) of section 49, the Government may, on the recommendations of the Council, prescribe the order and manner of utilisation of the input tax credit on account of integrated tax, central tax, State tax or Union territory tax, as the case may be, towards payment of any such tax.]

Interest on delayed payment of tax.

50. (1) Every person who is liable to pay tax in accordance with the provisions of this Act or the rules made thereunder, but fails to pay the tax or any part thereof to the Government within the period prescribed, shall for the period for which the tax or any part thereof remains unpaid, pay, on his own, interest at such rate, not exceeding eighteen per cent, as may be notified by the Government on the recommendations of the Council:

[36][**Provided** that the interest on tax payable in respect of supplies made during a tax period and declared in the return for the said period furnished after the due date in accordance with the provisions of section 39, except where such return is furnished after commencement of any proceedings under section 73 or section 74 [37]**[***or section 74A***]** in respect of the said period, shall be payable on that portion of the tax which is paid by debiting the electronic cash ledger.]

36. Substituted by the Finance Act, 2021, w.r.e.f. 1-7-2017 [However, Notification No. 16/2021-Central Tax, dated 1-6-2021 appoints 1-6-2021 as the date of enforcement].

37. Inserted by the Finance (No. 2) Act, 2024, w.e.f. **1-11-2024**.

(2) The interest under sub-section (1) shall be calculated, in such manner as may be prescribed, from the day succeeding the day on which such tax was due to be paid.

[38][(3) Where the input tax credit has been wrongly availed and utilised, the registered person shall pay interest on such input tax credit wrongly availed and utilised, at such rate not exceeding twenty-four per cent as may be notified by the Government, on the recommendations of the Council, and the interest shall be calculated, in such manner as may be prescribed.]

Tax deduction at source.

51. (1) Notwithstanding anything to the contrary contained in this Act, the Government may mandate,—

(*a*) a department or establishment of the Central Government or State Government; or

(*b*) local authority; or

(*c*) Governmental agencies; or

(*d*) such persons or category of persons as may be notified by the Government on the recommendations of the Council,

(hereafter in this section referred to as "the deductor"), to deduct tax at the rate of one per cent from the payment made or credited to the supplier (hereafter in this section referred to as "the deductee") of taxable goods or services or both, where the total value of such supply, under a contract, exceeds two lakh and fifty thousand rupees:

Provided that no deduction shall be made if the location of the supplier and the place of supply is in a State or Union territory which is different from the State or as the case may be, Union territory of registration of the recipient.

38. Substituted by the Finance Act, 2022, w.r.e.f. 1-7-2017. [However, Notification No. 9/2022-Central Tax, dated 5-7-2022 appoints 5-7-2022 as the date of enforcement].

Explanation.—For the purpose of deduction of tax specified above, the value of supply shall be taken as the amount excluding the central tax, State tax, Union territory tax, integrated tax and cess indicated in the invoice.

(2) The amount deducted as tax under this section shall be paid to the Government by the deductor within ten days after the end of the month in which such deduction is made, in such manner as may be prescribed.

[39][(3) A certificate of tax deduction at source shall be issued in such form and in such manner as may be prescribed.]

(4) [40][***]

(5) The deductee shall claim credit, in his electronic cash ledger, of the tax deducted and reflected in the return of the deductor furnished under sub-section (3) of section 39, in such manner as may be prescribed.

(6) If any deductor fails to pay to the Government the amount deducted as tax under sub-section (1), he shall pay interest in accordance with the provisions of sub-section (1) of section 50, in addition to the amount of tax deducted.

(7) The determination of the amount in default under this section shall be made in the manner specified in section 73 or section 74 [41][*or section 74A*].

(8) The refund to the deductor or the deductee arising on account of excess or erroneous deduction shall be dealt with in accordance with the provisions of section 54:

Provided that no refund to the deductor shall be granted, if the amount deducted has been credited to the electronic cash ledger of the deductee.

39. Substituted by the Finance Act, 2020, w.e.f. 1-1-2021.

40. Omitted, *ibid.*

41. Inserted by the Finance (No. 2) Act, 2024, w.e.f. **1-11-2024**.

Collection of tax at source.

52. (1) Notwithstanding anything to the contrary contained in this Act, every electronic commerce operator (hereafter in this section referred to as the "operator"), not being an agent, shall collect an amount calculated at such rate not exceeding one per cent, as may be notified by the Government on the recommendations of the Council, of the net value of taxable supplies made through it by other suppliers where the consideration with respect to such supplies is to be collected by the operator.

Explanation.—For the purposes of this sub-section, the expression "net value of taxable supplies" shall mean the aggregate value of taxable supplies of goods or services or both, other than services notified under sub-section (5) of section 9, made during any month by all registered persons through the operator reduced by the aggregate value of taxable supplies returned to the suppliers during the said month.

(2) The power to collect the amount specified in sub-section (1) shall be without prejudice to any other mode of recovery from the operator.

(3) The amount collected under sub-section (1) shall be paid to the Government by the operator within ten days after the end of the month in which such collection is made, in such manner as may be prescribed.

(4) Every operator who collects the amount specified in sub-section (1) shall furnish a statement, electronically, containing the details of outward supplies of goods or services or both effected through it, including the supplies of goods or services or both returned through it, and the amount collected under sub-section (1) during a month, in such form and manner as may be prescribed, within ten days after the end of such month:

[42][**Provided** that the Commissioner may, for reasons to be recorded in writing, by notification, extend the

42. Inserted by the Finance (No. 2) Act, 2019, w.e.f. 1-1-2020.

time limit for furnishing the statement for such class of registered persons as may be specified therein:

Provided further that any extension of time limit notified by the Commissioner of State tax or the Commissioner of Union territory tax shall be deemed to be notified by the Commissioner.]

[43][*Explanation.*—For the purposes of this sub-section, it is hereby declared that the due date for furnishing the said statement for the months of October, November and December, 2018 shall be the [44][7th February, 2019].]

(5) Every operator who collects the amount specified in sub-section (1) shall furnish an annual statement, electronically, containing the details of outward supplies of goods or services or both effected through it, including the supplies of goods or services or both returned through it, and the amount collected under the said sub-section during the financial year, in such form and manner as may be prescribed, before the thirty first day of December following the end of such financial year:

[45][**Provided** that the Commissioner may, on the recommendations of the Council and for reasons to be recorded in writing, by notification, extend the time limit for furnishing the annual statement for such class of registered persons as may be specified therein:

Provided further that any extension of time limit notified by the Commissioner of State tax or the Commissioner of Union territory tax shall be deemed to be notified by the Commissioner.]

(6) If any operator after furnishing a statement under sub-section (4) discovers any omission or incorrect

43. Inserted by the Central Goods and Services Tax (Fourth Removal of Difficulties) Order, 2018, w.e.f. 31-12-2018.

44. Substituted for "31st January, 2019" by the Central Goods and Services Tax (Second Removal of Difficulties) Order, 2019, w.e.f. 1-2-2019.

45. Inserted by the Finance (No. 2) Act, 2019, w.e.f. 1-1-2020.

particulars therein, other than as a result of scrutiny, audit, inspection or enforcement activity by the tax authorities, he shall rectify such omission or incorrect particulars in the statement to be furnished for the month during which such omission or incorrect particulars are noticed, subject to payment of interest, as specified in sub-section (1) of section 50:

Provided that no such rectification of any omission or incorrect particulars shall be allowed after the [46][thirtieth day of November] following the end of the financial year or the actual date of furnishing of the relevant annual statement, whichever is earlier.

(7) The supplier who has supplied the goods or services or both through the operator shall claim credit, in his electronic cash ledger, of the amount collected and reflected in the statement of the operator furnished under sub-section (4), in such manner as may be prescribed.

(8) The details of supplies furnished by every operator under sub-section (4) shall be matched with the corresponding details of outward supplies furnished by the concerned supplier registered under this Act in such manner and within such time as may be prescribed.

(9) Where the details of outward supplies furnished by the operator under sub-section (4) do not match with the corresponding details furnished by the supplier under [47][section 37 or section 39], the discrepancy shall be communicated to both persons in such manner and within such time as may be prescribed.

(10) The amount in respect of which any discrepancy is communicated under sub-section (9) and which is not rectified by the supplier in his valid return or the operator in his statement for the month in which

46. Substituted for "due date for furnishing of statement for the month of September" by the Finance Act, 2022, w.e.f. 1-10-2022.

47. Substituted for "section 37" by the Central Goods and Services Tax (Amendment) Act, 2018, w.e.f. 1-2-2019.

discrepancy is communicated, shall be added to the output tax liability of the said supplier, where the value of outward supplies furnished by the operator is more than the value of outward supplies furnished by the supplier, in his return for the month succeeding the month in which the discrepancy is communicated in such manner as may be prescribed.

(11) The concerned supplier, in whose output tax liability any amount has been added under sub-section (10), shall pay the tax payable in respect of such supply along with interest, at the rate specified under sub-section (1) of section 50 on the amount so added from the date such tax was due till the date of its payment.

(12) Any authority not below the rank of Deputy Commissioner may serve a notice, either before or during the course of any proceedings under this Act, requiring the operator to furnish such details relating to—

(*a*) supplies of goods or services or both effected through such operator during any period; or

(*b*) stock of goods held by the suppliers making supplies through such operator in the godowns or warehouses, by whatever name called, managed by such operator and declared as additional places of business by such suppliers,

as may be specified in the notice.

(13) Every operator on whom a notice has been served under sub-section (12) shall furnish the required information within fifteen working days of the date of service of such notice.

(14) Any person who fails to furnish the information required by the notice served under sub-section (12) shall, without prejudice to any action that may be taken under section 122, be liable to a penalty which may extend to twenty-five thousand rupees.

[48][(15) The operator shall not be allowed to furnish a statement under sub-section (4) after the expiry of a period of three years from the due date of furnishing the said statement:

Provided that the Government may, on the recommendations of the Council, by notification, subject to such conditions and restrictions as may be specified therein, allow an operator or a class of operators to furnish a statement under sub-section (4), even after the expiry of the said period of three years from the due date of furnishing the said statement.]

Explanation.—For the purposes of this section, the expression "concerned supplier" shall mean the supplier of goods or services or both making supplies through the operator.

Transfer of input tax credit.

53. On utilisation of input tax credit availed under this Act for payment of tax dues under the Integrated Goods and Services Tax Act in accordance with the provisions of sub-section (5) of section 49, as reflected in the valid return furnished under sub-section (1) of section 39, the amount collected as central tax shall stand reduced by an amount equal to such credit so utilised and the Central Government shall transfer an amount equal to the amount so reduced from the central tax account to the integrated tax account in such manner and within such time as may be prescribed.

[49][Transfer of certain amounts.

53A. Where any amount has been transferred from the electronic cash ledger under this Act to the electronic cash ledger under the State Goods and Services Tax Act or the Union Territory Goods and Services Tax Act, the Government shall, transfer to the State tax account or the Union territory tax account, an amount

48. Inserted by the Finance Act, 2023, w.e.f. 1-10-2023.
49. Inserted by the Finance (No. 2) Act, 2019, w.e.f. 1-1-2020.

equal to the amount transferred from the electronic cash ledger, in such manner and within such time as may be prescribed.]

CHAPTER XI

REFUNDS

Refund of tax.

54. (1) Any person claiming refund of any tax and interest, if any, paid on such tax or any other amount paid by him, may make an application before the expiry of two years from the relevant date in such form and manner as may be prescribed:

Provided that a registered person, claiming refund of any balance in the electronic cash ledger in accordance with the provisions of sub-section (6) of section 49, may claim such refund in [50][such form and] manner as may be prescribed.

(2) A specialised agency of the United Nations Organisation or any Multilateral Financial Institution and Organisation notified under the United Nations (Privileges and Immunities) Act, 1947 (46 of 1947), Consulate or Embassy of foreign countries or any other person or class of persons, as notified under section 55, entitled to a refund of tax paid by it on inward supplies of goods or services or both, may make an application for such refund, in such form and manner as may be prescribed, before the expiry of [51][two years] from the last day of the quarter in which such supply was received.

(3) Subject to the provisions of sub-section (10), a registered person may claim refund of any unutilised input tax credit at the end of any tax period:

Provided that no refund of unutilised input tax credit shall be allowed in cases other than—

---

50. Substituted for "the return furnished under section 39 in such" by the Finance Act, 2022, w.e.f. 1-10-2022.

51. Substituted, *ibid*.

(*i*) zero-rated supplies made without payment of tax;

(*ii*) where the credit has accumulated on account of rate of tax on inputs being higher than the rate of tax on output supplies (other than *nil* rated or fully exempt supplies), except supplies of goods or services or both as may be notified by the Government on the recommendations of the Council:

[52][***]

Provided also* that no refund of input tax credit shall be allowed, if the supplier of goods or services or both avails of drawback in respect of central tax or claims refund of the integrated tax paid on such supplies.

(4) The application shall be accompanied by—

(*a*) such documentary evidence as may be prescribed to establish that a refund is due to the applicant; and

(*b*) such documentary or other evidence (including the documents referred to in section 33) as the applicant may furnish to establish that the amount of tax and interest, if any, paid on such tax or any other amount paid in relation to which such refund is claimed was collected from, or paid by, him and the incidence of such tax and interest had not been passed on to any other person:

Provided that where the amount claimed as refund is less than two lakh rupees, it shall not be necessary for the applicant to furnish any documentary and other evidences but he may file a declaration, based on the documentary or other evidences available with him, certifying that the incidence of such tax and interest had not been passed on to any other person.

---

52. Omitted by the Finance (No. 2) Act, 2024, w.e.f. **1-11-2024**.

* Word 'also' should be read as 'further'.

(5) If, on receipt of any such application, the proper officer is satisfied that the whole or part of the amount claimed as refund is refundable, he may make an order accordingly and the amount so determined shall be credited to the Fund referred to in section 57.

(6) Notwithstanding anything contained in sub-section (5), the proper officer may, in the case of any claim for refund on account of zero-rated supply of goods or services or both made by registered persons, other than such category of registered persons as may be notified by the Government on the recommendations of the Council, refund on a provisional basis, ninety per cent of the total amount so claimed, [53][***] in such manner and subject to such conditions, limitations and safeguards as may be prescribed and thereafter make an order under sub-section (5) for final settlement of the refund claim after due verification of documents furnished by the applicant.

(7) The proper officer shall issue the order under sub-section (5) within sixty days from the date of receipt of application complete in all respects.

(8) Notwithstanding anything contained in sub-section (5), the refundable amount shall, instead of being credited to the Fund, be paid to the applicant, if such amount is relatable to—

(*a*) refund of tax paid on [54][export] of goods or services or both or on inputs or input services used in making such [54][exports];

(*b*) refund of unutilised input tax credit under sub-section (3);

(*c*) refund of tax paid on a supply which is not provided, either wholly or partially, and for

53. Words "excluding the amount of input tax credit provisionally accepted," omitted by the Finance Act, 2023, w.e.f. 1-10-2023.

54. Substituted for "zero-rated supplies" by the Central Goods and Services Tax (Amendment) Act, 2018, w.e.f. 1-2-2019.

which invoice has not been issued, or where a refund voucher has been issued;

(*d*) refund of tax in pursuance of section 77;

(*e*) the tax and interest, if any, or any other amount paid by the applicant, if he had not passed on the incidence of such tax and interest to any other person; or

(*f*) the tax or interest borne by such other class of applicants as the Government may, on the recommendations of the Council, by notification, specify.

[55][(8A) The Government may disburse the refund of the State tax in such manner as may be prescribed.]

(9) Notwithstanding anything to the contrary contained in any judgment, decree, order or direction of the Appellate Tribunal or any court or in any other provisions of this Act or the rules made thereunder or in any other law for the time being in force, no refund shall be made except in accordance with the provisions of sub-section (8).

(10) Where any refund is due [56][***] to a registered person who has defaulted in furnishing any return or who is required to pay any tax, interest or penalty, which has not been stayed by any court, Tribunal or Appellate Authority by the specified date, the proper officer may—

(*a*) withhold payment of refund due until the said person has furnished the return or paid the tax, interest or penalty, as the case may be;

(*b*) deduct from the refund due, any tax, interest, penalty, fee or any other amount which the taxable person is liable to pay but which remains unpaid under this Act or under the existing law.

---

55. Inserted by the Finance (No. 2) Act, 2019, w.e.f. 1-9-2019.

56. Words "under sub-section (3)" omitted by the Finance Act, 2022, w.e.f. 1-10-2022.

Explanation.—For the purposes of this sub-section, the expression "specified date" shall mean the last date for filing an appeal under this Act.

(11) Where an order giving rise to a refund is the subject matter of an appeal or further proceedings or where any other proceedings under this Act is pending and the Commissioner is of the opinion that grant of such refund is likely to adversely affect the revenue in the said appeal or other proceedings on account of malfeasance or fraud committed, he may, after giving the taxable person an opportunity of being heard, withhold the refund till such time as he may determine.

(12) Where a refund is withheld under sub-section (11), the taxable person shall, notwithstanding anything contained in section 56, be entitled to interest at such rate not exceeding six per cent as may be notified on the recommendations of the Council, if as a result of the appeal or further proceedings he becomes entitled to refund.

(13) Notwithstanding anything to the contrary contained in this section, the amount of advance tax deposited by a casual taxable person or a non-resident taxable person under sub-section (2) of section 27, shall not be refunded unless such person has, in respect of the entire period for which the certificate of registration granted to him had remained in force, furnished all the returns required under section 39.

(14) Notwithstanding anything contained in this section, no refund under sub-section (5) or sub-section (6) shall be paid to an applicant, if the amount is less than one thousand rupees.

[57]**[***(15) Notwithstanding anything contained in this section, no refund of unutilised input tax credit on account of zero rated supply of goods or of integrated*

57. Inserted by the Finance (No. 2) Act, 2024, w.e.f. **1-11-2024**.

tax paid on account of zero rated supply of goods shall be allowed where such zero rated supply of goods is subjected to export duty.]

Explanation.—For the purposes of this section,—

(*1*) "refund" includes refund of tax paid on zero-rated supplies of goods or services or both or on inputs or input services used in making such zero-rated supplies, or refund of tax on the supply of goods regarded as deemed exports, or refund of unutilised input tax credit as provided under sub-section (3).

(*2*) "relevant date" means—

(*a*) in the case of goods exported out of India where a refund of tax paid is available in respect of goods themselves or, as the case may be, the inputs or input services used in such goods,—

(*i*) if the goods are exported by sea or air, the date on which the ship or the aircraft in which such goods are loaded, leaves India; or

(*ii*) if the goods are exported by land, the date on which such goods pass the frontier; or

(*iii*) if the goods are exported by post, the date of despatch of goods by the Post Office concerned to a place outside India;

(*b*) in the case of supply of goods regarded as deemed exports where a refund of tax paid is available in respect of the goods, the date on which the return relating to such deemed exports is furnished;

[58][(*ba*) in case of zero-rated supply of goods or services or both to a Special Economic Zone developer or a Special Economic Zone unit where a refund of tax paid is available in respect of such supplies themselves, or as the case may be, the inputs or input services used in such supplies, the due date for furnishing of return under section 39 in respect of such supplies;]

(*c*) in the case of services exported out of India where a refund of tax paid is available in respect of services themselves or, as the case may be, the inputs or input services used in such services, the date of—

(*i*) receipt of payment in convertible foreign exchange [59][or in Indian rupees wherever permitted by the Reserve Bank of India], where the supply of services had been completed prior to the receipt of such payment; or

(*ii*) issue of invoice, where payment for the services had been received in advance prior to the date of issue of the invoice;

(*d*) in case where the tax becomes refundable as a consequence of judgment, decree, order or direction of the Appellate Authority, Appellate Tribunal or any court, the date of communication of such judgment, decree, order or direction;

58. Inserted by the Finance Act, 2022, w.e.f. 1-10-2022.

59. Inserted by the Central Goods and Services Tax (Amendment) Act, 2018, w.e.f. 1-2-2019.

[60][(*e*) in the case of refund of unutilised input tax credit under clause (*ii*) of the first proviso to sub-section (3), the due date for furnishing of return under section 39 for the period in which such claim for refund arises;]

(*f*) in the case where tax is paid provisionally under this Act or the rules made thereunder, the date of adjustment of tax after the final assessment thereof;

(*g*) in the case of a person, other than the supplier, the date of receipt of goods or services or both by such person; and

(*h*) in any other case, the date of payment of tax.

Refund in certain cases.

55. The Government may, on the recommendations of the Council, by notification, specify any specialised agency of the United Nations Organisation or any Multilateral Financial Institution and Organisation notified under the United Nations (Privileges and Immunities) Act, 1947 (46 of 1947), Consulate or Embassy of foreign countries and any other person or class of persons as may be specified in this behalf, who shall, subject to such conditions and restrictions as may be prescribed, be entitled to claim a refund of taxes paid on the notified supplies of goods or services or both received by them.

Interest on delayed refunds.

56. If any tax ordered to be refunded under sub-section (5) of section 54 to any applicant is not refunded within sixty days from the date of receipt of application under sub-section (1) of that section, interest at such rate not exceeding six per cent as may be specified

60. Substituted by the Central Goods and Services Tax (Amendment) Act, 2018, w.e.f. 1-2-2019.

in the notification issued by the Government on the recommendations of the Council shall be payable in respect of such refund [61][for the period of delay beyond sixty days from the date of receipt of such application till the date of refund of such tax, to be computed in such manner and subject to such conditions and restrictions as may be prescribed]:

Provided that where any claim of refund arises from an order passed by an adjudicating authority or Appellate Authority or Appellate Tribunal or court which has attained finality and the same is not refunded within sixty days from the date of receipt of application filed consequent to such order, interest at such rate not exceeding nine per cent as may be notified by the Government on the recommendations of the Council shall be payable in respect of such refund from the date immediately after the expiry of sixty days from the date of receipt of application till the date of refund.

Explanation.—For the purposes of this section, where any order of refund is made by an Appellate Authority, Appellate Tribunal or any court against an order of the proper officer under sub-section (5) of section 54, the order passed by the Appellate Authority, Appellate Tribunal or by the court shall be deemed to be an order passed under the said sub-section (5).

Consumer Welfare Fund.

57. The Government shall constitute a Fund, to be called the Consumer Welfare Fund and there shall be credited to the Fund,—

(*a*) the amount referred to in sub-section (5) of section 54;

---

61. Substituted for "from the date immediately after the expiry of sixty days from the date of receipt of application under the said sub-section till the date of refund of such tax" by the Finance Act, 2023, w.e.f. 1-10-2023.

(*b*) any income from investment of the amount credited to the Fund; and

(*c*) such other monies received by it,

in such manner as may be prescribed.

Utilisation of Fund.

58. (1) All sums credited to the Fund shall be utilised by the Government for the welfare of the consumers in such manner as may be prescribed.

(2) The Government or the authority specified by it shall maintain proper and separate account and other relevant records in relation to the Fund and prepare an annual statement of accounts in such form as may be prescribed in consultation with the Comptroller and Auditor General of India.

CHAPTER XII

ASSESSMENT

Self-assessment.

59. Every registered person shall self assess the taxes payable under this Act and furnish a return for each tax period as specified under section 39.

Provisional assessment.

60. (1) Subject to the provisions of sub-section (2), where the taxable person is unable to determine the value of goods or services or both or determine the rate of tax applicable thereto, he may request the proper officer in writing giving reasons for payment of tax on a provisional basis and the proper officer shall pass an order, within a period not later than ninety days from the date of receipt of such request, allowing payment of tax on provisional basis at such rate or on such value as may be specified by him.

(2) The payment of tax on provisional basis may be allowed, if the taxable person executes a bond in such form as may be prescribed, and with such surety or

security as the proper officer may deem fit, binding the taxable person for payment of the difference between the amount of tax as may be finally assessed and the amount of tax provisionally assessed.

(3) The proper officer shall, within a period not exceeding six months from the date of the communication of the order issued under sub-section (1), pass the final assessment order after taking into account such information as may be required for finalizing the assessment:

Provided that the period specified in this sub-section may, on sufficient cause being shown and for reasons to be recorded in writing, be extended by the Joint Commissioner or Additional Commissioner for a further period not exceeding six months and by the Commissioner for such further period not exceeding four years.

(4) The registered person shall be liable to pay interest on any tax payable on the supply of goods or services or both under provisional assessment but not paid on the due date specified under sub-section (7) of section 39 or the rules made thereunder, at the rate specified under sub-section (1) of section 50, from the first day after the due date of payment of tax in respect of the said supply of goods or services or both till the date of actual payment, whether such amount is paid before or after the issuance of order for final assessment.

(5) Where the registered person is entitled to a refund consequent to the order of final assessment under sub-section (3), subject to the provisions of sub-section (8) of section 54, interest shall be paid on such refund as provided in section 56.

Scrutiny of returns.

61. (1) The proper officer may scrutinize the return and related particulars furnished by the registered person to verify the correctness of the return and inform him of the discrepancies noticed, if any, in such manner as may be prescribed and seek his explanation thereto.

(2) In case the explanation is found acceptable, the registered person shall be informed accordingly and no further action shall be taken in this regard.

(3) In case no satisfactory explanation is furnished within a period of thirty days of being informed by the proper officer or such further period as may be permitted by him or where the registered person, after accepting the discrepancies, fails to take the corrective measure in his return for the month in which the discrepancy is accepted, the proper officer may initiate appropriate action including those under section 65 or section 66 or section 67, or proceed to determine the tax and other dues under section 73 or section 74 [62]**[*or section 74A*]**.

Assessment of non-filers of returns.

62. (1) Notwithstanding anything to the contrary contained in section 73 or section 74 [62]**[*or section 74A*]**, where a registered person fails to furnish the return under section 39 or section 45, even after the service of a notice under section 46, the proper officer may proceed to assess the tax liability of the said person to the best of his judgment taking into account all the relevant material which is available or which he has gathered and issue an assessment order within a period of five years from the date specified under section 44 for furnishing of the annual return for the financial year to which the tax not paid relates.

(2) Where the registered person furnishes a valid return within [63][sixty days] of the service of the assessment order under sub-section (1), the said assessment order shall be deemed to have been withdrawn but the

---

62. Inserted by the Finance (No. 2) Act, 2024, w.e.f. **1-11-2024**.

63. Substituted for "thirty days" by the Finance Act, 2023, w.e.f. 1-10-2023.

liability for payment of interest under sub-section (1) of section 50 or for payment of late fee under section 47 shall continue:

[64][**Provided** that where the registered person fails to furnish a valid return within sixty days of the service of the assessment order under sub-section (1), he may furnish the same within a further period of sixty days on payment of an additional late fee of one hundred rupees for each day of delay beyond sixty days of the service of the said assessment order and in case he furnishes valid return within such extended period, the said assessment order shall be deemed to have been withdrawn, but the liability to pay interest under sub-section (1) of section 50 or to pay late fee under section 47 shall continue.]

Assessment of unregistered persons.

63. Notwithstanding anything to the contrary contained in section 73 or section 74 [65]**[***or section 74A***]**, where a taxable person fails to obtain registration even though liable to do so or whose registration has been cancelled under sub-section (2) of section 29 but who was liable to pay tax, the proper officer may proceed to assess the tax liability of such taxable person to the best of his judgment for the relevant tax periods and issue an assessment order within a period of five years from the date specified under section 44 for furnishing of the annual return for the financial year to which the tax not paid relates:

Provided that no such assessment order shall be passed without giving the person an opportunity of being heard.

Summary assessment in certain special cases.

64. (1) The proper officer may, on any evidence showing a tax liability of a person coming to his

64. Inserted by the Finance Act, 2023, w.e.f. 1-10-2023.

65. Inserted by the Finance (No. 2) Act, 2024, w.e.f. **1-11-2024**.

notice, with the previous permission of Additional Commissioner or Joint Commissioner, proceed to assess the tax liability of such person to protect the interest of revenue and issue an assessment order, if he has sufficient grounds to believe that any delay in doing so may adversely affect the interest of revenue:

Provided that where the taxable person to whom the liability pertains is not ascertainable and such liability pertains to supply of goods, the person in charge of such goods shall be deemed to be the taxable person liable to be assessed and liable to pay tax and any other amount due under this section.

(2) On an application made by the taxable person within thirty days from the date of receipt of order passed under sub-section (1) or on his own motion, if the Additional Commissioner or Joint Commissioner considers that such order is erroneous, he may withdraw such order and follow the procedure laid down in section 73 or section 74 [65a][*or section 74A*].

CHAPTER XIII

AUDIT

Audit by tax authorities.

65. (1) The Commissioner or any officer authorised by him, by way of a general or a specific order, may undertake audit of any registered person for such period, at such frequency and in such manner as may be prescribed.

(2) The officers referred to in sub-section (1) may conduct audit at the place of business of the registered person or in their office.

(3) The registered person shall be informed by way of a notice not less than fifteen working days prior to the conduct of audit in such manner as may be prescribed.

65a. Inserted by the Finance (No. 2) Act, 2024, w.e.f. **1-11-2024**.

(4) The audit under sub-section (1) shall be completed within a period of three months from the date of commencement of the audit:

Provided that where the Commissioner is satisfied that audit in respect of such registered person cannot be completed within three months, he may, for the reasons to be recorded in writing, extend the period by a further period not exceeding six months.

Explanation.—For the purposes of this sub-section, the expression "commencement of audit" shall mean the date on which the records and other documents, called for by the tax authorities, are made available by the registered person or the actual institution of audit at the place of business, whichever is later.

(5) During the course of audit, the authorised officer may require the registered person,—

(*i*) to afford him the necessary facility to verify the books of account or other documents as he may require;

(*ii*) to furnish such information as he may require and render assistance for timely completion of the audit.

(6) On conclusion of audit, the proper officer shall, within thirty days, inform the registered person, whose records are audited, about the findings, his rights and obligations and the reasons for such findings.

(7) Where the audit conducted under sub-section (1) results in detection of tax not paid or short paid or erroneously refunded, or input tax credit wrongly availed or utilised, the proper officer may initiate action under section 73 or section 74 [66]**[***or section 74A***]**.

Special audit.

66. (1) If at any stage of scrutiny, inquiry, investigation or any other proceedings before him, any officer not

66. Inserted by the Finance (No. 2) Act, 2024, w.e.f. **1-11-2024**.

below the rank of Assistant Commissioner, having regard to the nature and complexity of the case and the interest of revenue, is of the opinion that the value has not been correctly declared or the credit availed is not within the normal limits, he may, with the prior approval of the Commissioner, direct such registered person by a communication in writing to get his records including books of account examined and audited by a chartered accountant or a cost accountant as may be nominated by the Commissioner.

(2) The chartered accountant or cost accountant so nominated shall, within the period of ninety days, submit a report of such audit duly signed and certified by him to the said Assistant Commissioner mentioning therein such other particulars as may be specified:

Provided that the Assistant Commissioner may, on an application made to him in this behalf by the registered person or the chartered accountant or cost accountant or for any material and sufficient reason, extend the said period by a further period of ninety days.

(3) The provisions of sub-section (1) shall have effect notwithstanding that the accounts of the registered person have been audited under any other provisions of this Act or any other law for the time being in force.

(4) The registered person shall be given an opportunity of being heard in respect of any material gathered on the basis of special audit under sub-section (1) which is proposed to be used in any proceedings against him under this Act or the rules made thereunder.

(5) The expenses of the examination and audit of records under sub-section (1), including the remuneration of such chartered accountant or cost accountant, shall be determined and paid by the Commissioner and such determination shall be final.

(6) Where the special audit conducted under sub-section (1) results in detection of tax not paid or short paid or erroneously refunded, or input tax credit

wrongly availed or utilised, the proper officer may initiate action under section 73 or section 74 [67][*or section 74A*].

CHAPTER XIV

INSPECTION, SEARCH, SEIZURE AND ARREST

Power of inspection, search and seizure.

67. (1) Where the proper officer, not below the rank of Joint Commissioner, has reasons to believe that—

(*a*) a taxable person has suppressed any transaction relating to supply of goods or services or both or the stock of goods in hand, or has claimed input tax credit in excess of his entitlement under this Act or has indulged in contravention of any of the provisions of this Act or the rules made thereunder to evade tax under this Act; or

(*b*) any person engaged in the business of transporting goods or an owner or operator of a warehouse or a godown or any other place is keeping goods which have escaped payment of tax or has kept his accounts or goods in such a manner as is likely to cause evasion of tax payable under this Act,

he may authorise in writing any other officer of central tax to inspect any places of business of the taxable person or the persons engaged in the business of transporting goods or the owner or the operator of warehouse or godown or any other place.

(2) Where the proper officer, not below the rank of Joint Commissioner, either pursuant to an inspection carried out under sub-section (1) or otherwise, has reasons to believe that any goods liable to confiscation or any documents or books or things, which in his

---

67. Inserted by the Finance (No. 2) Act, 2024, w.e.f. **1-11-2024**.

opinion shall be useful for or relevant to any proceedings under this Act, are secreted in any place, he may authorise in writing any other officer of central tax to search and seize or may himself search and seize such goods, documents or books or things:

Provided that where it is not practicable to seize any such goods, the proper officer, or any officer authorized by him, may serve on the owner or the custodian of the goods an order that he shall not remove, part with, or otherwise deal with the goods except with the previous permission of such officer:

Provided further that the documents or books or things so seized shall be retained by such officer only for so long as may be necessary for their examination and for any inquiry or proceedings under this Act.

(3) The documents, books or things referred to in sub-section (2) or any other documents, books or things produced by a taxable person or any other person, which have not been relied upon for the issue of notice under this Act or the rules made thereunder, shall be returned to such person within a period not exceeding thirty days of the issue of the said notice.

(4) The officer authorised under sub-section (2) shall have the power to seal or break open the door of any premises or to break open any *almirah,* electronic devices, box, receptacle in which any goods, accounts, registers or documents of the person are suspected to be concealed, where access to such premises, *almirah,* electronic devices, box or receptacle is denied.

(5) The person from whose custody any documents are seized under sub-section (2) shall be entitled to make copies thereof or take extracts therefrom in the presence of an authorised officer at such place and time as such officer may indicate in this behalf except where making such copies or taking such extracts may, in the opinion of the proper officer, prejudicially affect the investigation.

(6) The goods so seized under sub-section (2) shall be released, on a provisional basis, upon execution of a bond and furnishing of a security, in such manner and of such quantum, respectively, as may be prescribed or on payment of applicable tax, interest and penalty payable, as the case may be.

(7) Where any goods are seized under sub-section (2) and no notice in respect thereof is given within six months of the seizure of the goods, the goods shall be returned to the person from whose possession they were seized:

Provided that the period of six months may, on sufficient cause being shown, be extended by the proper officer for a further period not exceeding six months.

(8) The Government may, having regard to the perishable or hazardous nature of any goods, depreciation in the value of the goods with the passage of time, constraints of storage space for the goods or any other relevant considerations, by notification, specify the goods or class of goods which shall, as soon as may be after its seizure under sub-section (2), be disposed of by the proper officer in such manner as may be prescribed.

(9) Where any goods, being goods specified under sub-section (8), have been seized by a proper officer, or any officer authorised by him under sub-section (2), he shall prepare an inventory of such goods in such manner as may be prescribed.

(10) The provisions of the Code of Criminal Procedure, 1973 (2 of 1974), relating to search and seizure, shall, so far as may be, apply to search and seizure under this section subject to the modification that sub-section (5) of section 165 of the said Code shall have effect as if for the word "Magistrate", wherever it occurs, the word "Commissioner" were substituted.

(11) Where the proper officer has reasons to believe that any person has evaded or is attempting to evade the payment of any tax, he may, for reasons to be

recorded in writing, seize the accounts, registers or documents of such person produced before him and shall grant a receipt for the same, and shall retain the same for so long as may be necessary in connection with any proceedings under this Act or the rules made thereunder for prosecution.

(12) The Commissioner or an officer authorised by him may cause purchase of any goods or services or both by any person authorised by him from the business premises of any taxable person, to check the issue of tax invoices or bills of supply by such taxable person, and on return of goods so purchased by such officer, such taxable person or any person in charge of the business premises shall refund the amount so paid towards the goods after cancelling any tax invoice or bill of supply issued earlier.

Inspection of goods in movement.

68. (1) The Government may require the person in charge of a conveyance carrying any consignment of goods of value exceeding such amount as may be specified to carry with him such documents and such devices as may be prescribed.

(2) The details of documents required to be carried under sub-section (1) shall be validated in such manner as may be prescribed.

(3) Where any conveyance referred to in sub-section (1) is intercepted by the proper officer at any place, he may require the person in charge of the said conveyance to produce the documents prescribed under the said sub-section and devices for verification, and the said person shall be liable to produce the documents and devices and also allow the inspection of goods.

Power to arrest.

69. (1) Where the Commissioner has reasons to believe that a person has committed any offence specified in clause (*a*) or clause (*b*) or clause (*c*) or clause (*d*) of sub-section (1) of section 132 which is punishable under clause (*i*) or (*ii*) of sub-section (1), or sub-section (2) of the said section, he may, by order, authorise any officer of central tax to arrest such person.

(2) Where a person is arrested under sub-section (1) for an offence specified under sub-section (5) of section 132, the officer authorised to arrest the person shall inform such person of the grounds of arrest and produce him before a Magistrate within twenty four hours.

(3) Subject to the provisions of the Code of Criminal Procedure, 1973 (2 of 1974),—

(*a*) where a person is arrested under sub-section (1) for any offence specified under sub-section (4) of section 132, he shall be admitted to bail or in default of bail, forwarded to the custody of the Magistrate;

(*b*) in the case of a non-cognizable and bailable offence, the Deputy Commissioner or the Assistant Commissioner shall, for the purpose of releasing an arrested person on bail or otherwise, have the same powers and be subject to the same provisions as an officer-in-charge of a police station.

Power to summon person to give evidence and produce documents.

70. (1) The proper officer under this Act shall have power to summon any person whose attendance he considers necessary either to give evidence or to produce a document or any other thing in any inquiry in the same manner, as provided in the case of a civil court under the provisions of the Code of Civil Procedure, 1908 (5 of 1908).

[68]**[***(1A) All persons summoned under sub-section (1) shall be bound to attend, either in person or by an authorised representative, as such officer may direct,*

68. Inserted by the Finance (No. 2) Act, 2024, w.e.f. **1-11-2024**.

and the person so appearing shall state the truth during examination or make statements or produce such documents and other things as may be required.]

(2) Every such inquiry referred to in sub-section (1) shall be deemed to be a "judicial proceedings" within the meaning of section 193 and section 228 of the Indian Penal Code (45 of 1860).

Access to business premises.

71. (1) Any officer under this Act, authorised by the proper officer not below the rank of Joint Commissioner, shall have access to any place of business of a registered person to inspect books of account, documents, computers, computer programs, computer software whether installed in a computer or otherwise and such other things as he may require and which may be available at such place, for the purposes of carrying out any audit, scrutiny, verification and checks as may be necessary to safeguard the interest of revenue.

(2) Every person in charge of place referred to in sub-section (1) shall, on demand, make available to the officer authorised under sub-section (1) or the audit party deputed by the proper officer or a cost accountant or chartered accountant nominated under section 66—

(*i*) such records as prepared or maintained by the registered person and declared to the proper officer in such manner as may be prescribed;

(*ii*) trial balance or its equivalent;

(*iii*) statements of annual financial accounts, duly audited, wherever required;

(*iv*) cost audit report, if any, under section 148 of the Companies Act, 2013 (18 of 2013);

(*v*) the income-tax audit report, if any, under section 44AB of the Income-tax Act, 1961 (43 of 1961); and

(*vi*) any other relevant record,

for the scrutiny by the officer or audit party or the chartered accountant or cost accountant within a period not exceeding fifteen working days from the day when such demand is made, or such further period as may be allowed by the said officer or the audit party or the chartered accountant or cost accountant.

Officers to assist proper officers.

72. (1) All officers of Police, Railways, Customs, and those officers engaged in the collection of land revenue, including village officers, officers of State tax and officers of Union territory tax shall assist the proper officers in the implementation of this Act.

(2) The Government may, by notification, empower and require any other class of officers to assist the proper officers in the implementation of this Act when called upon to do so by the Commissioner.

CHAPTER XV

DEMANDS AND RECOVERY

Determination of tax [69][, *pertaining to the period up to Financial Year 2023-24,*] not paid or short paid or erroneously refunded or input tax credit wrongly availed or utilised for any reason other than fraud or any wilful misstatement or suppression of facts.

73. (1) Where it appears to the proper officer that any tax has not been paid or short paid or erroneously refunded, or where input tax credit has been wrongly availed or utilised for any reason, other than the reason of fraud or any wilful-misstatement or suppression of facts to evade tax, he shall serve notice on the person chargeable with tax which has not been so paid or which has been so short paid or to whom the refund has erroneously been made, or who has wrongly availed or utilised input tax credit,

69. Inserted by the Finance (No. 2) Act, 2024, w.e.f. **1-11-2024**.

requiring him to show cause as to why he should not pay the amount specified in the notice along with interest payable thereon under section 50 and a penalty leviable under the provisions of this Act or the rules made thereunder.

(2) The proper officer shall issue the notice under sub-section (1) at least three months prior to the time limit specified in sub-section (10) for issuance of order.

(3) Where a notice has been issued for any period under sub-section (1), the proper officer may serve a statement, containing the details of tax not paid or short paid or erroneously refunded or input tax credit wrongly availed or utilised for such periods other than those covered under sub-section (1), on the person chargeable with tax.

(4) The service of such statement shall be deemed to be service of notice on such person under sub-section (1), subject to the condition that the grounds relied upon for such tax periods other than those covered under sub-section (1) are the same as are mentioned in the earlier notice.

(5) The person chargeable with tax may, before service of notice under sub-section (1) or, as the case may be, the statement under sub-section (3), pay the amount of tax along with interest payable thereon under section 50 on the basis of his own ascertainment of such tax or the tax as ascertained by the proper officer and inform the proper officer in writing of such payment.

(6) The proper officer, on receipt of such information, shall not serve any notice under sub-section (1) or, as the case may be, the statement under sub-section (3), in respect of the tax so paid or any penalty payable under the provisions of this Act or the rules made thereunder.

(7) Where the proper officer is of the opinion that the amount paid under sub-section (5) falls short of the amount actually payable, he shall proceed to

issue the notice as provided for in sub-section (1) in respect of such amount which falls short of the amount actually payable.

(8) Where any person chargeable with tax under sub-section (1) or sub-section (3) pays the said tax along with interest payable under section 50 within thirty days of issue of show cause notice, no penalty shall be payable and all proceedings in respect of the said notice shall be deemed to be concluded.

(9) The proper officer shall, after considering the representation, if any, made by person chargeable with tax, determine the amount of tax, interest and a penalty equivalent to ten per cent of tax or ten thousand rupees, whichever is higher, due from such person and issue an order.

(10) The proper officer shall issue the order under sub-section (9) within three years from the due date for furnishing of annual return for the financial year to which the tax not paid or short paid or input tax credit wrongly availed or utilised relates to or within three years from the date of erroneous refund.

(11) Notwithstanding anything contained in sub-section (6) or sub-section (8), penalty under sub-section (9) shall be payable where any amount of self-assessed tax or any amount collected as tax has not been paid within a period of thirty days from the due date of payment of such tax.

[70-71][*(12) The provisions of this section shall be applicable for determination of tax pertaining to the period up to Financial Year 2023-24.*]

Determination of tax [70-71][, *pertaining to the period up to Financial Year 2023-24,*] not paid or short paid or erroneously refunded or input tax credit

70-71. Inserted by the Finance (No. 2) Act, 2024, w.e.f. **1-11-2024**.

wrongly availed or utilized by reason of fraud or any wilful-misstatement or suppression of facts.

74. (1) Where it appears to the proper officer that any tax has not been paid or short paid or erroneously refunded or where input tax credit has been wrongly availed or utilised by reason of fraud, or any wilful-misstatement or suppression of facts to evade tax, he shall serve notice on the person chargeable with tax which has not been so paid or which has been so short paid or to whom the refund has erroneously been made, or who has wrongly availed or utilised input tax credit, requiring him to show cause as to why he should not pay the amount specified in the notice along with interest payable thereon under section 50 and a penalty equivalent to the tax specified in the notice.

(2) The proper officer shall issue the notice under sub-section (1) at least six months prior to the time limit specified in sub-section (10) for issuance of order.

(3) Where a notice has been issued for any period under sub-section (1), the proper officer may serve a statement, containing the details of tax not paid or short paid or erroneously refunded or input tax credit wrongly availed or utilised for such periods other than those covered under sub-section (1), on the person chargeable with tax.

(4) The service of statement under sub-section (3) shall be deemed to be service of notice under sub-section (1) of section 73, subject to the condition that the grounds relied upon in the said statement, except the ground of fraud, or any wilful-misstatement or suppression of facts to evade tax, for periods other than those covered under sub-section (1) are the same as are mentioned in the earlier notice.

(5) The person chargeable with tax may, before service of notice under sub-section (1), pay the amount of tax along with interest payable under section 50 and a penalty equivalent to fifteen per cent of such tax on

the basis of his own ascertainment of such tax or the tax as ascertained by the proper officer and inform the proper officer in writing of such payment.

(6) The proper officer, on receipt of such information, shall not serve any notice under sub-section (1), in respect of the tax so paid or any penalty payable under the provisions of this Act or the rules made thereunder.

(7) Where the proper officer is of the opinion that the amount paid under sub-section (5) falls short of the amount actually payable, he shall proceed to issue the notice as provided for in sub-section (1) in respect of such amount which falls short of the amount actually payable.

(8) Where any person chargeable with tax under sub-section (1) pays the said tax along with interest payable under section 50 and a penalty equivalent to twenty-five per cent of such tax within thirty days of issue of the notice, all proceedings in respect of the said notice shall be deemed to be concluded.

(9) The proper officer shall, after considering the representation, if any, made by the person chargeable with tax, determine the amount of tax, interest and penalty due from such person and issue an order.

(10) The proper officer shall issue the order under sub-section (9) within a period of five years from the due date for furnishing of annual return for the financial year to which the tax not paid or short paid or input tax credit wrongly availed or utilised relates to or within five years from the date of erroneous refund.

(11) Where any person served with an order issued under sub-section (9) pays the tax along with interest payable thereon under section 50 and a penalty equivalent to fifty per cent of such tax within thirty days of communication of the order, all proceedings in respect of the said notice shall be deemed to be concluded.

[72]**[***(12) The provisions of this section shall be applicable for determination of tax pertaining to the period up to Financial Year 2023-24.***]**

Explanation 1.— For the purposes of section 73 and this section,—

(*i*) the expression "all proceedings in respect of the said notice" shall not include proceedings under section 132;

(*ii*) where the notice under the same proceedings is issued to the main person liable to pay tax and some other persons, and such proceedings against the main person have been concluded under section 73 or section 74, the proceedings against all the persons liable to pay penalty under [73][sections 122 and 125] are deemed to be concluded.

Explanation 2.—[74]**[*****]**

[75]**[Determination of tax not paid or short paid or erroneously refunded or input tax credit wrongly availed or utilised for any reason pertaining to Financial Year 2024-25 onward.**

74A. *(1) Where it appears to the proper officer that any tax has not been paid or short paid or erroneously refunded, or where input tax credit has been wrongly availed or utilised, he shall serve notice on the person chargeable with tax which has not been so paid or which has been so short paid or to whom the refund has erroneously been made, or who has wrongly availed or utilised input tax credit, requiring him to show cause as to why he should not pay the amount specified in*

72. Inserted by the Finance (No. 2) Act, 2024, w.e.f. **1-11-2024**.

73. Substituted for "sections 122, 125, 129 and 130" by the Finance Act, 2021, w.e.f. 1-1-2022.

74. Omitted by the Finance (No. 2) Act, 2024, w.e.f. **1-11-2024**.

75. Inserted, *ibid.*

the notice along with interest payable thereon under section 50 and a penalty leviable under the provisions of this Act or the rules made thereunder:

Provided *that no notice shall be issued, if the tax which has not been paid or short paid or erroneously refunded or where input tax credit has been wrongly availed or utilised in a financial year is less than one thousand rupees.*

(2) The proper officer shall issue the notice under sub-section (1) within forty-two months from the due date for furnishing of annual return for the financial year to which the tax not paid or short paid or input tax credit wrongly availed or utilised relates to or within forty-two months from the date of erroneous refund.

(3) Where a notice has been issued for any period under sub-section (1), the proper officer may serve a statement, containing the details of tax not paid or short paid or erroneously refunded or input tax credit wrongly availed or utilised for such periods other than those covered under sub-section (1), on the person chargeable with tax.

(4) The service of such statement shall be deemed to be service of notice on such person under sub-section (1), subject to the condition that the grounds relied upon for such tax periods other than those covered under sub-section (1) are the same as are mentioned in the earlier notice.

(5) The penalty in case where any tax which has not been paid or short paid or erroneously refunded, or where input tax credit has been wrongly availed or utilised,—

- (i) *for any reason, other than the reason of fraud or any wilful-misstatement or suppression of facts to evade tax, shall be equivalent to ten per cent of tax due from such person or ten thousand rupees, whichever is higher;*
- (ii) *for the reason of fraud or any wilful-misstatement or suppression of facts to evade tax shall be equivalent to the tax due from such person.*

(6) The proper officer shall, after considering the representation, if any, made by the person chargeable with tax, determine the amount of tax, interest and penalty due from such person and issue an order.

(7) The proper officer shall issue the order under sub-section (6) within twelve months from the date of issuance of notice specified in sub-section (2):

Provided *that where the proper officer is not able to issue the order within the specified period, the Commissioner, or an officer authorised by the Commissioner senior in rank to the proper officer but not below the rank of Joint Commissioner of Central Tax, may, having regard to the reasons for delay in issuance of the order under sub-section (6), to be recorded in writing, before the expiry of the specified period, extend the said period further by a maximum of six months.*

(8) The person chargeable with tax where any tax has not been paid or short paid or erroneously refunded, or where input tax credit has been wrongly availed or utilised for any reason, other than the reason of fraud or any wilful misstatement or suppression of facts to evade tax, may, —

(i) *before service of notice under sub-section (1), pay the amount of tax along with interest payable under section 50 of such tax on the basis of his own ascertainment of such tax or the tax as ascertained by the proper officer and inform the proper officer in writing of such payment, and the proper officer, on receipt of such information shall not serve any notice under sub-section (1) or the statement under sub-section (3), as the case may be, in respect of the tax so paid or any penalty payable under the provisions of this Act or the rules made thereunder;*

(ii) *pay the said tax along with interest payable under section 50 within sixty days of issue of show cause notice, and on doing so, no penalty shall be payable and all proceedings in respect of the said notice shall be deemed to be concluded.*

(9) The person chargeable with tax, where any tax has not been paid or short paid or erroneously refunded or where input tax credit has been wrongly availed or utilised by reason of fraud, or any wilful-misstatement or suppression of facts to evade tax, may,—

(i) *before service of notice under sub-section (1), pay the amount of tax along with interest payable under section 50 and a penalty equivalent to fifteen per cent of such tax on the basis of his own ascertainment of such tax or the tax as ascertained by the proper officer and inform the proper officer in writing of such payment, and the proper officer, on receipt of such information, shall not serve any notice under sub-section (1), in respect of the tax so paid or any penalty payable under the provisions of this Act or the rules made thereunder;*

(ii) *pay the said tax along with interest payable under section 50 and a penalty equivalent to twenty-five per cent of such tax within sixty days of issue of the notice, and on doing so, all proceedings in respect of the said notice shall be deemed to be concluded;*

(iii) *pay the tax along with interest payable thereon under section 50 and a penalty equivalent to fifty per cent of such tax within sixty days of communication of the order, and on doing so, all proceedings in respect of the said notice shall be deemed to be concluded.*

(10) Where the proper officer is of the opinion that the amount paid under clause (i) *of sub-section (8) or clause* (i) *of sub-section (9) falls short of the amount actually payable, he shall proceed to issue the notice as provided for in sub-section (1) in respect of such amount which falls short of the amount actually payable.*

(11) Notwithstanding anything contained in clause (i) *or clause* (ii) *of sub-section (8), penalty under clause* (i) *of sub-section (5) shall be payable where any amount of self-assessed tax or any amount collected as tax has not been paid within a period of thirty days from the due date of payment of such tax.*

(12) The provisions of this section shall be applicable for determination of tax pertaining to the Financial Year 2024-25 onwards.

Explanation 1.—*For the purposes of this section,—*

- (i) *the expression "all proceedings in respect of the said notice" shall not include proceedings under section 132;*
- (ii) *where the notice under the same proceedings is issued to the main person liable to pay tax and some other persons, and such proceedings against the main person have been concluded under this section, the proceedings against all the persons liable to pay penalty under sections 122 and 125 are deemed to be concluded.*

Explanation 2.—*For the purposes of this Act, the expression "suppression" shall mean non-declaration of facts or information which a taxable person is required to declare in the return, statement, report or any other document furnished under this Act or the rules made thereunder, or failure to furnish any information on being asked for, in writing, by the proper officer.*]

General provisions relating to determination of tax.

75. (1) Where the service of notice or issuance of order is stayed by an order of a court or Appellate Tribunal, the period of such stay shall be excluded in computing the period specified in sub-sections (2) and (10) of section 73 or sub-sections (2) and (10) of section 74 [76][*or sub-sections (2) and (7) of section 74A*], as the case may be.

76. Inserted by the Finance (No. 2) Act, 2024, w.e.f. **1-11-2024**.

(2) Where any Appellate Authority or Appellate Tribunal or court concludes that the notice issued under sub-section (1) of section 74 is not sustainable for the reason that the charges of fraud or any wilful-misstatement or suppression of facts to evade tax has not been established against the person to whom the notice was issued, the proper officer shall determine the tax payable by such person, deeming as if the notice were issued under sub-section (1) of section 73.

[76a]**[***(2A) Where any Appellate Authority or Appellate Tribunal or court concludes that the penalty under clause* (ii) *of sub-section (5) of section 74A is not sustainable for the reason that the charges of fraud or any wilful misstatement or suppression of facts to evade tax has not been established against the person to whom the notice was issued, the penalty shall be payable by such person, under clause* (i) *of sub-section (5) of section 74A.***]**

(3) Where any order is required to be issued in pursuance of the direction of the Appellate Authority or Appellate Tribunal or a court, such order shall be issued within two years from the date of communication of the said direction.

(4) An opportunity of hearing shall be granted where a request is received in writing from the person chargeable with tax or penalty, or where any adverse decision is contemplated against such person.

(5) The proper officer shall, if sufficient cause is shown by the person chargeable with tax, grant time to the said person and adjourn the hearing for reasons to be recorded in writing:

Provided that no such adjournment shall be granted for more than three times to a person during the proceedings.

(6) The proper officer, in his order, shall set out the relevant facts and the basis of his decision.

76a. Inserted by the Finance (No. 2) Act, 2024, w.e.f. **1-11-2024**.

(7) The amount of tax, interest and penalty demanded in the order shall not be in excess of the amount specified in the notice and no demand shall be confirmed on the grounds other than the grounds specified in the notice.

(8) Where the Appellate Authority or Appellate Tribunal or court modifies the amount of tax determined by the proper officer, the amount of interest and penalty shall stand modified accordingly, taking into account the amount of tax so modified.

(9) The interest on the tax short paid or not paid shall be payable whether or not specified in the order determining the tax liability.

[77]**[***(10) The adjudication proceedings shall be deemed to be concluded, if the order is not issued within the period specified in sub-section (10) of section 73 or in sub-section (10) of section 74 or in sub-section (7) of section 74A.***]**

(11) An issue on which the Appellate Authority or the Appellate Tribunal or the High Court has given its decision which is prejudicial to the interest of revenue in some other proceedings and an appeal to the Appellate Tribunal or the High Court or the Supreme Court against such decision of the Appellate Authority or the Appellate Tribunal or the High Court is pending, the period spent between the date of the decision of the Appellate Authority and that of the Appellate Tribunal or the date of decision of the Appellate Tribunal and that of the High Court or the date of the decision of the High Court and that of the Supreme Court shall be excluded in computing the period referred to in sub-section (10) of section 73 or sub-section (10) of section 74 [78]**[***or sub-section (7) of section 74A***]** where proceedings are initiated by way of issue of a show cause notice under the said sections.

77. Substituted by the Finance (No. 2) Act, 2024, w.e.f. **1-11-2024.**

78. Inserted, *ibid.*

(12) Notwithstanding anything contained in section 73 or section 74 [79][*or section 74A*], where any amount of self-assessed tax in accordance with a return furnished under section 39 remains unpaid, either wholly or partly, or any amount of interest payable on such tax remains unpaid, the same shall be recovered under the provisions of section 79.

[80][*Explanation*.—For the purposes of this sub-section, the expression "self-assessed tax" shall include the tax payable in respect of details of outward supplies furnished under section 37, but not included in the return furnished under section 39.]

(13) Where any penalty is imposed under section 73 or section 74 [79][*or section 74A*], no penalty for the same act or omission shall be imposed on the same person under any other provision of this Act.

Tax collected but not paid to Government.

76. (1) Notwithstanding anything to the contrary contained in any order or direction of any Appellate Authority or Appellate Tribunal or court or in any other provisions of this Act or the rules made thereunder or any other law for the time being in force, every person who has collected from any other person any amount as representing the tax under this Act, and has not paid the said amount to the Government, shall forthwith pay the said amount to the Government, irrespective of whether the supplies in respect of which such amount was collected are taxable or not.

(2) Where any amount is required to be paid to the Government under sub-section (1), and which has not been so paid, the proper officer may serve on the person liable to pay such amount a notice requiring him to show cause as to why the said amount as specified in the notice, should not be paid by him to the Government and why a penalty equivalent to the

---

79. Inserted by the Finance (No. 2) Act, 2024, w.e.f. **1-11-2024**.

80. Inserted by the Finance Act, 2021, w.e.f. 1-1-2022.

amount specified in the notice should not be imposed on him under the provisions of this Act.

(3) The proper officer shall, after considering the representation, if any, made by the person on whom the notice is served under sub-section (2), determine the amount due from such person and thereupon such person shall pay the amount so determined.

(4) The person referred to in sub-section (1) shall in addition to paying the amount referred to in sub-section (1) or sub-section (3) also be liable to pay interest thereon at the rate specified under section 50 from the date such amount was collected by him to the date such amount is paid by him to the Government.

(5) An opportunity of hearing shall be granted where a request is received in writing from the person to whom the notice was issued to show cause.

(6) The proper officer shall issue an order within one year from the date of issue of the notice.

(7) Where the issuance of order is stayed by an order of the court or Appellate Tribunal, the period of such stay shall be excluded in computing the period of one year.

(8) The proper officer, in his order, shall set out the relevant facts and the basis of his decision.

(9) The amount paid to the Government under sub-section (1) or sub-section (3) shall be adjusted against the tax payable, if any, by the person in relation to the supplies referred to in sub-section (1).

(10) Where any surplus is left after the adjustment under sub-section (9), the amount of such surplus shall either be credited to the Fund or refunded to the person who has borne the incidence of such amount.

(11) The person who has borne the incidence of the amount, may apply for the refund of the same in accordance with the provisions of section 54.

Tax wrongfully collected and paid to Central Government or State Government.

77. (1) A registered person who has paid the Central tax and State tax or, as the case may be, the central tax and the Union territory tax on a transaction considered by him to be an intra-State supply, but which is subsequently held to be an inter-State supply, shall be refunded the amount of taxes so paid in such manner and subject to such conditions as may be prescribed.

(2) A registered person who has paid integrated tax on a transaction considered by him to be an inter-State supply, but which is subsequently held to be an intra-State supply, shall not be required to pay any interest on the amount of Central tax and State tax or, as the case may be, the Central tax and the Union territory tax payable.

Initiation of recovery proceedings.

78. Any amount payable by a taxable person in pursuance of an order passed under this Act shall be paid by such person within a period of three months from the date of service of such order failing which recovery proceedings shall be initiated:

Provided that where the proper officer considers it expedient in the interest of revenue, he may, for reasons to be recorded in writing, require the said taxable person to make such payment within such period less than a period of three months as may be specified by him.

Recovery of tax.

79. (1) Where any amount payable by a person to the Government under any of the provisions of this Act or the rules made thereunder is not paid, the proper officer shall proceed to recover the amount by one or more of the following modes, namely:—

(*a*) the proper officer may deduct or may require any other specified officer to deduct the amount so payable from any money owing to such person which may be under the control of the proper officer or such other specified officer;

(*b*) the proper officer may recover or may require any other specified officer to recover the amount so payable by detaining and selling any goods belonging to such person which are under the control of the proper officer or such other specified officer;

(*c*) (*i*) the proper officer may, by a notice in writing, require any other person from whom money is due or may become due to such person or who holds or may subsequently hold money for or on account of such person, to pay to the Government either forthwith upon the money becoming due or being held, or within the time specified in the notice not being before the money becomes due or is held, so much of the money as is sufficient to pay the amount due from such person or the whole of the money when it is equal to or less than that amount;

(*ii*) every person to whom the notice is issued under sub-clause (*i*) shall be bound to comply with such notice, and in particular, where any such notice is issued to a post office, banking company or an insurer, it shall not be necessary to produce any pass book, deposit receipt, policy or any other document for the purpose of any entry, endorsement or the like being made before payment is made, notwithstanding any rule, practice or requirement to the contrary;

(*iii*) in case the person to whom a notice under sub-clause (*i*) has been issued, fails to make the payment in pursuance thereof to the Government, he shall be deemed to be a defaulter in respect of the amount specified in the notice and all the consequences of this Act or the rules made thereunder shall follow;

(*iv*) the officer issuing a notice under sub-clause (*i*) may, at any time, amend or revoke such notice or extend the time for making any payment in pursuance of the notice;

(*v*) any person making any payment in compliance with a notice issued under sub-clause (*i*) shall be deemed to have made the payment under the authority of the person in default and such payment being credited to the Government shall be deemed to constitute a good and sufficient discharge of the liability of such person to the person in default to the extent of the amount specified in the receipt;

(*vi*) any person discharging any liability to the person in default after service on him of the notice issued under sub-clause (*i*) shall be personally liable to the Government to the extent of the liability discharged or to the extent of the liability of the person in default for tax, interest and penalty, whichever is less;

(*vii*) where a person on whom a notice is served under sub-clause (*i*) proves to the satisfaction of the officer issuing the notice that the money demanded or any part thereof was not due to the person in default or that he did not hold any money for or on account of the person in default, at the time the notice was served on him, nor is the money demanded or any part thereof, likely to become due to the said person or be held for or on account of such person, nothing contained in this section shall be deemed to require the person on whom the notice has been served to pay to the Government any such money or part thereof;

(*d*) the proper officer may, in accordance with the rules to be made in this behalf, distrain any movable or immovable property belonging to or under the control of such person, and detain the same until the amount payable is paid; and in case, any part of the said amount payable or of the cost of the distress or keeping of the property, remains unpaid for a period of thirty days next after any such distress, may cause the said property to be sold and with the proceeds of such sale, may satisfy the amount payable and the costs including cost of sale remaining unpaid and shall render the surplus amount, if any, to such person;

(*e*) the proper officer may prepare a certificate signed by him specifying the amount due from such person and send it to the Collector of the district in which such person owns any property or resides or carries on his business or to any officer authorised by the Government and the said Collector or the said officer, on receipt of such certificate, shall proceed to recover from such person the amount specified thereunder as if it were an arrear of land revenue;

(*f*) notwithstanding anything contained in the Code of Criminal Procedure, 1973 (2 of 1974), the proper officer may file an application to the appropriate Magistrate and such Magistrate shall proceed to recover from such person the amount specified thereunder as if it were a fine imposed by him.

(2) Where the terms of any bond or other instrument executed under this Act or any rules or regulations made thereunder provide that any amount due under such instrument may be recovered in the manner laid down in sub-section (1), the amount may, without prejudice to any other mode of recovery, be recovered in accordance with the provisions of that sub-section.

(3) Where any amount of tax, interest or penalty is payable by a person to the Government under any of the provisions of this Act or the rules made thereunder and which remains unpaid, the proper officer of State tax or Union territory tax, during the course of recovery of said tax arrears, may recover the amount from the said person as if it were an arrear of State tax or Union territory tax and credit the amount so recovered to the account of the Government.

(4) Where the amount recovered under sub-section (3) is less than the amount due to the Central Government and State Government, the amount to be credited to the account of the respective Governments shall be in proportion to the amount due to each such Government.

[81][*Explanation.*—For the purposes of this section, the word person shall include "distinct persons" as referred to in sub-section (4) or, as the case may be, sub-section (5) of section 25.]

Payment of tax and other amount in instalments.

80. On an application filed by a taxable person, the Commissioner may, for reasons to be recorded in writing, extend the time for payment or allow payment of any amount due under this Act, other than the amount due as per the liability self-assessed in any return, by such person in monthly instalments not exceeding twenty four, subject to payment of interest under section 50 and subject to such conditions and limitations as may be prescribed:

Provided that where there is default in payment of any one instalment on its due date, the whole outstanding balance payable on such date shall become due and payable forthwith and shall, without any further notice being served on the person, be liable for recovery.

81. Inserted by the Central Goods and Services Tax (Amendment) Act, 2018, w.e.f. 1-2-2019.

Transfer of property to be void in certain cases.

81. Where a person, after any amount has become due from him, creates a charge on or parts with the property belonging to him or in his possession by way of sale, mortgage, exchange, or any other mode of transfer whatsoever of any of his properties in favour of any other person with the intention of defrauding the Government revenue, such charge or transfer shall be void as against any claim in respect of any tax or any other sum payable by the said person:

Provided that, such charge or transfer shall not be void if it is made for adequate consideration, in good faith and without notice of the pendency of such proceedings under this Act or without notice of such tax or other sum payable by the said person, or with the previous permission of the proper officer.

Tax to be first charge on property.

82. Notwithstanding anything to the contrary contained in any law for the time being in force, save as otherwise provided in the Insolvency and Bankruptcy Code, 2016 (31 of 2016), any amount payable by a taxable person or any other person on account of tax, interest or penalty which he is liable to pay to the Government shall be a first charge on the property of such taxable person or such person.

Provisional attachment to protect revenue in certain cases.

83. [82][(1) Where, after the initiation of any proceeding under Chapter XII, Chapter XIV or Chapter XV, the Commissioner is of the opinion that for the purpose of protecting the interest of the Government revenue it is necessary so to do, he may, by order in writing, attach provisionally, any property, including bank account, belonging to the taxable person or any person specified in sub-section (1A) of section 122, in such manner as may be prescribed.]

---

82. Substituted by the Finance Act, 2021, w.e.f. 1-1-2022.

(2) Every such provisional attachment shall cease to have effect after the expiry of a period of one year from the date of the order made under sub-section (1).

Continuation and validation of certain recovery proceedings.

84. Where any notice of demand in respect of any tax, penalty, interest or any other amount payable under this Act, (hereafter in this section referred to as "Government dues"), is served upon any taxable person or any other person and any appeal or revision application is filed or any other proceeding is initiated in respect of such Government dues, then—

(*a*) where such Government dues are enhanced in such appeal, revision or other proceedings, the Commissioner shall serve upon the taxable person or any other person another notice of demand in respect of the amount by which such Government dues are enhanced and any recovery proceedings in relation to such Government dues as are covered by the notice of demand served upon him before the disposal of such appeal, revision or other proceedings may, without the service of any fresh notice of demand, be continued from the stage at which such proceedings stood immediately before such disposal;

(*b*) where such Government dues are reduced in such appeal, revision or in other proceedings—

(*i*) it shall not be necessary for the Commissioner to serve upon the taxable person a fresh notice of demand;

(*ii*) the Commissioner shall give intimation of such reduction to him and to the appropriate authority with whom recovery proceedings is pending;

(*iii*) any recovery proceedings initiated on the basis of the demand served upon him prior to the disposal of such appeal, revision or other proceedings may be continued in relation to the amount so reduced from the stage at which such proceedings stood immediately before such disposal.

CHAPTER XVI

LIABILITY TO PAY IN CERTAIN CASES

Liability in case of transfer of business.

85. (1) Where a taxable person, liable to pay tax under this Act, transfers his business in whole or in part, by sale, gift, lease, leave and license, hire or in any other manner whatsoever, the taxable person and the person to whom the business is so transferred shall, jointly and severally, be liable wholly or to the extent of such transfer, to pay the tax, interest or any penalty due from the taxable person upto the time of such transfer, whether such tax, interest or penalty has been determined before such transfer, but has remained unpaid or is determined thereafter.

(2) Where the transferee of a business referred to in sub-section (1) carries on such business either in his own name or in some other name, he shall be liable to pay tax on the supply of goods or services or both effected by him with effect from the date of such transfer and shall, if he is a registered person under this Act, apply within the prescribed time for amendment of his certificate of registration.

Liability of agent and principal.

86. Where an agent supplies or receives any taxable goods on behalf of his principal, such agent and his principal shall, jointly and severally, be liable to pay the tax payable on such goods under this Act.

Liability in case of amalgamation or merger of companies.

87. (1) When two or more companies are amalgamated or merged in pursuance of an order of court or of Tribunal or otherwise and the order is to take effect from a date earlier to the date of the order and any two or more of such companies have supplied or received any goods or services or both to or from each other during the period commencing on the date from which the order takes effect till the date of the order, then such transactions of supply and receipt shall be included in the turnover of supply or receipt of the respective companies and they shall be liable to pay tax accordingly.

(2) Notwithstanding anything contained in the said order, for the purposes of this Act, the said two or more companies shall be treated as distinct companies for the period up to the date of the said order and the registration certificates of the said companies shall be cancelled with effect from the date of the said order.

Liability in case of company in liquidation.

88. (1) When any company is being wound up whether under the orders of a court or Tribunal or otherwise, every person appointed as receiver of any assets of a company (hereafter in this section referred to as the "liquidator"), shall, within thirty days after his appointment, give intimation of his appointment to the Commissioner.

(2) The Commissioner shall, after making such inquiry or calling for such information as he may deem fit, notify the liquidator within three months from the date on which he receives intimation of the appointment of the liquidator, the amount which in the opinion of the Commissioner would be sufficient to provide for any tax, interest or penalty which is then, or is likely thereafter to become, payable by the company.

(3) When any private company is wound up and any tax, interest or penalty determined under this Act on the company for any period, whether before or in the course of or after its liquidation, cannot be recovered, then every person who was a director of such company at any time during the period for which the tax was due shall, jointly and severally, be liable for the

payment of such tax, interest or penalty, unless he proves to the satisfaction of the Commissioner that such non-recovery cannot be attributed to any gross neglect, misfeasance or breach of duty on his part in relation to the affairs of the company.

Liability of directors of private company.

89. (1) Notwithstanding anything contained in the Companies Act, 2013 (18 of 2013), where any tax, interest or penalty due from a private company in respect of any supply of goods or services or both for any period cannot be recovered, then, every person who was a director of the private company during such period shall, jointly and severally, be liable for the payment of such tax, interest or penalty unless he proves that the non-recovery cannot be attributed to any gross neglect, misfeasance or breach of duty on his part in relation to the affairs of the company.

(2) Where a private company is converted into a public company and the tax, interest or penalty in respect of any supply of goods or services or both for any period during which such company was a private company cannot be recovered before such conversion, then, nothing contained in sub-section (1) shall apply to any person who was a director of such private company in relation to any tax, interest or penalty in respect of such supply of goods or services or both of such private company:

Provided that nothing contained in this sub-section shall apply to any personal penalty imposed on such director.

Liability of partners of firm to pay tax.

90. Notwithstanding any contract to the contrary and any other law for the time being in force, where any firm is liable to pay any tax, interest or penalty under this Act, the firm and each of the partners of the firm shall, jointly and severally, be liable for such payment:

Provided that where any partner retires from the firm, he or the firm, shall intimate the date of retirement of the said partner to the Commissioner by a notice in that behalf in writing and such partner shall be liable to pay tax, interest or penalty due up to the date of his retirement whether determined or not, on that date:

Provided further that if no such intimation is given within one month from the date of retirement, the liability of such partner under the first proviso shall continue until the date on which such intimation is received by the Commissioner.

Liability of guardians, trustees, etc.

91. Where the business in respect of which any tax, interest or penalty is payable under this Act is carried on by any guardian, trustee or agent of a minor or other incapacitated person on behalf of and for the benefit of such minor or other incapacitated person, the tax, interest or penalty shall be levied upon and recoverable from such guardian, trustee or agent in like manner and to the same extent as it would be determined and recoverable from any such minor or other incapacitated person, as if he were a major or capacitated person and as if he were conducting the business himself, and all the provisions of this Act or the rules made thereunder shall apply accordingly.

Liability of Court of Wards, etc.

92. Where the estate or any portion of the estate of a taxable person owning a business in respect of which any tax, interest or penalty is payable under this Act is under the control of the Court of Wards, the Administrator General, the Official Trustee or any receiver or manager (including any person, whatever be his designation, who in fact manages the business) appointed by or under any order of a court, the tax, interest or penalty shall be levied upon and be recoverable from such Court of Wards, Administrator General, Official Trustee, receiver or manager in like manner and to the same extent as it would be determined and be recoverable from the taxable person as if he were conducting the business himself, and all the provisions of this Act or the rules made thereunder shall apply accordingly.

Special provisions regarding liability to pay tax, interest or penalty in certain cases.

93. (1) Save as otherwise provided in the Insolvency and Bankruptcy Code, 2016 (31 of 2016), where a person, liable to pay tax, interest or penalty under this Act, dies, then—

(*a*) if a business carried on by the person is continued after his death by his legal representative or any other person, such legal representative or other person, shall be liable to pay tax, interest or penalty due from such person under this Act; and

(*b*) if the business carried on by the person is discontinued, whether before or after his death, his legal representative shall be liable to pay, out of the estate of the deceased, to the extent to which the estate is capable of meeting the charge, the tax, interest or penalty due from such person under this Act,

whether such tax, interest or penalty has been determined before his death but has remained unpaid or is determined after his death.

(2) Save as otherwise provided in the Insolvency and Bankruptcy Code, 2016 (31 of 2016), where a taxable person, liable to pay tax, interest or penalty under this Act, is a Hindu Undivided Family or an association of persons and the property of the Hindu Undivided Family or the association of persons is partitioned amongst the various members or groups of members, then, each member or group of members shall, jointly and severally, be liable to pay the tax, interest or penalty due from the taxable person under this Act up to the time of the partition whether such tax, penalty or interest has been determined before partition but has remained unpaid or is determined after the partition.

(3) Save as otherwise provided in the Insolvency and Bankruptcy Code, 2016 (31 of 2016), where a taxable person, liable to pay tax, interest or penalty under this Act, is a firm, and the firm is dissolved, then, every person who was a partner shall, jointly and severally, be liable to pay the tax, interest or penalty due from the firm under this Act up to the time of dissolution whether such tax, interest or penalty has been determined before the dissolution, but has remained unpaid or is determined after dissolution.

(4) Save as otherwise provided in the Insolvency and Bankruptcy Code, 2016 (31 of 2016), where a taxable person liable to pay tax, interest or penalty under this Act,—

(*a*) is the guardian of a ward on whose behalf the business is carried on by the guardian; or

(*b*) is a trustee who carries on the business under a trust for a beneficiary,

then, if the guardianship or trust is terminated, the ward or the beneficiary shall be liable to pay the tax, interest or penalty due from the taxable person upto the time of the termination of the guardianship or trust, whether such tax, interest or penalty has been determined before the termination of guardianship or trust but has remained unpaid or is determined thereafter.

Liability in other cases.

94. (1) Where a taxable person is a firm or an association of persons or a Hindu Undivided Family and such firm, association or family has discontinued business—

(*a*) the tax, interest or penalty payable under this Act by such firm, association or family up to the date of such discontinuance may be determined as if no such discontinuance had taken place; and (*b*) every person who, at the time of such discontinuance, was a partner of such firm, or a member of such association or family, shall, notwithstanding such discontinuance, jointly and severally, be liable for the payment of tax and interest determined and penalty imposed and payable by such firm, association or family, whether such tax and interest has been determined or penalty imposed prior to or after such discontinuance and subject as aforesaid, the provisions of this Act shall, so far as may be, apply as if every such person or partner or member were himself a taxable person.

(2) Where a change has occurred in the constitution of a firm or an association of persons, the partners of the firm or members of association, as it existed before and as it exists after the reconstitution, shall, without prejudice to the provisions of section 90, jointly and severally, be liable to pay tax, interest or penalty due from such firm or association for any period before its reconstitution.

(3) The provisions of sub-section (1) shall, so far as may be, apply where the taxable person, being a firm or association of persons is dissolved or where the taxable person, being a Hindu Undivided Family, has effected partition with respect to the business carried on by it and accordingly references in that sub-section to discontinuance shall be construed as reference to dissolution or to partition.

Explanation.—For the purposes of this Chapter,—

(*i*) a "Limited Liability Partnership" formed and registered under the provisions of the Limited Liability Partnership Act, 2008 (6 of 2009) shall also be considered as a firm;

(*ii*) "court" means the District Court, High Court or Supreme Court.

CHAPTER XVII

ADVANCE RULING

Definitions.

95. In this Chapter, unless the context otherwise requires,—

(*a*) "advance ruling" means a decision provided by the Authority or the Appellate Authority [83-84]**[***or the National Appellate Authority***]** to an applicant on matters or on questions specified in sub-section (2) of section 97 or sub-section (1) of section 100 [83-84]**[***or of section 101C***]**, in relation to the supply of goods or services or both being undertaken or proposed to be undertaken by the applicant;

(*b*) "Appellate Authority" means the Appellate Authority for Advance Ruling referred to in section 99;

(*c*) "applicant" means any person registered or desirous of obtaining registration under this Act;

(*d*) "application" means an application made to the Authority under sub-section (1) of section 97;

(*e*) "Authority" means the Authority for Advance Ruling referred to in section 96;

[83-84]**[***(f) "National Appellate Authority" means the National Appellate Authority for Advance Ruling referred to in section 101A.***]**

Authority for advance ruling.

96. Subject to the provisions of this Chapter, for the purposes of this Act, the Authority for advance ruling constituted under the provisions of a State Goods

83-84. Inserted by the Finance (No. 2) Act, 2019, with effect from a date yet to be notified.

and Services Tax Act or Union Territory Goods and Services Tax Act shall be deemed to be the Authority for advance ruling in respect of that State or Union territory.

Application for advance ruling.

97. (1) An applicant desirous of obtaining an advance ruling under this Chapter may make an application in such form and manner and accompanied by such fee as may be prescribed, stating the question on which the advance ruling is sought.

(2) The question on which the advance ruling is sought under this Act, shall be in respect of,—

(*a*) classification of any goods or services or both;

(*b*) applicability of a notification issued under the provisions of this Act;

(*c*) determination of time and value of supply of goods or services or both;

(*d*) admissibility of input tax credit of tax paid or deemed to have been paid;

(*e*) determination of the liability to pay tax on any goods or services or both;

(*f*) whether applicant is required to be registered;

(*g*) whether any particular thing done by the applicant with respect to any goods or services or both amounts to or results in a supply of goods or services or both, within the meaning of that term.

Procedure on receipt of application.

98. (1) On receipt of an application, the Authority shall cause a copy thereof to be forwarded to the concerned officer and, if necessary, call upon him to furnish the relevant records:

Provided that where any records have been called for by the Authority in any case, such records shall, as soon as possible, be returned to the said concerned officer.

(2) The Authority may, after examining the application and the records called for and after hearing the applicant or his authorised representative and the concerned officer or his authorised representative, by order, either admit or reject the application:

Provided that the Authority shall not admit the application where the question raised in the application is already pending or decided in any proceedings in the case of an applicant under any of the provisions of this Act:

Provided further that no application shall be rejected under this sub-section unless an opportunity of hearing has been given to the applicant:

Provided also that where the application is rejected, the reasons for such rejection shall be specified in the order.

(3) A copy of every order made under sub-section (2) shall be sent to the applicant and to the concerned officer.

(4) Where an application is admitted under sub-section (2), the Authority shall, after examining such further material as may be placed before it by the applicant or obtained by the Authority and after providing an opportunity of being heard to the applicant or his authorised representative as well as to the concerned officer or his authorised representative, pronounce its advance ruling on the question specified in the application.

(5) Where the members of the Authority differ on any question on which the advance ruling is sought, they shall state the point or points on which they differ and make a reference to the Appellate Authority for hearing and decision on such question.

(6) The Authority shall pronounce its advance ruling in writing within ninety days from the date of receipt of application.

(7) A copy of the advance ruling pronounced by the Authority duly signed by the members and certified in such manner as may be prescribed shall be sent to the applicant, the concerned officer and the jurisdictional officer after such pronouncement.

Appellate Authority for Advance Ruling.

99. Subject to the provisions of this Chapter, for the purposes of this Act, the Appellate Authority for Advance Ruling constituted under the provisions of a State Goods and Services Tax Act or a Union Territory Goods and Services Tax Act shall be deemed to be the Appellate Authority in respect of that State or Union territory.

Appeal to Appellate Authority.

100. (1) The concerned officer, the jurisdictional officer or an applicant aggrieved by any advance ruling pronounced under sub-section (4) of section 98, may appeal to the Appellate Authority.

(2) Every appeal under this section shall be filed within a period of thirty days from the date on which the ruling sought to be appealed against is communicated to the concerned officer, the jurisdictional officer and the applicant:

Provided that the Appellate Authority may, if it is satisfied that the appellant was prevented by a sufficient cause from presenting the appeal within the said period of thirty days, allow it to be presented within a further period not exceeding thirty days.

(3) Every appeal under this section shall be in such form, accompanied by such fee and verified in such manner as may be prescribed.

Orders of Appellate Authority.

101. (1) The Appellate Authority may, after giving the parties to the appeal or reference an opportunity of being heard, pass such order as it thinks fit, confirming or modifying the ruling appealed against or referred to.

(2) The order referred to in sub-section (1) shall be passed within a period of ninety days from the date of filing of the appeal under section 100 or a reference under sub-section (5) of section 98.

(3) Where the members of the Appellate Authority differ on any point or points referred to in appeal or reference, it shall be deemed that no advance ruling can be issued in respect of the question under the appeal or reference.

(4) A copy of the advance ruling pronounced by the Appellate Authority duly signed by the Members and certified in such manner as may be prescribed shall be sent to the applicant, the concerned officer, the jurisdictional officer and to the Authority after such pronouncement.

[85][Constitution of National Appellate Authority for Advance Ruling.

101A. *(1) The Government shall, on the recommendations of the Council, by notification, constitute, with effect from such date as may be specified therein, an Authority known as the National Appellate Authority for Advance Ruling for hearing appeals made under section 101B.*

(2) The National Appellate Authority shall consist of—

- (i) *the President, who has been a Judge of the Supreme Court or is or has been the Chief Justice of a High Court, or is or has been a Judge of a High Court for a period not less than five years;*
- (ii) *a Technical Member (Centre) who is or has been a member of Indian Revenue (Customs and Central Excise) Service, Group A, and has completed at least fifteen years of service in Group A;*
- (iii) *a Technical Member (State) who is or has been an officer of the State Government not below*

85. Inserted by the Finance (No. 2) Act, 2019, with effect from a date yet to be notified.

the rank of Additional Commissioner of Value Added Tax or the Additional Commissioner of State tax with at least three years of experience in the administration of an existing law or the State Goods and Services Tax Act or in the field of finance and taxation.

(3) The President of the National Appellate Authority shall be appointed by the Government after consultation with the Chief Justice of India or his nominee:

Provided *that in the event of the occurrence of any vacancy in the office of the President by reason of his death, resignation or otherwise, the senior most Member of the National Appellate Authority shall act as the President until the date on which a new President, appointed in accordance with the provisions of this Act to fill such vacancy, enters upon his office:*

Provided further *that where the President is unable to discharge his functions owing to absence, illness or any other cause, the senior most Member of the National Appellate Authority shall discharge the functions of the President until the date on which the President resumes his duties.*

(4) The Technical Member (Centre) and Technical Member (State) of the National Appellate Authority shall be appointed by the Government on the recommendations of a Selection Committee consisting of such persons and in such manner as may be prescribed.

(5) No appointment of the Members of the National Appellate Authority shall be invalid merely by the reason of any vacancy or defect in the constitution of the Selection Committee.

(6) Before appointing any person as the President or Members of the National Appellate Authority, the Government shall satisfy itself that such person does not have any financial or other interests which are likely to prejudicially affect his functions as such President or Member.

(7) The salary, allowances and other terms and conditions of service of the President and the Members of the National Appellate Authority shall be such as may be prescribed:

Provided *that neither salary and allowances nor other terms and conditions of service of the President or Members of the National Appellate Authority shall be varied to their disadvantage after their appointment.*

(8) The President of the National Appellate Authority shall hold office for a term of three years from the date on which he enters upon his office, or until he attains the age of seventy years, whichever is earlier and shall also be eligible for reappointment.

(9) The Technical Member (Centre) or Technical Member (State) of the National Appellate Authority shall hold office for a term of five years from the date on which he enters upon his office, or until he attains the age of sixty-five years, whichever is earlier and shall also be eligible for reappointment.

(10) The President or any Member may, by notice in writing under his hand addressed to the Government, resign from his office:

Provided *that the President or Member shall continue to hold office until the expiry of three months from the date of receipt of such notice by the Government, or until a person duly appointed as his successor enters upon his office or until the expiry of his term of office, whichever is the earliest.*

(11) The Government may, after consultation with the Chief Justice of India, remove from the office such President or Member, who—

- (a) *has been adjudged an insolvent; or*
- (b) *has been convicted of an offence which, in the opinion of such Government involves moral turpitude; or*
- (c) *has become physically or mentally incapable of acting as such President or Member; or*

(d) *has acquired such financial or other interest as is likely to affect prejudicially his functions as such President or Member; or*

(e) *has so abused his position as to render his continuance in office prejudicial to the public interest:*

Provided *that the President or the Member shall not be removed on any of the grounds specified in clauses* (d) *and* (e)*, unless he has been informed of the charges against him and has been given an opportunity of being heard.*

(12) Without prejudice to the provisions of sub-section (11), the President and Technical Members of the National Appellate Authority shall not be removed from their office except by an order made by the Government on the ground of proven misbehaviour or incapacity after an inquiry made by a Judge of the Supreme Court nominated by the Chief Justice of India on a reference made to him by the Government and such President or Member had been given an opportunity of being heard.

(13) The Government, with the concurrence of the Chief Justice of India, may suspend from office, the President or Technical Members of the National Appellate Authority in respect of whom a reference has been made to the Judge of the Supreme Court under sub-section (12).

(14) Subject to the provisions of article 220 of the Constitution, the President or Members of the National Appellate Authority, on ceasing to hold their office, shall not be eligible to appear, act or plead before the National Appellate Authority where he was the President or, as the case may be, a Member.

Appeal to National Appellate Authority.

101B. *(1) Where, in respect of the questions referred to in sub-section (2) of section 97, conflicting advance rulings are given by the Appellate Authorities of two or more States or Union territories or both under sub-section (1) or sub-section (3) of section 101, any officer* *authorised by the Commissioner or an applicant, being distinct person referred to in section 25 aggrieved by such advance ruling, may prefer an appeal to National Appellate Authority:*

Provided *that the officer shall be from the States in which such advance rulings have been given.*

(2) Every appeal under this section shall be filed within a period of thirty days from the date on which the ruling sought to be appealed against is communicated to the applicants, concerned officers and jurisdictional officers:

Provided *that the officer authorised by the Commissioner may file appeal within a period of ninety days from the date on which the ruling sought to be appealed against is communicated to the concerned officer or the jurisdictional officer:*

Provided further *that the National Appellate Authority may, if it is satisfied that the appellant was prevented by a sufficient cause from presenting the appeal within the said period of thirty days, or as the case may be, ninety days, allow such appeal to be presented within a further period not exceeding thirty days.*

Explanation.—*For removal of doubts, it is clarified that the period of thirty days or as the case may be, ninety days shall be counted from the date of communication of the last of the conflicting rulings sought to be appealed against.*

(3) Every appeal under this section shall be in such form, accompanied by such fee and verified in such manner as may be prescribed.

Order of National Appellate Authority.

101C. *(1) The National Appellate Authority may, after giving an opportunity of being heard to the applicant, the officer authorised by the Commissioner, all Principal Chief Commissioners, Chief Commissioners of Central tax and Chief Commissioner and Commissioner of State tax of all States and Chief Commissioner and*

Commissioner of Union territory tax of all Union territories, pass such order as it thinks fit, confirming or modifying the rulings appealed against.

(2) If the members of the National Appellate Authority differ in opinion on any point, it shall be decided according to the opinion of the majority.

(3) The order referred to in sub-section (1) shall be passed as far as possible within a period of ninety days from the date of filing of the appeal under section 101B.

(4) A copy of the advance ruling pronounced by the National Appellate Authority shall be duly signed by the Members and certified in such manner as may be prescribed and shall be sent to the applicant, the officer authorised by the Commissioner, the Board, the Chief Commissioner and Commissioner of State tax of all States and Chief Commissioner and Commissioner of Union territory tax of all Union territories and to the Authority or Appellate Authority, as the case may be, after such pronouncement.]

Rectification of advance ruling.

102. The Authority or the Appellate Authority [86]**[***or the National Appellate Authority***]** may amend any order passed by it under section 98 or section 101 [86]**[***or section 101C, respectively,***]** so as to rectify any error apparent on the face of the record, if such error is noticed by the Authority or the Appellate Authority [86]**[***or the National Appellate Authority***]** on its own accord, or is brought to its notice by the concerned officer, the jurisdictional officer, the applicant [87]**[***, appellant, the Authority or the Appellate Authority***]** within a period of six months from the date of the order:

Provided that no rectification which has the effect of enhancing the tax liability or reducing the amount of admissible input tax credit shall be made unless

86. Inserted by the Finance (No. 2) Act, 2019, with effect from a date yet to be notified.

87. Substituted for "or the appellant", *ibid.*

the applicant or the appellant has been given an opportunity of being heard.

Applicability of advance ruling.

103. (1) The advance ruling pronounced by the Authority or the Appellate Authority under this Chapter shall be binding only—

(*a*) on the applicant who had sought it in respect of any matter referred to in sub-section (2) of section 97 for advance ruling;

(*b*) on the concerned officer or the jurisdictional officer in respect of the applicant.

[88]**[***(1A) The advance ruling pronounced by the National Appellate Authority under this Chapter shall be binding on—*

*(*a*) the applicants, being distinct persons, who had sought the ruling under sub-section (1) of section 101B and all registered persons having the same Permanent Account Number issued under the Income-tax Act, 1961 (43 of 1961);*

*(*b*) the concerned officers and the jurisdictional officers in respect of the applicants referred to in clause (*a*) and the registered persons having the same Permanent Account Number issued under the Income-tax Act, 1961 (43 of 1961).***]**

(2) The advance ruling referred to in sub-section (1) [88]**[***and sub-section (1A)***]** shall be binding unless the law, facts or circumstances supporting the original advance ruling have changed.

Advance ruling to be void in certain circumstances.

104. (1) Where the Authority or the Appellate Authority [88]**[***or the National Appellate Authority***]** finds that advance ruling pronounced by it under sub-section (4) of section 98 or under sub-section (1) of section 101 [88]**[***or under section 101C***]** has been obtained by the

88. Inserted by the Finance (No. 2) Act, 2019, with effect from a date yet to be notified.

applicant or the appellant by fraud or suppression of material facts or misrepresentation of facts, it may, by order, declare such ruling to be *void ab initio* and thereupon all the provisions of this Act or the rules made thereunder shall apply to the applicant or the appellant as if such advance ruling had never been made:

Provided that no order shall be passed under this sub-section unless an opportunity of being heard has been given to the applicant or the appellant.

Explanation.—The period beginning with the date of such advance ruling and ending with the date of order under this sub-section shall be excluded while computing the period specified in sub-sections (2) and (10) of section 73 or sub-sections (2) and (10) of section 74 [89]**[***or sub-sections (2) and (7) of section 74A***]**.

(2) A copy of the order made under sub-section (1) shall be sent to the applicant, the concerned officer and the jurisdictional officer.

[90]**[*Powers of Authority, Appellate Authority and National Appellate Authority*]**.

105. (1) The Authority or the Appellate Authority [91]**[***or the National Appellate Authority***]** shall, for the purpose of exercising its powers regarding—

(*a*) discovery and inspection;

(*b*) enforcing the attendance of any person and examining him on oath;

(*c*) issuing commissions and compelling production of books of account and other records,

89. Inserted by the Finance (No. 2) Act, 2024, w.e.f. **1-11-2024**.

90. Substituted for "Powers of Authority and Appellate Authority" by the Finance (No. 2) Act, 2019, with effect from a date yet to be notified.

91. Inserted, *ibid*.

have all the powers of a civil court under the Code of Civil Procedure, 1908 (5 of 1908).

(2) The Authority or the Appellate Authority [92][*or the National Appellate Authority*] shall be deemed to be a civil court for the purposes of section 195, but not for the purposes of Chapter XXVI of the Code of Criminal Procedure, 1973 (2 of 1974), and every proceeding before the Authority or the Appellate Authority [92][*or the National Appellate Authority*] shall be deemed to be a judicial proceedings within the meaning of sections 193 and 228, and for the purpose of section 196 of the Indian Penal Code (45 of 1860).

[93][*Procedure of Authority, Appellate Authority and National Appellate Authority*].

106. The Authority or the Appellate Authority [92][*or the National Appellate Authority*] shall, subject to the provisions of this Chapter, have power to regulate its own procedure.

CHAPTER XVIII

APPEALS AND REVISION

Appeals to Appellate Authority.

107. (1) Any person aggrieved by any decision or order passed under this Act or the State Goods and Services Tax Act or the Union Territory Goods and Services Tax Act by an adjudicating authority may appeal to such Appellate Authority as may be prescribed within three months from the date on which the said decision or order is communicated to such person.

(2) The Commissioner may, on his own motion, or upon request from the Commissioner of State tax or

92. Inserted by the Finance (No. 2) Act, 2019, with effect from a date yet to be notified.

93. Substituted for "Procedure of Authority and Appellate Authority", *ibid*.

the Commissioner of Union territory tax, call for and examine the record of any proceedings in which an adjudicating authority has passed any decision or order under this Act or the State Goods and Services Tax Act or the Union Territory Goods and Services Tax Act, for the purpose of satisfying himself as to the legality or propriety of the said decision or order and may, by order, direct any officer subordinate to him to apply to the Appellate Authority within six months from the date of communication of the said decision or order for the determination of such points arising out of the said decision or order as may be specified by the Commissioner in his order.

(3) Where, in pursuance of an order under sub-section (2), the authorised officer makes an application to the Appellate Authority, such application shall be dealt with by the Appellate Authority as if it were an appeal made against the decision or order of the adjudicating authority and such authorised officer were an appellant and the provisions of this Act relating to appeals shall apply to such application.

(4) The Appellate Authority may, if he is satisfied that the appellant was prevented by sufficient cause from presenting the appeal within the aforesaid period of three months or six months, as the case may be, allow it to be presented within a further period of one month.

(5) Every appeal under this section shall be in such form and shall be verified in such manner as may be prescribed.

(6) No appeal shall be filed under sub-section (1), unless the appellant has paid—

(*a*) in full, such part of the amount of tax, interest, fine, fee and penalty arising from the impugned order, as is admitted by him; and

(*b*) a sum equal to ten per cent of the remaining amount of tax in dispute arising from the said order, [94][subject to a maximum of [95][*twenty*] crore rupees,] in relation to which the appeal has been filed:

[96][**Provided** that no appeal shall be filed against an order under sub-section (3) of section 129, unless a sum equal to twenty-five per cent of the penalty has been paid by the appellant.]

(7) Where the appellant has paid the amount under sub-section (6), the recovery proceedings for the balance amount shall be deemed to be stayed.

(8) The Appellate Authority shall give an opportunity to the appellant of being heard.

(9) The Appellate Authority may, if sufficient cause is shown at any stage of hearing of an appeal, grant time to the parties or any of them and adjourn the hearing of the appeal for reasons to be recorded in writing:

Provided that no such adjournment shall be granted more than three times to a party during hearing of the appeal.

(10) The Appellate Authority may, at the time of hearing of an appeal, allow an appellant to add any ground of appeal not specified in the grounds of appeal, if it is satisfied that the omission of that ground from the grounds of appeal was not wilful or unreasonable.

(11) The Appellate Authority shall, after making such further inquiry as may be necessary, pass such order, as it thinks just and proper, confirming, modifying or annulling the decision or order appealed against but shall not refer the case back to the adjudicating authority that passed the said decision or order:

Provided that an order enhancing any fee or penalty or fine in lieu of confiscation or confiscating goods

94. Inserted by the Central Goods and Services Tax (Amendment) Act, 2018, w.e.f. 1-2-2019.

95. Substituted for "twenty-five" by the Finance (No. 2) Act, 2024, w.e.f. **1-11-2024.**

96. Inserted by the Finance Act, 2021, w.e.f. 1-1-2022.

of greater value or reducing the amount of refund or input tax credit shall not be passed unless the appellant has been given a reasonable opportunity of showing cause against the proposed order:

Provided further that where the Appellate Authority is of the opinion that any tax has not been paid or short-paid or erroneously refunded, or where input tax credit has been wrongly availed or utilised, no order requiring the appellant to pay such tax or input tax credit shall be passed unless the appellant is given notice to show cause against the proposed order and the order is passed within the time limit specified under section 73 or section 74 [97]**[***or section 74A***]**.

(12) The order of the Appellate Authority disposing of the appeal shall be in writing and shall state the points for determination, the decision thereon and the reasons for such decision.

(13) The Appellate Authority shall, where it is possible to do so, hear and decide every appeal within a period of one year from the date on which it is filed:

Provided that where the issuance of order is stayed by an order of a court or Tribunal, the period of such stay shall be excluded in computing the period of one year.

(14) On disposal of the appeal, the Appellate Authority shall communicate the order passed by it to the appellant, respondent and to the adjudicating authority.

(15) A copy of the order passed by the Appellate Authority shall also be sent to the jurisdictional Commissioner or the authority designated by him in this behalf and the jurisdictional Commissioner of State tax or Commissioner of Union Territory tax or an authority designated by him in this behalf.

97. Inserted by the Finance (No. 2) Act, 2024, w.e.f. **1-11-2024**.

(16) Every order passed under this section shall, subject to the provisions of section 108 or section 113 or section 117 or section 118 be final and binding on the parties.

Powers of Revisional Authority.

108. (1) Subject to the provisions of section 121 and any rules made thereunder, the Revisional Authority may, on his own motion, or upon information received by him or on request from the Commissioner of State tax, or the Commissioner of Union territory tax, call for and examine the record of any proceedings, and if he considers that any decision or order passed under this Act or under the State Goods and Services Tax Act or the Union Territory Goods and Services Tax Act by any officer subordinate to him is erroneous insofar as it is prejudicial to the interest of revenue and is illegal or improper or has not taken into account certain material facts, whether available at the time of issuance of the said order or not or in consequence of an observation by the Comptroller and Auditor General of India, he may, if necessary, stay the operation of such decision or order for such period as he deems fit and after giving the person concerned an opportunity of being heard and after making such further inquiry as may be necessary, pass such order, as he thinks just and proper, including enhancing or modifying or annulling the said decision or order.

(2) The Revisional Authority shall not exercise any power under sub-section (1), if—

(*a*) the order has been subject to an appeal under section 107 or section 112 or section 117 or section 118; or

(*b*) the period specified under sub-section (2) of section 107 has not yet expired or more than three years have expired after the passing of the decision or order sought to be revised; or

(*c*) the order has already been taken for revision under this section at an earlier stage; or (*d*) the order has been passed in exercise of the powers under sub-section (1):

Provided that the Revisional Authority may pass an order under sub-section (1) on any point which has not been raised and decided in an appeal referred to in clause (*a*) of sub-section (2), before the expiry of a period of one year from the date of the order in such appeal or before the expiry of a period of three years referred to in clause (*b*) of that sub-section, whichever is later.

(3) Every order passed in revision under sub-section (1) shall, subject to the provisions of section 113 or section 117 or section 118, be final and binding on the parties.

(4) If the said decision or order involves an issue on which the Appellate Tribunal or the High Court has given its decision in some other proceedings and an appeal to the High Court or the Supreme Court against such decision of the Appellate Tribunal or the High Court is pending, the period spent between the date of the decision of the Appellate Tribunal and the date of the decision of the High Court or the date of the decision of the High Court and the date of the decision of the Supreme Court shall be excluded in computing the period of limitation referred to in clause (*b*) of sub-section (2) where proceedings for revision have been initiated by way of issue of a notice under this section.

(5) Where the issuance of an order under sub-section (1) is stayed by the order of a court or Appellate Tribunal, the period of such stay shall be excluded in computing the period of limitation referred to in clause (*b*) of sub-section (2).

(6) For the purposes of this section, the term,—

(*i*) "record" shall include all records relating to any proceedings under this Act available at the time of examination by the Revisional Authority;

(*ii*) "decision" shall include intimation given by any officer lower in rank than the Revisional Authority.

[98][**Constitution of Appellate Tribunal and Benches thereof.**

109. (1) The Government shall, on the recommendations of the Council, by notification, establish with effect from such date as may be specified therein, an Appellate Tribunal known as the Goods and Services Tax Appellate Tribunal for hearing appeals against the orders passed by the Appellate Authority or the Revisional Authority [99][, *or for conducting an examination or adjudicating the cases referred to in sub-section (2) of section 171, if so notified under the said section*].

(2) The jurisdiction, powers and authority conferred on the Appellate Tribunal shall be exercised by the Principal Bench and the State Benches constituted under sub-section (3) and sub-section (4).

(3) The Government shall, by notification, constitute a Principal Bench of the Appellate Tribunal at New Delhi which shall consist of the President, a Judicial Member, a Technical Member (Centre) and a Technical Member (State).

(4) On the request of the State, the Government may, by notification, constitute such number of State Benches at such places and with such jurisdiction as may be recommended by the Council, which shall consist of two Judicial Members, a Technical Member (Centre) and a Technical Member (State).

(5) The Principal Bench and the State Bench shall hear appeals against the orders passed by the Appellate Authority or the Revisional Authority:

---

98. Substituted by the Finance Act, 2023, w.e.f. 1-8-2023.

99. Inserted by the Finance (No. 2) Act, 2024, w.e.f. **27-9-2024.**

Provided that the cases in which any one of the issues involved relates to the place of supply, shall be heard only by the Principal Bench:

[1]**[Provided further** *that the matters referred to in sub-section (2) of section 171 shall be examined or adjudicated only by the Principal Bench:*

Provided also *that the Government may, on the recommendations of the Council, notify other cases or class of cases which shall be heard only by the Principal Bench.***]**

(6) [2]**[***Subject to the provisions of sub-section (5), the President***]** shall, from time to time, by a general or special order, distribute the business of the Appellate Tribunal among the Benches and may transfer cases from one Bench to another.

(7) The senior-most Judicial Member within the State Benches, as may be notified, shall act as the Vice-President for such State Benches and shall exercise such powers of the President as may be prescribed, but for all other purposes be considered as a Member.

(8) Appeals, where the tax or input tax credit involved or the amount of fine, fee or penalty determined in any order appealed against, does not exceed fifty lakh rupees and which does not involve any question of law may, with the approval of the President, and subject to such conditions as may be prescribed on the recommendations of the Council, be heard by a single Member, and in all other cases, shall be heard together by one Judicial Member and one Technical Member.

(9) If, after hearing the case, the Members differ in their opinion on any point or points, such Member shall state the point or points on which they differ, and the President shall refer such case for hearing,—

---

1. Inserted by the Finance (No. 2) Act, 2024, w.e.f. **27-9-2024.**
2. Substituted for "The President", *ibid.*

(*a*) where the appeal was originally heard by Members of a State Bench, to another Member of a State Bench within the State or, where no such other State Bench is available within the State, to a Member of a State Bench in another State;

(*b*) where the appeal was originally heard by Members of the Principal Bench, to another Member from the Principal Bench or, where no such other Member is available, to a Member of any State Bench,

and such point or points shall be decided according to the majority opinion including the opinion of the Members who first heard the case.

(10) The Government may, in consultation with the President, for the administrative efficiency, transfer Members from one Bench to another Bench:

Provided that a Technical Member (State) of a State Bench may be transferred to a State Bench only of the same State in which he was originally appointed, in consultation with the State Government.

(11) No act or proceedings of the Appellate Tribunal shall be questioned or shall be invalid merely on the ground of the existence of any vacancy or defect in the constitution of the Appellate Tribunal.]

[3][**President and Members of Appellate Tribunal, their qualification, appointment, conditions of service, etc.**

110. (1) A person shall not be qualified for appointment as—

(*a*) the President, unless he has been a Judge of the Supreme Court or is or has been the Chief Justice of a High Court;

(*b*) a Judicial Member, unless he—

(*i*) has been a Judge of the High Court; or

3. Substituted by the Finance Act, 2023, w.e.f. 1-8-2023.

(*ii*) has, for a combined period of ten years, been a District Judge or an Additional District Judge;

[4][(*iii*) has been an advocate for ten years with substantial experience in litigation in matters relating to indirect taxes in the Appellate Tribunal, Customs, Excise and Service Tax Appellate Tribunal, State Value Added Tax Tribunal, by whatever name called, High Court or Supreme Court:]

[4][**Provided** that a person who has not completed the age of fifty years shall not be eligible for appointment as the President or Member;]

(*c*) a Technical Member (Centre), unless he is or has been a member of the Indian Revenue (Customs and Indirect Taxes) Service, Group A, or of the All India service with at least three years of experience in the administration of an existing law or goods and services tax in the Central Government, and has completed at least twenty-five years of service in Group A;

(*d*) a Technical Member (State), unless he is or has been an officer of the State Government or an officer of All India Service, not below the rank of Additional Commissioner of Value Added Tax or the State goods and services tax or such rank, not lower than that of the First Appellate Authority, as may be notified by the concerned State Government, on the recommendations of the Council and has completed twenty-five years of service in Group A, or equivalent, with at least three years of experience in the administration of

4. Inserted by the Central Goods and Services Tax (Second Amendment) Act, 2023, w.e.f. 28-12-2023.

an existing law or the goods and services tax or in the field of finance and taxation in the State Government:

Provided that the State Government may, on the recommendations of the Council, by notification, relax the requirement of completion of twenty-five years of service in Group A, or equivalent, in respect of officers of such State where no person has completed twenty-five years of service in Group A, or equivalent, but has completed twenty-five years of service in the Government, subject to such conditions, and till such period, as may be specified in the notification.

(2) The President, Judicial Member, Technical Member (Centre) and Technical Member (State) shall be appointed or re-appointed by the Government on the recommendations of a Search-cum-Selection Committee constituted under sub-section (4):

Provided that in the event of the occurrence of any vacancy in the office of the President by reason of his death, resignation or otherwise, the Judicial Member or, in his absence, the senior-most Technical Member of the Principal Bench shall act as the President until the date on which a new President, appointed in accordance with the provisions of this Act to fill such vacancy, enters upon his office:

Provided further that where the President is unable to discharge his functions owing to absence, illness or any other cause, the Judicial Member or, in his absence, the senior-most Technical Member of the Principal Bench, shall discharge the functions of the President until the date on which the President resumes his duties.

(3) While making selection for Technical Member (State) of a State Bench, first preference shall be given to officers who have worked in the State Government of the State to which the jurisdiction of the Bench extends.

(4)(*a*) The Search-cum-Selection Committee for Technical Member (State) of a State Bench shall consist of the following members, namely:—

(*i*) the Chief Justice of the High Court in whose jurisdiction the State Bench is located, to be the Chairperson of the Committee;

(*ii*) the senior-most Judicial Member in the State, and where no Judicial Member is available, a retired Judge of the High Court in whose jurisdiction the State Bench is located, as may be nominated by the Chief Justice of such High Court;

(*iii*) Chief Secretary of the State in which the State Bench is located;

(*iv*) one Additional Chief Secretary or Principal Secretary or Secretary of the State in which the State Bench is located, as may be nominated by such State Government, not in-charge of the Department responsible for administration of State tax; and

(*v*) Additional Chief Secretary or Principal Secretary or Secretary of the Department responsible for administration of State tax, of the State in which the State Bench is located — Member Secretary; and

(*b*) the Search-cum-Selection Committee for all other cases shall consist of the following members, namely:—

(*i*) the Chief Justice of India or a Judge of Supreme Court nominated by him, to be the Chairperson of the Committee;

(*ii*) Secretary of the Central Government nominated by the Cabinet Secretary — Member;

(*iii*) Chief Secretary of a State to be nominated by the Council — Member;

(*iv*) one Member, who—

(*A*) in case of appointment of a President of a Tribunal, shall be the outgoing President of the Tribunal; or

(*B*) in case of appointment of a Member of a Tribunal, shall be the sitting President of the Tribunal; or

(*C*) in case of the President of the Tribunal seeking re-appointment or where the outgoing President is unavailable or the removal of the President is being considered, shall be a retired Judge of the Supreme Court or a retired Chief Justice of a High Court nominated by the Chief Justice of India; and

(*v*) Secretary of the Department of Revenue in the Ministry of Finance of the Central Government — Member Secretary.

(5) The Chairperson shall have the casting vote and the Member Secretary shall not have a vote.

(6) Notwithstanding anything contained in any judgment, order, or decree of any court or any law for the time being in force, the Committee shall recommend a panel of two names for appointment or re-appointment to the post of the President or a Member, as the case may be.

(7) No appointment or re-appointment of the Members of the Appellate Tribunal shall be invalid merely by reason of any vacancy or defect in the constitution of the Search-cum-Selection Committee.

(8) Notwithstanding anything contained in any judgment, order, or decree of any court or any law for the time being in force, the salary of the President and the Members of the Appellate Tribunal shall be such as may be prescribed and their allowances and other terms and conditions of service shall be the same as applicable to Central Government officers carrying the same pay:

Provided that neither the salary and allowances nor other terms and conditions of service of the President of Members of the Appellate Tribunal shall be varied to their disadvantage after their appointment:

Provided further that, if the President or Member takes a house on rent, he may be reimbursed a house rent higher than the house rent allowance as are admissible to a Central Government officer holding the post carrying the same pay, subject to such limitations and conditions as may be prescribed.

(9) Notwithstanding anything contained in any judgment, order, or decree of any court or any law for the time being in force, the President of the Appellate Tribunal shall hold office for a term of four years from the date on which he enters upon his office, or until he attains the age of [5][seventy years, whichever is earlier and shall be eligible for re-appointment for a period not exceeding two years subject to the age-limit specified above].

(10) Notwithstanding anything contained in any judgment, order, or decree of any court or any law for the time being in force, the Judicial Member, Technical Member (Centre) or Technical Member (State) of the Appellate Tribunal shall hold office for a term of four years from the date on which he enters upon his office, or until he attains the age of [6][sixty-seven years, whichever is earlier and shall be eligible for re-appointment for a period not exceeding two years subject to the age-limit specified above].

(11) The President or any Member may, by notice in writing under his hand addressed to the Government, resign from his office:

---

5. Substituted for "sixty-seven years, whichever is earlier and shall be eligible for re-appointment for a period not exceeding two years" by the Central Goods and Services Tax (Second Amendment) Act, 2023, w.e.f. 28-12-2023.
6. Substituted for "sixty-five years, whichever is earlier and shall be eligible for re-appointment for a period not exceeding two years", *ibid.*

Provided that the President or Member shall continue to hold office until the expiry of three months from the date of receipt of such notice by the Government or until a person duly appointed as his successor enters upon his office or until the expiry of his term of office, whichever is the earliest.

(12) The Government may, on the recommendations of the Search-cum-Selection Committee, remove from the office President or a Member, who—

(*a*) has been adjudged an insolvent; or

(*b*) has been convicted of an offence which involves moral turpitude; or

(*c*) has become physically or mentally incapable of acting as such President or Member; or

(*d*) has acquired such financial or other interest as is likely to affect prejudicially his functions as such President or Member; or

(*e*) has so abused his position as to render his continuance in office prejudicial to the public interest;

Provided that the President or the Member shall not be removed on any of the grounds specified in clauses (*d*) and (*e*), unless he has been informed of the charges against him and has been given an opportunity of being heard.

(13) The Government, on the recommendations of the Search-cum-Selection Committee, may suspend from office, the President or a Judicial or technical Member in respect of whom proceedings for removal have been initiated under sub-section (12).

(14) Subject to the provisions of article 220 of the Constitution, the President or other Members, on ceasing to hold their office, shall not be eligible to appear, act or plead before the Principal Bench or the State Bench in which he was the President or, as the case may be, a Member.]

Procedure before Appellate Tribunal.

111. (1) The Appellate Tribunal shall not, while disposing of any proceedings before it or an appeal before it, be bound by the procedure laid down in the Code of Civil Procedure, 1908 (5 of 1908), but shall be guided by the principles of natural justice and subject to the other provisions of this Act and the rules made thereunder, the Appellate Tribunal shall have power to regulate its own procedure.

(2) The Appellate Tribunal shall, for the purposes of discharging its functions under this Act, have the same powers as are vested in a civil court under the Code of Civil Procedure, 1908 (5 of 1908) while trying a suit in respect of the following matters, namely:—

(*a*) summoning and enforcing the attendance of any person and examining him on oath;

(*b*) requiring the discovery and production of documents;

(*c*) receiving evidence on affidavits;

(*d*) subject to the provisions of sections 123 and 124 of the Indian Evidence Act, 1872 (1 of 1872), requisitioning any public record or document or a copy of such record or document from any office;

(*e*) issuing commissions for the examination of witnesses or documents;

(*f*) dismissing a representation for default or deciding it *ex parte;*

(*g*) setting aside any order of dismissal of any representation for default or any order passed by it *ex parte;* and

(*h*) any other matter which may be prescribed.

(3) Any order made by the Appellate Tribunal may be enforced by it in the same manner as if it were a decree made by a court in a suit pending therein, and it shall be lawful for the Appellate Tribunal to

send for execution of its orders to the court within the local limits of whose jurisdiction,—

(*a*) in the case of an order against a company, the registered office of the company is situated; or

(*b*) in the case of an order against any other person, the person concerned voluntarily resides or carries on business or personally works for gain.

(4) All proceedings before the Appellate Tribunal shall be deemed to be judicial proceedings within the meaning of sections 193 and 228, and for the purposes of section 196 of the Indian Penal Code (45 of 1860), and the Appellate Tribunal shall be deemed to be civil court for the purposes of section 195 and Chapter XXVI of the Code of Criminal Procedure, 1973 (2 of 1974).

Appeals to Appellate Tribunal.

112. (1) Any person aggrieved by an order passed against him under section 107 or section 108 of this Act or the State Goods and Services Tax Act or the Union Territory Goods and Services Tax Act may appeal to the Appellate Tribunal against such order within three months from the date on which the order sought to be appealed against is communicated to the person preferring the appeal [7]**[**; *or the date, as may be notified by the Government, on the recommendations of the Council, for filing appeal before the Appellate Tribunal under this Act, whichever is later*].

(2) The Appellate Tribunal may, in its discretion, refuse to admit any such appeal where the tax or input tax credit involved or the difference in tax or input tax credit involved or the amount of fine, fee or penalty determined by such order, does not exceed fifty thousand rupees.

---

7. Inserted by the Finance (No. 2) Act, 2024, w.r.e.f. **1-8-2024**. [However, Notification No. 17/2024-Central Tax, dated 27-9-2024 appoints 1-11-2024 as the date of enforcement].

(3) The Commissioner may, on his own motion, or upon request from the Commissioner of State tax or Commissioner of Union territory tax, call for and examine the record of any order passed by the Appellate Authority or the Revisional Authority under this Act or the State Goods and Services Tax Act or the Union Territory Goods and Services Tax Act for the purpose of satisfying himself as to the legality or propriety of the said order and may, by order, direct any officer subordinate to him to apply to the Appellate Tribunal within six months from the date on which the said order has been passed [8]**[***; or the date, as may be notified by the Government, on the recommendations of the Council, for the purpose of filing application before the Appellate Tribunal under this Act, whichever is later,*]** for determination of such points arising out of the said order as may be specified by the Commissioner in his order.

(4) Where in pursuance of an order under sub-section (3) the authorised officer makes an application to the Appellate Tribunal, such application shall be dealt with by the Appellate Tribunal as if it were an appeal made against the order under sub-section (11) of section 107 or under sub-section (1) of section 108 and the provisions of this Act shall apply to such application, as they apply in relation to appeals filed under sub-section (1).

(5) On receipt of notice that an appeal has been preferred under this section, the party against whom the appeal has been preferred may, notwithstanding that he may not have appealed against such order or any part thereof, file, within forty-five days of the receipt of notice, a memorandum of cross-objections, verified in the prescribed manner, against any part of the order appealed against and such memorandum shall be disposed of by the Appellate Tribunal, as if it were an appeal presented within the time specified in sub-section (1).

---

8. Inserted by the Finance (No. 2) Act, 2024, w.r.e.f. **1-8-2024**. [However, Notification No. 17/2024-Central Tax, dated 27-9-2024 appoints 1-11-2024 as the date of enforcement].

(6) The Appellate Tribunal may admit an appeal within three months after the expiry of the period referred to in sub-section (1) [9][*or permit the filing of an application within three months after the expiry of the period referred to in sub-section (3)*], or permit the filing of a memorandum of cross-objections within forty-five days after the expiry of the period referred to in sub-section (5) if it is satisfied that there was sufficient cause for not presenting it within that period.

(7) An appeal to the Appellate Tribunal shall be in such form, verified in such manner and shall be accompanied by such fee, as may be prescribed.

(8) No appeal shall be filed under sub-section (1), unless the appellant has paid—

(*a*) in full, such part of the amount of tax, interest, fine, fee and penalty arising from the impugned order, as is admitted by him, and

(*b*) a sum equal to [10][*ten per cent*] of the remaining amount of tax in dispute, in addition to the amount paid under sub-section (6) of section 107, arising from the said order, [11][subject to a maximum of [12][*twenty crore rupees*],] in relation to which the appeal has been filed.

(9) Where the appellant has paid the amount as per sub-section (8), the recovery proceedings for the balance amount shall be deemed to be stayed till the disposal of the appeal.

(10) Every application made before the Appellate Tribunal,—

9. Inserted by the Finance (No. 2) Act, 2024, w.e.f. **1-11-2024.**

10. Substituted for "twenty per cent", *ibid.*

11. Inserted by the Central Goods and Services Tax (Amendment) Act, 2018, w.e.f. 1-2-2019.

12. Substituted for "fifty crore rupees" by the Finance (No. 2) Act, 2024, w.e.f. **1-11-2024.**

(*a*) in an appeal for rectification of error or for any other purpose; or

(*b*) for restoration of an appeal or an application,

shall be accompanied by such fees as may be prescribed.

Orders of Appellate Tribunal.

113. (1) The Appellate Tribunal may, after giving the parties to the appeal an opportunity of being heard, pass such orders thereon as it thinks fit, confirming, modifying or annulling the decision or order appealed against or may refer the case back to the Appellate Authority, or the Revisional Authority or to the original adjudicating authority, with such directions as it may think fit, for a fresh adjudication or decision after taking additional evidence, if necessary.

(2) The Appellate Tribunal may, if sufficient cause is shown, at any stage of hearing of an appeal, grant time to the parties or any of them and adjourn the hearing of the appeal for reasons to be recorded in writing:

Provided that no such adjournment shall be granted more than three times to a party during hearing of the appeal.

(3) The Appellate Tribunal may amend any order passed by it under sub-section (1) so as to rectify any error apparent on the face of the record, if such error is noticed by it on its own accord, or is brought to its notice by the Commissioner or the Commissioner of State tax or the Commissioner of the Union territory tax or the other party to the appeal within a period of three months from the date of the order:

Provided that no amendment which has the effect of enhancing an assessment or reducing a refund or input tax credit or otherwise increasing the liability of the other party, shall be made under this sub-section, unless the party has been given an opportunity of being heard.

(4) The Appellate Tribunal shall, as far as possible, hear and decide every appeal within a period of one year from the date on which it is filed.

(5) The Appellate Tribunal shall send a copy of every order passed under this section to the Appellate Authority or the Revisional Authority, or the original adjudicating authority, as the case may be, the appellant and the jurisdictional Commissioner or the Commissioner of State tax or the Union territory tax.

(6) Save as provided in section 117 or section 118, orders passed by the Appellate Tribunal on an appeal shall be final and binding on the parties.

[13][**Financial and administrative powers of President.**

114. The President shall exercise such financial and administrative powers over the Appellate Tribunal as may be prescribed.]

Interest on refund of amount paid for admission of appeal.

115. Where an amount paid by the appellant under sub-section (6) of section 107 or sub-section (8) of section 112 is required to be refunded consequent to any order of the Appellate Authority or of the Appellate Tribunal, interest at the rate specified under section 56 shall be payable in respect of such refund from the date of payment of the amount till the date of refund of such amount.

Appearance by authorised representative.

116. (1) Any person who is entitled or required to appear before an officer appointed under this Act, or the Appellate Authority or the Appellate Tribunal in connection with any proceedings under this Act, may, otherwise than when required under this Act to appear personally for examination on oath or affirmation,

13. Substituted by the Finance Act, 2023, w.e.f. 1-8-2023.

subject to the other provisions of this section, appear by an authorised representative.

(2) For the purposes of this Act, the expression "authorised representative" shall mean a person authorised by the person referred to in sub-section (1) to appear on his behalf, being—

(*a*) his relative or regular employee; or

(*b*) an advocate who is entitled to practice in any court in India, and who has not been debarred from practicing before any court in India; or

(*c*) any chartered accountant, a cost accountant or a company secretary, who holds a certificate of practice and who has not been debarred from practice; or

(*d*) a retired officer of the Commercial Tax Department of any State Government or Union territory or of the Board who, during his service under the Government, had worked in a post not below the rank than that of a Group-B Gazetted officer for a period of not less than two years:

Provided that such officer shall not be entitled to appear before any proceedings under this Act for a period of one year from the date of his retirement or resignation; or

(*e*) any person who has been authorised to act as a goods and services tax practitioner on behalf of the concerned registered person.

(3) No person,—

(*a*) who has been dismissed or removed from Government service; or

(*b*) who is convicted of an offence connected with any proceedings under this Act, the State Goods and Services Tax Act, the Integrated Goods and Services Tax Act or the Union Territory Goods and Services Tax Act, or under the existing law or under any of the Acts passed by a State Legislature dealing with the imposition of taxes on sale of goods or supply of goods or services or both; or

(*c*) who is found guilty of misconduct by the prescribed authority; or

(*d*) who has been adjudged as an insolvent,

shall be qualified to represent any person under sub-section (1)—

(*i*) for all times in case of persons referred to in clauses (*a*), (*b*) and (*c*); and

(*ii*) for the period during which the insolvency continues in the case of a person referred to in clause (*d*).

(4) Any person who has been disqualified under the provisions of the State Goods and Services Tax Act or the Union Territory Goods and Services Tax Act shall be deemed to be disqualified under this Act.

Appeal to High Court.

117. (1) Any person aggrieved by any order passed by the [14][State Benches] of the Appellate Tribunal may file an appeal to the High Court and the High Court may admit such appeal, if it is satisfied that the case involves a substantial question of law.

(2) An appeal under sub-section (1) shall be filed within a period of one hundred and eighty days from the date on which the order appealed against is received by the aggrieved person and it shall be in such form, verified in such manner as may be prescribed:

Provided that the High Court may entertain an appeal after the expiry of the said period if it is satisfied that there was sufficient cause for not filing it within such period.

14. Substituted for "State Bench or Area Benches" by the Finance Act, 2023, w.e.f. 1-8-2023.

(3) Where the High Court is satisfied that a substantial question of law is involved in any case, it shall formulate that question and the appeal shall be heard only on the question so formulated, and the respondents shall, at the hearing of the appeal, be allowed to argue that the case does not involve such question:

Provided that nothing in this sub-section shall be deemed to take away or abridge the power of the court to hear, for reasons to be recorded, the appeal on any other substantial question of law not formulated by it, if it is satisfied that the case involves such question.

(4) The High Court shall decide the question of law so formulated and deliver such judgment thereon containing the grounds on which such decision is founded and may award such cost as it deems fit.

(5) The High Court may determine any issue which—

(*a*) has not been determined by the [15][State Benches]; or

(*b*) has been wrongly determined by the [15][State Benches], by reason of a decision on such question of law as herein referred to in sub-section (3).

(6) Where an appeal has been filed before the High Court, it shall be heard by a Bench of not less than two Judges of the High Court, and shall be decided in accordance with the opinion of such Judges or of the majority, if any, of such Judges.

(7) Where there is no such majority, the Judges shall state the point of law upon which they differ and the case shall, then, be heard upon that point only, by one or more of the other Judges of the High Court and such point shall be decided according to the opinion of the majority of the Judges who have heard the case including those who first heard it.

---

15. Substituted for "State Bench or Area Benches" by the Finance Act, 2023, w.e.f. 1-8-2023.

(8) Where the High Court delivers a judgment in an appeal filed before it under this section, effect shall be given to such judgment by either side on the basis of a certified copy of the judgment.

(9) Save as otherwise provided in this Act, the provisions of the Code of Civil Procedure, 1908 (5 of 1908), relating to appeals to the High Court shall, as far as may be, apply in the case of appeals under this section.

Appeal to Supreme Court.

118. (1) An appeal shall lie to the Supreme Court—

(*a*) from any order passed by the [16][Principal Bench] of the Appellate Tribunal; or

(*b*) from any judgment or order passed by the High Court in an appeal made under section 117 in any case which, on its own motion or on an application made by or on behalf of the party aggrieved, immediately after passing of the judgment or order, the High Court certifies to be a fit one for appeal to the Supreme Court.

(2) The provisions of the Code of Civil Procedure, 1908 (5 of 1908), relating to appeals to the Supreme Court shall, so far as may be, apply in the case of appeals under this section as they apply in the case of appeals from decrees of a High Court.

(3) Where the judgment of the High Court is varied or reversed in the appeal, effect shall be given to the order of the Supreme Court in the manner provided in section 117 in the case of a judgment of the High Court.

Sums due to be paid notwithstanding appeal, etc.

119. Notwithstanding that an appeal has been preferred to the High Court or the Supreme Court, sums due to the Government as a result of an order

16. Substituted for "National Bench or Regional Benches" by the Finance Act, 2023, w.e.f. 1-8-2023.

passed by the [17][Principal Bench] of the Appellate Tribunal under sub-section (1) of section 113 or an order passed by the [18][State Benches] of the Appellate Tribunal under sub-section (1) of section 113 or an order passed by the High Court under section 117, as the case may be, shall be payable in accordance with the order so passed.

Appeal not to be filed in certain cases.

120. (1) The Board may, on the recommendations of the Council, from time to time, issue orders or instructions or directions fixing such monetary limits, as it may deem fit, for the purposes of regulating the filing of appeal or application by the officer of the central tax under the provisions of this Chapter.

(2) Where, in pursuance of the orders or instructions or directions issued under sub-section (1), the officer of the central tax has not filed an appeal or application against any decision or order passed under the provisions of this Act, it shall not preclude such officer of the central tax from filing appeal or application in any other case involving the same or similar issues or questions of law.

(3) Notwithstanding the fact that no appeal or application has been filed by the officer of the central tax pursuant to the orders or instructions or directions issued under sub-section (1), no person, being a party in appeal or application shall contend that the officer of the central tax has acquiesced in the decision on the disputed issue by not filing an appeal or application.

(4) The Appellate Tribunal or court hearing such appeal or application shall have regard to the circumstances under which appeal or application was not filed by the officer of the central tax in pursuance of the orders or instructions or directions issued under sub-section (1).

17. Substituted for "National or Regional Benches" by the Finance Act, 2023, w.e.f. 1-8-2023.

18. Substituted for "State Bench or Area Benches", *ibid.*

Non-appealable decisions and orders.

121. Notwithstanding anything to the contrary in any provisions of this Act, no appeal shall lie against any decision taken or order passed by an officer of central tax if such decision taken or order passed relates to any one or more of the following matters, namely:—

(*a*) an order of the Commissioner or other authority empowered to direct transfer of proceedings from one officer to another officer; or

(*b*) an order pertaining to the seizure or retention of books of account, register and other documents; or

(*c*) an order sanctioning prosecution under this Act; or

(*d*) an order passed under section 80.

CHAPTER XIX

OFFENCES AND PENALTIES

Penalty for certain offences.

122. (1) Where a taxable person who—

(*i*) supplies any goods or services or both without issue of any invoice or issues an incorrect or false invoice with regard to any such supply;

(*ii*) issues any invoice or bill without supply of goods or services or both in violation of the provisions of this Act or the rules made thereunder;

(*iii*) collects any amount as tax but fails to pay the same to the Government beyond a period of three months from the date on which such payment becomes due;

(*iv*) collects any tax in contravention of the provisions of this Act but fails to pay the same to the Government beyond a period of three months from the date on which such payment becomes due;

(*v*) fails to deduct the tax in accordance with the provisions of sub-section (1) of section 51, or deducts an amount which is less than the amount required to be deducted under the said sub-section, or where he fails to pay to the Government under sub-section (2) thereof, the amount deducted as tax;

(*vi*) fails to collect tax in accordance with the provisions of sub-section (1) of section 52, or collects an amount which is less than the amount required to be collected under the said sub-section or where he fails to pay to the Government the amount collected as tax under sub-section (3) of section 52;

(*vii*) takes or utilizes input tax credit without actual receipt of goods or services or both either fully or partially, in contravention of the provisions of this Act or the rules made thereunder;

(*viii*) fraudulently obtains refund of tax under this Act;

(*ix*) takes or distributes input tax credit in contravention of section 20, or the rules made thereunder;

(*x*) falsifies or substitutes financial records or produces fake accounts or documents or furnishes any false information or return with an intention to evade payment of tax due under this Act;

(*xi*) is liable to be registered under this Act but fails to obtain registration;

(*xii*) furnishes any false information with regard to registration particulars, either at the time of applying for registration, or subsequently;

(*xiii*) obstructs or prevents any officer in discharge of his duties under this Act;

(*xiv*) transports any taxable goods without the cover of documents as may be specified in this behalf;

(*xv*) suppresses his turnover leading to evasion of tax under this Act;

(*xvi*) fails to keep, maintain or retain books of account and other documents in accordance with the provisions of this Act or the rules made thereunder;

(*xvii*) fails to furnish information or documents called for by an officer in accordance with the provisions of this Act or the rules made thereunder or furnishes false information or documents during any proceedings under this Act;

(*xviii*) supplies, transports or stores any goods which he has reasons to believe are liable to confiscation under this Act;

(*xix*) issues any invoice or document by using the registration number of another registered person;

(*xx*) tampers with, or destroys any material evidence or document;

(*xxi*) disposes off or tampers with any goods that have been detained, seized, or attached under this Act,

shall be liable to pay a penalty of ten thousand rupees or an amount equivalent to the tax evaded or the tax not deducted under section 51 or short deducted or deducted but not paid to the Government or tax not collected under section 52 or short collected or collected but not paid to the Government or input tax credit availed of or passed on or distributed irregularly, or the refund claimed fraudulently, whichever is higher.

[19][(1A) Any person who retains the benefit of a transaction covered under clauses (*i*), (*ii*), (*vii*) or

19. Inserted by the Finance Act, 2020, w.e.f. 1-1-2021.

clause (*ix*) of sub-section (1) and at whose instance such transaction is conducted, shall be liable to a penalty of an amount equivalent to the tax evaded or input tax credit availed of or passed on.]

[20][(1B) [21]**[***Any electronic commerce operator, who is liable to collect tax at source under section 52,***]**—

(*i*) allows a supply of goods or services or both through it by an unregistered person other than a person exempted from registration by a notification issued under this Act to make such supply;

(*ii*) allows an inter-State supply of goods or services or both through it by a person who is not eligible to make such inter-State supply; or

(*iii*) fails to furnish the correct details in the statement to be furnished under sub-section (4) of section 52 of any outward supply of goods effected through it by a person exempted from obtaining registration under this Act,

shall be liable to pay a penalty of ten thousand rupees, or an amount equivalent to the amount of tax involved had such supply been made by a registered person other than a person paying tax under section 10, whichever is higher.]

(2) Any registered person who supplies any goods or services or both on which any tax has not been paid or short-paid or erroneously refunded, or where the input tax credit has been wrongly availed or utilised,—

(*a*) for any reason, other than the reason of fraud or any wilful misstatement or suppression of facts to evade tax, shall be liable to a penalty of ten thousand rupees or ten per cent of the tax due from such person, whichever is higher;

20. Inserted by the Finance Act, 2023, w.e.f. 1-10-2023.

21. Substituted for "Any electronic commerce operator who" by the Finance (No. 2) Act, 2024, w.r.e.f. **1-10-2023**. [However, Notification No. 17/2024-Central Tax, dated 27-9-2024 appoints 1-11-2024 as the date of enforcement].

(*b*) for reason of fraud or any wilful misstatement or suppression of facts to evade tax, shall be liable to a penalty equal to ten thousand rupees or the tax due from such person, whichever is higher.

(3) Any person who—

(*a*) aids or abets any of the offences specified in clauses (*i*) to (*xxi*) of sub-section (1);

(*b*) acquires possession of, or in any way concerns himself in transporting, removing, depositing, keeping, concealing, supplying, or purchasing or in any other manner deals with any goods which he knows or has reasons to believe are liable to confiscation under this Act or the rules made thereunder;

(*c*) receives or is in any way concerned with the supply of, or in any other manner deals with any supply of services which he knows or has reasons to believe are in contravention of any provisions of this Act or the rules made thereunder;

(*d*) fails to appear before the officer of central tax, when issued with a summon for appearance to give evidence or produce a document in an inquiry;

(*e*) fails to issue invoice in accordance with the provisions of this Act or the rules made thereunder or fails to account for an invoice in his books of account,

shall be liable to a penalty which may extend to twenty five thousand rupees.

[22]**[Penalty for failure to register certain machines used in manufacture of goods as per special procedure.**

122A. *(1) Notwithstanding anything contained in this Act, where any person, who is engaged in the manufac-*

22. Inserted by the Finance Act, 2024, w.e.f. **1-10-2024**.

ture of goods in respect of which any special procedure relating to registration of machines has been notified under section 148, acts in contravention of the said special procedure, he shall, in addition to any penalty that is paid or is payable by him under Chapter XV or any other provisions of this Chapter, be liable to pay a penalty equal to an amount of one lakh rupees for every machine not so registered.

(2) In addition to the penalty under sub-section (1), every machine not so registered shall be liable for seizure and confiscation:

Provided *that such machine shall not be confiscated where—*

(a) *the penalty so imposed is paid; and*

(b) *the registration of such machine is made in accordance with the special procedure within three days of the receipt of communication of the order of penalty.*]

Penalty for failure to furnish information return.

123. If a person who is required to furnish an information return under section 150 fails to do so within the period specified in the notice issued under sub-section (3) thereof, the proper officer may direct that such person shall be liable to pay a penalty of one hundred rupees for each day of the period during which the failure to furnish such return continues:

Provided that the penalty imposed under this section shall not exceed five thousand rupees.

Fine for failure to furnish statistics.

124. If any person required to furnish any information or return under section 151,—

(*a*) without reasonable cause fails to furnish such information or return as may be required under that section, or (*b*) wilfully furnishes or causes to furnish any information or return which he knows to be false,

he shall be punishable with a fine which may extend to ten thousand rupees and in case of a continuing offence to a further fine which may extend to one hundred rupees for each day after the first day during which the offence continues subject to a maximum limit of twenty five thousand rupees.

General penalty.

125. Any person, who contravenes any of the provisions of this Act or any rules made thereunder for which no penalty is separately provided for in this Act, shall be liable to a penalty which may extend to twenty five thousand rupees.

General disciplines related to penalty.

126. (1) No officer under this Act shall impose any penalty for minor breaches of tax regulations or procedural requirements and in particular, any omission or mistake in documentation which is easily rectifiable and made without fraudulent intent or gross negligence.

Explanation.—For the purpose of this sub-section,—

(*a*) a breach shall be considered a 'minor breach' if the amount of tax involved is less than five thousand rupees;

(*b*) an omission or mistake in documentation shall be considered to be easily rectifiable if the same is an error apparent on the face of record.

(2) The penalty imposed under this Act shall depend on the facts and circumstances of each case and shall be commensurate with the degree and severity of the breach.

(3) No penalty shall be imposed on any person without giving him an opportunity of being heard.

(4) The officer under this Act shall while imposing penalty in an order for a breach of any law, regulation or procedural requirement, specify the nature of the breach and the applicable law, regulation or procedure under which the amount of penalty for the breach has been specified.

(5) When a person voluntarily discloses to an officer under this Act the circumstances of a breach of the tax law, regulation or procedural requirement prior to the discovery of the breach by the officer under this Act, the proper officer may consider this fact as a mitigating factor when quantifying a penalty for that person.

(6) The provisions of this section shall not apply in such cases where the penalty specified under this Act is either a fixed sum or expressed as a fixed percentage.

Power to impose penalty in certain cases.

127. Where the proper officer is of the view that a person is liable to a penalty and the same is not covered under any proceedings under section 62 or section 63 or section 64 or section 73 or section 74 [23]**[***or section 74A***]** or section 129 or section 130, he may issue an order levying such penalty after giving a reasonable opportunity of being heard to such person.

Power to waive penalty or fee or both.

128. The Government may, by notification, waive in part or full, any penalty referred to in section 122 or section 123 or section 125 or any late fee referred to in section 47 for such class of taxpayers and under such mitigating circumstances as may be specified therein on the recommendations of the Council.

[23]**[Waiver of interest or penalty or both relating to demands raised under section 73, for certain tax periods.**

128A. *(1) Notwithstanding anything to the contrary contained in this Act, where any amount of tax is*

---

23. Inserted by the Finance (No. 2) Act, 2024, w.e.f. **1-11-2024.**

payable by a person chargeable with tax in accordance with,—

(a) *a notice issued under sub-section (1) of section 73 or a statement issued under sub-section (3) of section 73, and where no order under sub-section (9) of section 73 has been issued; or*

(b) *an order passed under sub-section (9) of section 73, and where no order under sub-section (11) of section 107 or sub-section (1) of section 108 has been passed; or*

(c) *an order passed under sub-section (11) of section 107 or sub-section (1) of section 108, and where no order under sub-section (1) of section 113 has been passed,*

pertaining to the period from 1st July, 2017 to 31st March, 2020, or a part thereof, and the said person pays the full amount of tax payable as per the notice or statement or the order referred to in clause (a), *clause* (b) *or clause* (c), *as the case may be, on or before the date, as may be notified by the Government on the recommendations of the Council, no interest under section 50 and penalty under this Act, shall be payable and all the proceedings in respect of the said notice or order or statement, as the case may be, shall be deemed to be concluded, subject to such conditions as may be prescribed:*

Provided *that where a notice has been issued under sub-section (1) of section 74, and an order is passed or required to be passed by the proper officer in pursuance of the direction of the Appellate Authority or Appellate Tribunal or a court in accordance with the provisions of sub-section (2) of section 75, the said notice or order shall be considered to be a notice or order, as the case may be, referred to in clause* (a) *or clause* (b) *of this sub-section:*

Provided further *that the conclusion of the proceedings under this sub-section, in cases where an applica-*

*tion is filed under sub-section (3) of section 107 or under sub-section (3) of section 112 or an appeal is filed by an officer of central tax under sub-section (1) of section 117 or under sub-section (1) of section 118 or where any proceedings are initiated under sub-section (1) of section 108, against an order referred to in clause (*b*) or clause (*c*) or against the directions of the Appellate Authority or the Appellate Tribunal or the court referred to in the first proviso, shall be subject to the condition that the said person pays the additional amount of tax payable, if any, in accordance with the order of the Appellate Authority or the Appellate Tribunal or the court or the Revisional Authority, as the case may be, within three months from the date of the said order:*

Provided also *that where such interest and penalty has already been paid, no refund of the same shall be available.*

(2) Nothing contained in sub-section (1) shall be applicable in respect of any amount payable by the person on account of erroneous refund.

(3) Nothing contained in sub-section (1) shall be applicable in respect of cases where an appeal or writ petition filed by the said person is pending before Appellate Authority or Appellate Tribunal or a court, as the case may be, and has not been withdrawn by the said person on or before the date notified under sub-section (1).

*(4) Notwithstanding anything contained in this Act, where any amount specified under sub-section (1) has been paid and the proceedings are deemed to be concluded under the said sub-section, no appeal under sub-section (1) of section 107 or sub-section (1) of section 112 shall lie against an order referred to in clause (*b*) or clause (*c*) of sub-section (1), as the case may be.***]**

Detention, seizure and release of goods and conveyances in transit.

129. (1) Notwithstanding anything contained in this Act, where any person transports any goods or stores any goods while they are in transit in contravention of the provisions of this Act or the rules made thereunder, all such goods and conveyance used as a means of transport for carrying the said goods and documents relating to such goods and conveyance shall be liable to detention or seizure and after detention or seizure, shall be released,—

[24][(*a*) on payment of penalty equal to two hundred per cent of the tax payable on such goods and, in case of exempted goods, on payment of an amount equal to two per cent of the value of goods or twenty-five thousand rupees, whichever is less, where the owner of the goods comes forward for payment of such penalty;

(*b*) on payment of penalty equal to fifty per cent of the value of the goods or two hundred per cent of the tax payable on such goods, whichever is higher, and in case of exempted goods, on payment of an amount equal to five per cent of the value of goods or twenty-five thousand rupees, whichever is less, where the owner of the goods does not come forward for payment of such penalty;]

(*c*) upon furnishing a security equivalent to the amount payable under clause (*a*) or clause (*b*) in such form and manner as may be prescribed:

Provided that no such goods or conveyance shall be detained or seized without serving an order of detention or seizure on the person transporting the goods.

(2) [25][***]

[26][(3) The proper officer detaining or seizing goods or conveyance shall issue a notice within seven days

24. Substituted by the Finance Act, 2021, w.e.f. 1-1-2022.
25. Omitted, *ibid*.
26. Substituted, *ibid*.

of such detention or seizure, specifying the penalty payable, and thereafter, pass an order within a period of seven days from the date of service of such notice, for payment of penalty under clause (*a*) or clause (*b*) of sub-section (1).]

(4) [27][No penalty] shall be determined under sub-section (3) without giving the person concerned an opportunity of being heard.

(5) On payment of amount referred in sub-section (1), all proceedings in respect of the notice specified in sub-section (3) shall be deemed to be concluded.

[28][(6) Where the person transporting any goods or the owner of such goods fails to pay the amount of penalty under sub-section (1) within fifteen days from the date of receipt of the copy of the order passed under sub-section (3), the goods or conveyance so detained or seized shall be liable to be sold or disposed of otherwise, in such manner and within such time as may be prescribed, to recover the penalty payable under sub-section (3):

Provided that the conveyance shall be released on payment by the transporter of penalty under sub-section (3) or one lakh rupees, whichever is less:

Provided further that where the detained or seized goods are perishable or hazardous in nature or are likely to depreciate in value with passage of time, the said period of fifteen days may be reduced by the proper officer.]

Confiscation of goods or conveyances and levy of penalty.

130. (1) [29][Where] any person—

(*i*) supplies or receives any goods in contravention of any of the provisions of this Act or the

27. Substituted for "No tax, interest or penalty" by the Finance Act, 2021, w.e.f. 1-1-2022.
28. Substituted, *ibid*.
29. Substituted for "Notwithstanding anything contained in this Act, if", *ibid*.

rules made thereunder with intent to evade payment of tax; or

(*ii*) does not account for any goods on which he is liable to pay tax under this Act; or

(*iii*) supplies any goods liable to tax under this Act without having applied for registration; or

(*iv*) contravenes any of the provisions of this Act or the rules made thereunder with intent to evade payment of tax; or

(*v*) uses any conveyance as a means of transport for carriage of goods in contravention of the provisions of this Act or the rules made thereunder unless the owner of the conveyance proves that it was so used without the knowledge or connivance of the owner himself, his agent, if any, and the person in charge of the conveyance,

then, all such goods or conveyances shall be liable to confiscation and the person shall be liable to penalty under section 122.

(2) Whenever confiscation of any goods or conveyance is authorised by this Act, the officer adjudging it shall give to the owner of the goods an option to pay in lieu of confiscation, such fine as the said officer thinks fit:

Provided that such fine leviable shall not exceed the market value of the goods confiscated, less the tax chargeable thereon:

Provided further that the aggregate of such fine and penalty leviable shall not be less than the [30][penalty equal to hundred per cent of the tax payable on such goods]:

Provided also that where any such conveyance is used for the carriage of the goods or passengers for

30. Substituted for "amount of penalty leviable under sub-section (1) of section 129" by the Finance Act, 2021, we.f. 1-1-2022.

hire, the owner of the conveyance shall be given an option to pay in lieu of the confiscation of the conveyance a fine equal to the tax payable on the goods being transported thereon.

(3) [31][***]

(4) No order for confiscation of goods or conveyance or for imposition of penalty shall be issued without giving the person an opportunity of being heard.

(5) Where any goods or conveyance are confiscated under this Act, the title of such goods or conveyance shall thereupon vest in the Government.

(6) The proper officer adjudging confiscation shall take and hold possession of the things confiscated and every officer of Police, on the requisition of such proper officer, shall assist him in taking and holding such possession.

(7) The proper officer may, after satisfying himself that the confiscated goods or conveyance are not required in any other proceedings under this Act and after giving reasonable time not exceeding three months to pay fine in lieu of confiscation, dispose of such goods or conveyance and deposit the sale proceeds thereof with the Government.

Confiscation or penalty not to interfere with other punishments.

131. Without prejudice to the provisions contained in the Code of Criminal Procedure, 1973 (2 of 1974), no confiscation made or penalty imposed under the provisions of this Act or the rules made thereunder shall prevent the infliction of any other punishment to which the person affected thereby is liable under the provisions of this Act or under any other law for the time being in force.

31. Omitted by the Finance Act, 2021, w.e.f. 1-1-2022.

Punishment for certain offences.

132. (1) [32][Whoever commits, or causes to commit and retain the benefits arising out of, any of the following offences], namely:—

(*a*) supplies any goods or services or both without issue of any invoice, in violation of the provisions of this Act or the rules made thereunder, with the intention to evade tax;

(*b*) issues any invoice or bill without supply of goods or services or both in violation of the provisions of this Act, or the rules made thereunder leading to wrongful availment or utilisation of input tax credit or refund of tax;

[33][(*c*) avails input tax credit using the invoice or bill referred to in clause (*b*) or fraudulently avails input tax credit without any invoice or bill;]

(*d*) collects any amount as tax but fails to pay the same to the Government beyond a period of three months from the date on which such payment becomes due;

(*e*) evades tax [34][***] or fraudulently obtains refund and where such offence is not covered under clauses (*a*) to (*d*);

(*f*) falsifies or substitutes financial records or produces fake accounts or documents or furnishes any false information with an intention to evade payment of tax due under this Act;

(*g*) [35][***]

(*h*) acquires possession of, or in any way concerns himself in transporting, removing,

---

32. Substituted for "Whoever commits any of the following offences" by the Finance Act, 2020, w.e.f. 1-1-2021.
33. Substituted, *ibid.*
34. Words ", fraudulently avails input tax credit" omitted, *ibid.*
35. Omitted by the Finance Act, 2023, w.e.f. 1-10-2023.

depositing, keeping, concealing, supplying, or purchasing or in any other manner deals with, any goods which he knows or has reasons to believe are liable to confiscation under this Act or the rules made thereunder;

(*i*) receives or is in any way concerned with the supply of, or in any other manner deals with any supply of services which he knows or has reasons to believe are in contravention of any provisions of this Act or the rules made thereunder;

(*j*) [36][***]

(*k*) [36][***]

(*l*) attempts to commit, or abets the commission of any of the offences mentioned in [37][clauses (*a*) to (*f*) and clauses (*h*) and (*i*)] of this section,

shall be punishable—

(*i*) in cases where the amount of tax evaded or the amount of input tax credit wrongly availed or utilised or the amount of refund wrongly taken exceeds five hundred lakh rupees, with imprisonment for a term which may extend to five years and with fine;

(*ii*) in cases where the amount of tax evaded or the amount of input tax credit wrongly availed or utilised or the amount of refund wrongly taken exceeds two hundred lakh rupees but does not exceed five hundred lakh rupees, with imprisonment for a term which may extend to three years and with fine;

(*iii*) in the case of [38][an offence specified in clause (b),] where the amount of tax evaded or the

---

36. Omitted by the Finance Act, 2023, w.e.f. 1-10-2023.

37. Substituted for "clauses (*a*) to (*k*)", *ibid.*

38. Substituted for "any other offence", *ibid.*

amount of input tax credit wrongly availed or utilised or the amount of refund wrongly taken exceeds one hundred lakh rupees but does not exceed two hundred lakh rupees, with imprisonment for a term which may extend to one year and with fine;

(*iv*) in cases where he commits or abets the commission of an offence specified in clause (*f*) [39][***], he shall be punishable with imprisonment for a term which may extend to six months or with fine or with both.

(2) Where any person convicted of an offence under this section is again convicted of an offence under this section, then, he shall be punishable for the second and for every subsequent offence with imprisonment for a term which may extend to five years and with fine.

(3) The imprisonment referred to in clauses (*i*), (*ii*) and (*iii*) of sub-section (1) and sub-section (2) shall, in the absence of special and adequate reasons to the contrary to be recorded in the judgment of the Court, be for a term not less than six months.

(4) Notwithstanding anything contained in the Code of Criminal Procedure, 1973 (2 of 1974), all offences under this Act, except the offences referred to in sub-section (5) shall be non-cognizable and bailable.

(5) The offences specified in clause (*a*) or clause (*b*) or clause (*c*) or clause (*d*) of sub-section (1) and punishable under clause (*i*) of that sub-section shall be cognizable and non-bailable.

(6) A person shall not be prosecuted for any offence under this section except with the previous sanction of the Commissioner.

Explanation.— For the purposes of this section, the term "tax" shall include the amount of tax evaded or the amount of input tax credit wrongly availed or

39. Words "or clause (*g*) or clause (*j*)" omitted by the Finance Act, 2023, w.e.f. 1-10-2023.

utilised or refund wrongly taken under the provisions of this Act, the State Goods and Services Tax Act, the Integrated Goods and Services Tax Act or the Union Territory Goods and Services Tax Act and cess levied under the Goods and Services Tax (Compensation to States) Act.

Liability of officers and certain other persons.

133. (1) Where any person engaged in connection with the collection of statistics under section 151 or compilation or computerisation thereof or if any officer of central tax having access to information specified under sub-section (1) of section 150, or if any person engaged in connection with the provision of service on the common portal or the agent of common portal, wilfully discloses any information or the contents of any return furnished under this Act or rules made thereunder otherwise than in execution of his duties under the said sections or for the purposes of prosecution for an offence under this Act or under any other Act for the time being in force, he shall be punishable with imprisonment for a term which may extend to six months or with fine which may extend to twenty-five thousand rupees, or with both.

(2) Any person—

(*a*) who is a Government servant shall not be prosecuted for any offence under this section except with the previous sanction of the Government;

(*b*) who is not a Government servant shall not be prosecuted for any offence under this section except with the previous sanction of the Commissioner.

Cognizance of offences.

134. No court shall take cognizance of any offence punishable under this Act or the rules made thereunder except with the previous sanction of the Commissioner, and no court inferior to that of a Magistrate of the First Class, shall try any such offence.

Presumption of culpable mental state.

135. In any prosecution for an offence under this Act which requires a culpable mental state on the part of the accused, the court shall presume the existence of such mental state but it shall be a defence for the accused to prove the fact that he had no such mental state with respect to the act charged as an offence in that prosecution.

Explanation.—For the purposes of this section,—

(*i*) the expression "culpable mental state" includes intention, motive, knowledge of a fact, and belief in, or reason to believe, a fact;

(*ii*) a fact is said to be proved only when the court believes it to exist beyond reasonable doubt and not merely when its existence is established by a preponderance of probability.

Relevancy of statements under certain circumstances.

136. A statement made and signed by a person on appearance in response to any summons issued under section 70 during the course of any inquiry or proceedings under this Act shall be relevant, for the purpose of proving, in any prosecution for an offence under this Act, the truth of the facts which it contains,—

(*a*) when the person who made the statement is dead or cannot be found, or is incapable of giving evidence, or is kept out of the way by the adverse party, or whose presence cannot be obtained without an amount of delay or expense which, under the circumstances of the case, the court considers unreasonable; or

(*b*) when the person who made the statement is examined as a witness in the case before the court and the court is of the opinion that, having regard to the circumstances of the case, the statement should be admitted in evidence in the interest of justice.

Offences by companies.

137. (1) Where an offence committed by a person under this Act is a company, every person who, at the time the offence was committed was in charge of, and was responsible to, the company for the conduct of business of the company, as well as the company, shall be deemed to be guilty of the offence and shall be liable to be proceeded against and punished accordingly.

(2) Notwithstanding anything contained in sub-section (1), where an offence under this Act has been committed by a company and it is proved that the offence has been committed with the consent or connivance of, or is attributable to any negligence on the part of, any director, manager, secretary or other officer of the company, such director, manager, secretary or other officer shall also be deemed to be guilty of that offence and shall be liable to be proceeded against and punished accordingly.

(3) Where an offence under this Act has been committed by a taxable person being a partnership firm or a Limited Liability Partnership or a Hindu undivided family or a trust, the partner or *karta* or managing trustee shall be deemed to be guilty of that offence and shall be liable to be proceeded against and punished accordingly and the provisions of sub-section (2) shall, *mutatis mutandis,* apply to such persons.

(4) Nothing contained in this section shall render any such person liable to any punishment provided in this Act, if he proves that the offence was committed without his knowledge or that he had exercised all due diligence to prevent the commission of such offence.

Explanation.—For the purposes of this section,—

(*i*) "company" means a body corporate and includes a firm or other association of individuals; and (*ii*) "director", in relation to a firm, means a partner in the firm.

Compounding of offences.

138. (1) Any offence under this Act may, either before or after the institution of prosecution, be compounded by the Commissioner on payment, by the person accused of the offence, to the Central Government or the State Government, as the case may be, of such compounding amount in such manner as may be prescribed:

Provided that nothing contained in this section shall apply to—

[40][(*a*) a person who has been allowed to compound once in respect of any of the offences specified in clauses (*a*) to (*f*), (*h*), (*i*) and (*l*) of sub-section (1) of section 132;]

(*b*) [41][***]

[42][(*c*) a person who has been accused of committing an offence under clause (*b*) of sub-section (1) of section 132;]

(*d*) a person who has been convicted for an offence under this Act by a court;

(*e*) [43][***]

(*f*) any other class of persons or offences as may be prescribed:

Provided further that any compounding allowed under the provisions of this section shall not affect the proceedings, if any, instituted under any other law:

Provided also that compounding shall be allowed only after making payment of tax, interest and penalty involved in such offences.

40. Substituted by the Finance Act, 2023, w.e.f. 1-10-2023.

41. Omitted, *ibid.*

42. Substituted, *ibid.*

43. Omitted, *ibid.*

(2) The amount for compounding of offences under this section shall be such as may be prescribed, subject to the minimum amount not being less than [44][twenty-five per cent of the tax involved and the maximum amount not being more than one hundred per cent of the tax involved].

(3) On payment of such compounding amount as may be determined by the Commissioner, no further proceedings shall be initiated under this Act against the accused person in respect of the same offence and any criminal proceedings, if already initiated in respect of the said offence, shall stand abated.

CHAPTER XX

TRANSITIONAL PROVISIONS

Migration of existing taxpayers.

139. (1) On and from the appointed day, every person registered under any of the existing laws and having a valid Permanent Account Number shall be issued a certificate of registration on provisional basis, subject to such conditions and in such form and manner as may be prescribed, which unless replaced by a final certificate of registration under sub-section (2), shall be liable to be cancelled if the conditions so prescribed are not complied with.

(2) The final certificate of registration shall be granted in such form and manner and subject to such conditions as may be prescribed.

(3) The certificate of registration issued to a person under sub-section (1) shall be deemed to have not been issued if the said registration is cancelled in pursuance of an application filed by such person

44. Substituted for "ten thousand rupees or fifty per cent of the tax involved, whichever is higher, and the maximum amount not being less than thirty thousand rupees or one hundred and fifty per cent of the tax, whichever is higher" by the Finance Act, 2023, w.e.f. 1-10-2023.

that he was not liable to registration under section 22 or section 24.

Transitional arrangements for input tax credit.

140. (1) A registered person, other than a person opting to pay tax under section 10, shall be entitled to take, in his electronic credit ledger, the amount of CENVAT credit [45][of eligible duties] carried forward in the return relating to the period ending with the day immediately preceding the appointed day, furnished by him under the existing law [46][within such time and] in such manner as may be prescribed:

Provided that the registered person shall not be allowed to take credit in the following circumstances, namely:—

(*i*) where the said amount of credit is not admissible as input tax credit under this Act; or

(*ii*) where he has not furnished all the returns required under the existing law for the period of six months immediately preceding the appointed date; or

(*iii*) where the said amount of credit relates to goods manufactured and cleared under such exemption notifications as are notified by the Government.

(2) A registered person, other than a person opting to pay tax under section 10, shall be entitled to take, in his electronic credit ledger, credit of the unavailed CENVAT credit in respect of capital goods, not carried forward in a return, furnished under the existing law by him, for the period ending with the day immediately

45. Inserted by the Central Goods and Services Tax (Amendment) Act, 2018, w.r.e.f. 1-7-2017.

46. Inserted by the Finance Act, 2020, w.r.e.f. 1-7-2017 [However, Notification No. 43/2020-Central Tax, dated 16-5-2020 appoints 18-5-2020 as the date of enforcement].

preceding the appointed day [47][within such time and] in such manner as may be prescribed:

Provided that the registered person shall not be allowed to take credit unless the said credit was admissible as CENVAT credit under the existing law and is also admissible as input tax credit under this Act.

Explanation.—For the purposes of this sub-section, the expression "unavailed CENVAT credit" means the amount that remains after subtracting the amount of CENVAT credit already availed in respect of capital goods by the taxable person under the existing law from the aggregate amount of CENVAT credit to which the said person was entitled in respect of the said capital goods under the existing law.

(3) A registered person, who was not liable to be registered under the existing law, or who was engaged in the manufacture of exempted goods or provision of exempted services, or who was providing works contract service and was availing of the benefit of Notification No. 26/2012-Service Tax, dated the 20th June, 2012 or a first stage dealer or a second stage dealer or a registered importer or a depot of a manufacturer, shall be entitled to take, in his electronic credit ledger, credit of eligible duties in respect of inputs held in stock and inputs contained in semi-finished or finished [48][goods held in stock on the appointed day, within such time and in such manner as may be prescribed, subject to] the following conditions, namely:—

(*i*) such inputs or goods are used or intended to be used for making taxable supplies under this Act;

47. Inserted by the Finance Act, 2020, w.r.e.f. 1-7-2017 [However, Notification No. 43/2020-Central Tax, dated 16-5-2020 appoints 18-5-2020 as the date of enforcement].

48. Substituted for "goods held in stock on the appointed day subject to" by the Finance Act, 2020, w.r.e.f. 1-7-2017 [However, Notification No. 43/2020-Central Tax, dated 16-5-2020 appoints 18-5-2020 as the date of enforcement].

(*ii*) the said registered person is eligible for input tax credit on such inputs under this Act;

(*iii*) the said registered person is in possession of invoice or other prescribed documents evidencing payment of duty under the existing law in respect of such inputs;

(*iv*) such invoices or other prescribed documents were issued not earlier than twelve months immediately preceding the appointed day; and

(*v*) the supplier of services is not eligible for any abatement under this Act:

Provided that where a registered person, other than a manufacturer or a supplier of services, is not in possession of an invoice or any other documents evidencing payment of duty in respect of inputs, then, such registered person shall, subject to such conditions, limitations and safeguards as may be prescribed, including that the said taxable person shall pass on the benefit of such credit by way of reduced prices to the recipient, be allowed to take credit at such rate and in such manner as may be prescribed.

(4) A registered person, who was engaged in the manufacture of taxable as well as exempted goods under the Central Excise Act, 1944 (1 of 1944) or provision of taxable as well as exempted services under Chapter V of the Finance Act, 1994 (32 of 1994), but which are liable to tax under this Act, shall be entitled to take, in his electronic credit ledger,—

(*a*) the amount of CENVAT credit carried forward in a return furnished under the existing law by him in accordance with the provisions of sub-section (1); and

(*b*) the amount of CENVAT credit of eligible duties in respect of inputs held in stock and inputs contained in semi-finished or finished goods held in stock on the appointed day, relating to such exempted goods or services, in accordance with the provisions of sub-section (3).

(5) A registered person shall be entitled to take, in his electronic credit ledger, credit of eligible duties and taxes in respect of inputs or input services received on or after the appointed day but the duty or tax in respect of which has been paid by the supplier under the [49][existing law, within such time and in such manner as may be prescribed], subject to the condition that the invoice or any other duty or tax paying document of the same was recorded in the books of account of such person within a period of thirty days from the appointed day:

Provided that the period of thirty days may, on sufficient cause being shown, be extended by the Commissioner for a further period not exceeding thirty days:

Provided further that said registered person shall furnish a statement, in such manner as may be prescribed, in respect of credit that has been taken under this sub-section.

(6) A registered person, who was either paying tax at a fixed rate or paying a fixed amount in lieu of the tax payable under the existing law shall be entitled to take, in his electronic credit ledger, credit of eligible duties in respect of inputs held in stock and inputs contained in semi-finished or finished [50][goods held in stock on the appointed day, within such time and in such manner as may be prescribed, subject to] the following conditions, namely:—

49. Substituted for "existing law" by the Finance Act, 2020, w.r.e.f. 1-7-2017 [However, Notification No. 43/2020-Central Tax, dated 16-5-2020 appoints 18-5-2020 as the date of enforcement].

50. Substituted for "goods held in stock on the appointed day subject to", *ibid.*

(*i*) such inputs or goods are used or intended to be used for making taxable supplies under this Act;

(*ii*) the said registered person is not paying tax under section 10;

(*iii*) the said registered person is eligible for input tax credit on such inputs under this Act;

(*iv*) the said registered person is in possession of invoice or other prescribed documents evidencing payment of duty under the existing law in respect of inputs; and

(*v*) such invoices or other prescribed documents were issued not earlier than twelve months immediately preceding the appointed day.

(7) Notwithstanding anything to the contrary contained in this Act, the input tax credit on account of any services received prior to the appointed day by an Input Service Distributor shall be eligible for distribution as [51][credit under this Act, within such time and in such manner as may be prescribed, [52]**[***whether the invoices relating to such services are received prior to, on or after, the appointed day***]**].

(8) Where a registered person having centralised registration under the existing law has obtained a registration under this Act, such person shall be allowed to take, in his electronic credit ledger, credit of the amount of CENVAT credit carried forward in a return, furnished under the existing law by him, in respect of the period ending with the day immediately

51. Substituted for "credit under this Act even if" by the Finance Act, 2020, w.r.e.f. 1-7-2017 [However, Notification No. 43/2020-Central Tax, dated 16-5-2020 appoints 18-5-2020 as the date of enforcement].

52. Substituted for "even if the invoices relating to such services are received on or after the appointed day" by the Finance (No. 2) Act, 2024, w.r.e.f. **1-7-2017**. [However, Notification No. 17/2024-Central Tax, dated 27-9-2024 appoints 1-11-2024 as the date of enforcement].

preceding the appointed day [53][within such time and in such manner] as may be prescribed:

Provided that if the registered person furnishes his return for the period ending with the day immediately preceding the appointed day within three months of the appointed day, such credit shall be allowed subject to the condition that the said return is either an original return or a revised return where the credit has been reduced from that claimed earlier:

Provided further that the registered person shall not be allowed to take credit unless the said amount is admissible as input tax credit under this Act:

Provided also that such credit may be transferred to any of the registered persons having the same Permanent Account Number for which the centralised registration was obtained under the existing law.

(9) Where any CENVAT credit availed for the input services provided under the existing law has been reversed due to non-payment of the consideration within a period of three months, such [54][credit can be reclaimed within such time and in such manner as may be prescribed, subject to] the condition that the registered person has made the payment of the consideration for that supply of services within a period of three months from the appointed day.

(10) The amount of credit under sub-sections (3), (4) and (6) shall be calculated in such manner as may be prescribed.

---

53. Substituted for "in such manner" by the Finance Act, 2020, w.r.e.f. 1-7-2017 [However, Notification No. 43/2020-Central Tax, dated 16-5-2020 appoints 18-5-2020 as the date of enforcement].

54. Substituted for "credit can be reclaimed subject to" by the Finance Act, 2020, w.r.e.f. 1-7-2017 [However, Notification No. 43/2020-Central Tax, dated 16-5-2020 appoints 18-5-2020 as the date of enforcement].

Explanation 1.—For the purposes of [55][sub-sections (1), (3), (4)] and (6), the expression "eligible duties" means—

(*i*) the additional duty of excise leviable under section 3 of the Additional Duties of Excise (Goods of Special Importance) Act, 1957 (58 of 1957);

(*ii*) the additional duty leviable under sub-section (1) of section 3 of the Customs Tariff Act, 1975 (51 of 1975);

(*iii*) the additional duty leviable under sub-section (5) of section 3 of the Customs Tariff Act, 1975 (51 of 1975);

(*iv*) [56][***]

(*v*) the duty of excise specified in the First Schedule to the Central Excise Tariff Act, 1985 (5 of 1986);

(*vi*) the duty of excise specified in the Second Schedule to the Central Excise Tariff Act, 1985 (5 of 1986); and

(*vii*) the National Calamity Contingent Duty leviable under section 136 of the Finance Act, 2001 (14 of 2001),

in respect of inputs held in stock and inputs contained in semi-finished or finished goods held in stock on the appointed day.

Explanation 2.—For the purposes of [57][sub-sections (1) and (5)], the expression "eligible duties and taxes" means—

---

55. Substituted for "sub-sections (3), (4)" by the Central Goods and Services Tax (Amendment) Act, 2018, w.r.e.f. 1-7-2017.

56. Omitted, *ibid.*

57. Substituted for "sub-section (5)", *ibid.*

(*i*) the additional duty of excise leviable under section 3 of the Additional Duties of Excise (Goods of Special Importance) Act, 1957 (58 of 1957);

(*ii*) the additional duty leviable under sub-section (1) of section 3 of the Customs Tariff Act, 1975 (51 of 1975);

(*iii*) the additional duty leviable under sub-section (5) of section 3 of the Customs Tariff Act, 1975 (51 of 1975);

(*iv*) [58][***]

(*v*) the duty of excise specified in the First Schedule to the Central Excise Tariff Act, 1985 (5 of 1986);

(*vi*) the duty of excise specified in the Second Schedule to the Central Excise Tariff Act, 1985 (5 of 1986);

(*vii*) the National Calamity Contingent Duty leviable under section 136 of the Finance Act, 2001 (14 of 2001); and

(*viii*) the service tax leviable under section 66B of the Finance Act, 1994 (32 of 1994),

in respect of inputs and input services received on or after the appointed day.

[59][*Explanation 3.*—For removal of doubts, it is hereby clarified that the expression "eligible duties and taxes" excludes any cess which has not been specified in *Explanation 1* or *Explanation 2* and any cess which is collected as additional duty of customs under sub-section (1) of section 3 of the Customs Tariff Act, 1975 (51 of 1975).]

58. Omitted by the Central Goods and Services Tax (Amendment) Act, 2018, w.r.e.f. 1-7-2017.

59. Inserted, *ibid.*

Transitional provisions relating to job work.

141. (1) Where any inputs received at a place of business had been removed as such or removed after being partially processed to a job worker for further processing, testing, repair, reconditioning or any other purpose in accordance with the provisions of existing law prior to the appointed day and such inputs are returned to the said place on or after the appointed day, no tax shall be payable if such inputs, after completion of the job work or otherwise, are returned to the said place within six months from the appointed day:

Provided that the period of six months may, on sufficient cause being shown, be extended by the Commissioner for a further period not exceeding two months:

Provided further that if such inputs are not returned within the period specified in this sub-section, the input tax credit shall be liable to be recovered in accordance with the provisions of clause (*a*) of sub-section (8) of section 142.

(2) Where any semi-finished goods had been removed from the place of business to any other premises for carrying out certain manufacturing processes in accordance with the provisions of existing law prior to the appointed day and such goods (hereafter in this section referred to as "the said goods") are returned to the said place on or after the appointed day, no tax shall be payable, if the said goods, after undergoing manufacturing processes or otherwise, are returned to the said place within six months from the appointed day:

Provided that the period of six months may, on sufficient cause being shown, be extended by the Commissioner for a further period not exceeding two months:

Provided further that if the said goods are not returned within the period specified in this sub-section, the input tax credit shall be liable to be recovered in accordance with the provisions of clause (*a*) of sub-section (8) of section 142:

Provided also that the manufacturer may, in accordance with the provisions of the existing law, transfer the said goods to the premises of any registered person for the purpose of supplying therefrom on payment of tax in India or without payment of tax for exports within the period specified in this sub-section.

(3) Where any excisable goods manufactured at a place of business had been removed without payment of duty for carrying out tests or any other process not amounting to manufacture, to any other premises, whether registered or not, in accordance with the provisions of existing law prior to the appointed day and such goods, are returned to the said place on or after the appointed day, no tax shall be payable if the said goods, after undergoing tests or any other process, are returned to the said place within six months from the appointed day:

Provided that the period of six months may, on sufficient cause being shown, be extended by the Commissioner for a further period not exceeding two months:

Provided further that if the said goods are not returned within the period specified in this sub-section, the input tax credit shall be liable to be recovered in accordance with the provisions of clause (*a*) of sub-section (8) of section 142:

Provided also that the manufacturer may, in accordance with the provisions of the existing law, transfer the said goods from the said other premises on payment of tax in India or without payment of tax for exports within the period specified in this sub-section.

(4) The tax under sub-sections (1), (2) and (3) shall not be payable, only if the manufacturer and the job worker declare the details of the inputs or goods held

in stock by the job worker on behalf of the manufacturer on the appointed day in such form and manner and within such time as may be prescribed.

Miscellaneous transitional provisions.

142. (1) Where any goods on which duty, if any, had been paid under the existing law at the time of removal thereof, not being earlier than six months prior to the appointed day, are returned to any place of business on or after the appointed day, the registered person shall be eligible for refund of the duty paid under the existing law where such goods are returned by a person, other than a registered person, to the said place of business within a period of six months from the appointed day and such goods are identifiable to the satisfaction of the proper officer:

Provided that if the said goods are returned by a registered person, the return of such goods shall be deemed to be a supply.

(2) (*a*) Where, in pursuance of a contract entered into prior to the appointed day, the price of any goods or services or both is revised upwards on or after the appointed day, the registered person who had removed or provided such goods or services or both shall issue to the recipient a supplementary invoice or debit note, containing such particulars as may be prescribed, within thirty days of such price revision and for the purposes of this Act such supplementary invoice or debit note shall be deemed to have been issued in respect of an outward supply made under this Act;

(*b*) Where, in pursuance of a contract entered into prior to the appointed day, the price of any goods or services or both is revised downwards on or after the appointed day, the registered person who had removed or provided such goods or services or both may issue to the recipient a credit note, containing such particulars as may be prescribed, within thirty days of such price revision and for the purposes of this Act such credit note shall be deemed to have been issued in respect of an outward supply made under this Act:

Provided that the registered person shall be allowed to reduce his tax liability on account of issue of the credit note only if the recipient of the credit note has reduced his input tax credit corresponding to such reduction of tax liability.

(3) Every claim for refund filed by any person before, on or after the appointed day, for refund of any amount of CENVAT credit, duty, tax, interest or any other amount paid under the existing law, shall be disposed of in accordance with the provisions of existing law and any amount eventually accruing to him shall be paid in cash, notwithstanding anything to the contrary contained under the provisions of existing law other than the provisions of sub-section (2) of section 11B of the Central Excise Act, 1944 (1 of 1944):

Provided that where any claim for refund of CENVAT credit is fully or partially rejected, the amount so rejected shall lapse:

Provided further that no refund shall be allowed of any amount of CENVAT credit where the balance of the said amount as on the appointed day has been carried forward under this Act.

(4) Every claim for refund filed after the appointed day for refund of any duty or tax paid under existing law in respect of the goods or services exported before or after the appointed day, shall be disposed of in accordance with the provisions of the existing law:

Provided that where any claim for refund of CENVAT credit is fully or partially rejected, the amount so rejected shall lapse:

Provided further that no refund shall be allowed of any amount of CENVAT credit where the balance of the said amount as on the appointed day has been carried forward under this Act.

(5) Every claim filed by a person after the appointed day for refund of tax paid under the existing law in respect of services not provided shall be disposed of in accordance with the provisions of existing law and any amount eventually accruing to him shall be paid in cash, notwithstanding anything to the contrary contained under the provisions of existing law other than the provisions of sub-section (2) of section 11B of the Central Excise Act, 1944 (1 of 1944).

(6) (*a*) Every proceeding of appeal, review or reference relating to a claim for CENVAT credit initiated whether before, on or after the appointed day under the existing law shall be disposed of in accordance with the provisions of existing law, and any amount of credit found to be admissible to the claimant shall be refunded to him in cash, notwithstanding anything to the contrary contained under the provisions of existing law other than the provisions of sub-section (2) of section 11B of the Central Excise Act, 1944 (1 of 1944) and the amount rejected, if any, shall not be admissible as input tax credit under this Act:

Provided that no refund shall be allowed of any amount of CENVAT credit where the balance of the said amount as on the appointed day has been carried forward under this Act;

(*b*) Every proceeding of appeal, review or reference relating to recovery of CENVAT credit initiated whether before, on or after the appointed day under the existing law shall be disposed of in accordance with the provisions of existing law and if any amount of credit becomes recoverable as a result of such appeal, review or reference, the same shall, unless recovered under the existing law, be recovered as an arrear of tax under this Act and the amount so recovered shall not be admissible as input tax credit under this Act.

(7) (*a*) Every proceeding of appeal, review or reference relating to any output duty or tax liability initiated whether before, on or after the appointed day under the existing law, shall be disposed of in accordance

with the provisions of the existing law, and if any amount becomes recoverable as a result of such appeal, review or reference, the same shall, unless recovered under the existing law, be recovered as an arrear of duty or tax under this Act and the amount so recovered shall not be admissible as input tax credit under this Act.

(*b*) Every proceeding of appeal, review or reference relating to any output duty or tax liability initiated whether before, on or after the appointed day under the existing law, shall be disposed of in accordance with the provisions of the existing law, and any amount found to be admissible to the claimant shall be refunded to him in cash, notwithstanding anything to the contrary contained under the provisions of existing law other than the provisions of sub-section (2) of section 11B of the Central Excise Act, 1944 (1 of 1944) and the amount rejected, if any, shall not be admissible as input tax credit under this Act.

(8) (*a*) Where in pursuance of an assessment or adjudication proceedings instituted, whether before, on or after the appointed day, under the existing law, any amount of tax, interest, fine or penalty becomes recoverable from the person, the same shall, unless recovered under the existing law, be recovered as an arrear of tax under this Act and the amount so recovered shall not be admissible as input tax credit under this Act;

(*b*) Where in pursuance of an assessment or adjudication proceedings instituted, whether before, on or after the appointed day, under the existing law, any amount of tax, interest, fine or penalty becomes refundable to the taxable person, the same shall be refunded to him in cash under the said law, notwithstanding anything to the contrary contained in the said law other than the provisions of sub-section (2) of section 11B of the Central Excise Act, 1944 (1 of 1944) and the amount rejected, if any, shall not be admissible as input tax credit under this Act.

(9) (*a*) Where any return, furnished under the existing law, is revised after the appointed day and if, pursuant to such revision, any amount is found to be recoverable or any amount of CENVAT credit is found to be inadmissible, the same shall, unless recovered under the existing law, be recovered as an arrear of tax under this Act and the amount so recovered shall not be admissible as input tax credit under this Act;

(*b*) Where any return, furnished under the existing law, is revised after the appointed day but within the time limit specified for such revision under the existing law and if, pursuant to such revision, any amount is found to be refundable or CENVAT credit is found to be admissible to any taxable person, the same shall be refunded to him in cash under the existing law, notwithstanding anything to the contrary contained in the said law other than the provisions of sub-section (2) of section 11B of the Central Excise Act, 1944 (1 of 1944) and the amount rejected, if any, shall not be admissible as input tax credit under this Act.

(10) Save as otherwise provided in this Chapter, the goods or services or both supplied on or after the appointed day in pursuance of a contract entered into prior to the appointed day shall be liable to tax under the provisions of this Act.

(11) (*a*) Notwithstanding anything contained in section 12, no tax shall be payable on goods under this Act to the extent the tax was leviable on the said goods under the Value Added Tax Act of the State;

(*b*) Notwithstanding anything contained in section 13, no tax shall be payable on services under this Act to the extent the tax was leviable on the said services under Chapter V of the Finance Act, 1994 (32 of 1994);

(*c*) Where tax was paid on any supply both under the Value Added Tax Act and under Chapter V of the Finance Act, 1994 (32 of 1994), tax shall be leviable under this Act and the taxable person shall be entitled to take credit of value added tax or service tax paid under the existing law to the extent of supplies made after the appointed day and such credit shall be calculated in such manner as may be prescribed.

(12) Where any goods sent on approval basis, not earlier than six months before the appointed day, are rejected or not approved by the buyer and returned to the seller on or after the appointed day, no tax shall be payable thereon if such goods are returned within six months from the appointed day:

Provided that the said period of six months may, on sufficient cause being shown, be extended by the Commissioner for a further period not exceeding two months:

Provided further that the tax shall be payable by the person returning the goods if such goods are liable to tax under this Act, and are returned after a period specified in this sub-section:

Provided also that tax shall be payable by the person who has sent the goods on approval basis if such goods are liable to tax under this Act, and are not returned within a period specified in this sub-section.

(13) Where a supplier has made any sale of goods in respect of which tax was required to be deducted at source under any law of a State or Union territory relating to Value Added Tax and has also issued an invoice for the same before the appointed day, no deduction of tax at source under section 51 shall be made by the deductor under the said section where payment to the said supplier is made on or after the appointed day.

Explanation.—For the purposes of this Chapter, the expressions "capital goods", "Central Value Added Tax (CENVAT) credit", "first stage dealer", "second stage dealer", or "manufacture" shall have the same meaning as respectively assigned to them in the Central Excise Act, 1944 (1 of 1944) or the rules made thereunder.

CHAPTER XXI

MISCELLANEOUS

Job work procedure.

143. (1) A registered person (hereafter in this section referred to as the "principal") may under intimation and subject to such conditions as may be prescribed, send any inputs or capital goods, without payment of tax, to a job worker for job work and from there subsequently send to another job worker and likewise, and shall,—

(*a*) bring back inputs, after completion of job work or otherwise, or capital goods, other than moulds and dies, jigs and fixtures, or tools, within one year and three years, respectively, of their being sent out, to any of his place of business, without payment of tax;

(*b*) supply such inputs, after completion of job work or otherwise, or capital goods, other than moulds and dies, jigs and fixtures, or tools, within one year and three years, respectively, of their being sent out from the place of business of a job worker on payment of tax within India, or with or without payment of tax for export, as the case may be:

Provided that the principal shall not supply the goods from the place of business of a job worker in accordance with the provisions of this clause unless the said principal declares the place of business of the job worker as his additional place of business except in a case—

(*i*) where the job worker is registered under section 25; or

(*ii*) where the principal is engaged in the supply of such goods as may be notified by the Commissioner:

[60][**Provided further** that the period of one year and three years may, on sufficient cause being shown, be extended by the Commissioner for a further period not exceeding one year and two years respectively.]

(2) The responsibility for keeping proper accounts for the inputs or capital goods shall lie with the principal.

(3) Where the inputs sent for job work are not received back by the principal after completion of job work or otherwise in accordance with the provisions of clause (*a*) of sub-section (1) or are not supplied from the place of business of the job worker in accordance with the provisions of clause (*b*) of sub-section (1) within a period of one year of their being sent out, it shall be deemed that such inputs had been supplied by the principal to the job worker on the day when the said inputs were sent out.

(4) Where the capital goods, other than moulds and dies, jigs and fixtures, or tools, sent for job work are not received back by the principal in accordance with the provisions of clause (*a*) of sub-section (1) or are not supplied from the place of business of the job worker in accordance with the provisions of clause (*b*) of sub-section (1) within a period of three years of their being sent out, it shall be deemed that such capital goods had been supplied by the principal to the job worker on the day when the said capital goods were sent out.

(5) Notwithstanding anything contained in sub-sections (1) and (2), any waste and scrap generated during the job work may be supplied by the job worker directly from his place of business on payment of tax, if such job worker is registered, or by the principal, if the job worker is not registered.

Explanation.—For the purposes of job work, input includes intermediate goods arising from any treat-

60. Inserted by the Central Goods and Services Tax (Amendment) Act, 2018, w.e.f. 1-2-2019.

ment or process carried out on the inputs by the principal or the job worker.

Presumption as to documents in certain cases.

144. Where any document—

(*i*) is produced by any person under this Act or any other law for the time being in force; or

(*ii*) has been seized from the custody or control of any person under this Act or any other law for the time being in force; or

(*iii*) has been received from any place outside India in the course of any proceedings under this Act or any other law for the time being in force,

and such document is tendered by the prosecution in evidence against him or any other person who is tried jointly with him, the court shall—

(*a*) unless the contrary is proved by such person, presume—

(*i*) the truth of the contents of such document;

(*ii*) that the signature and every other part of such document which purports to be in the handwriting of any particular person or which the court may reasonably assume to have been signed by, or to be in the handwriting of, any particular person, is in that person's handwriting, and in the case of a document executed or attested, that it was executed or attested by the person by whom it purports to have been so executed or attested;

(*b*) admit the document in evidence notwithstanding that it is not duly stamped, if such document is otherwise admissible in evidence.

Admissibility of micro films, facsimile copies of documents and computer printouts as documents and as evidence.

145. (1) Notwithstanding anything contained in any other law for the time being in force,—

(*a*) a micro film of a document or the reproduction of the image or images embodied in such micro film (whether enlarged or not); or

(*b*) a facsimile copy of a document; or

(*c*) a statement contained in a document and included in a printed material produced by a computer, subject to such conditions as may be prescribed; or

(*d*) any information stored electronically in any device or media, including any hard copies made of such information,

shall be deemed to be a document for the purposes of this Act and the rules made thereunder and shall be admissible in any proceedings thereunder, without further proof or production of the original, as evidence of any contents of the original or of any fact stated therein of which direct evidence would be admissible.

(2) In any proceedings under this Act or the rules made thereunder, where it is desired to give a statement in evidence by virtue of this section, a certificate,—

(*a*) identifying the document containing the statement and describing the manner in which it was produced;

(*b*) giving such particulars of any device involved in the production of that document as may be appropriate for the purpose of showing that the document was produced by a computer,

shall be evidence of any matter stated in the certificate and for the purposes of this sub-section it shall be sufficient for a matter to be stated to the best of the knowledge and belief of the person stating it.

Common Portal.

146. The Government may, on the recommendations of the Council, notify the Common Goods and Services Tax Electronic Portal for facilitating registration, payment of tax, furnishing of returns, computation and settlement of integrated tax, electronic way bill and for carrying out such other functions and for such purposes as may be prescribed.

Deemed Exports.

147. The Government may, on the recommendations of the Council, notify certain supplies of goods as deemed exports, where goods supplied do not leave India, and payment for such supplies is received either in Indian rupees or in convertible foreign exchange, if such goods are manufactured in India.

Special procedure for certain processes.

148. The Government may, on the recommendations of the Council, and subject to such conditions and safeguards as may be prescribed, notify certain classes of registered persons, and the special procedures to be followed by such persons including those with regard to registration, furnishing of return, payment of tax and administration of such persons.

Goods and services tax compliance rating.

149. (1) Every registered person may be assigned a goods and services tax compliance rating score by the Government based on his record of compliance with the provisions of this Act.

(2) The goods and services tax compliance rating score may be determined on the basis of such parameters as may be prescribed.

(3) The goods and services tax compliance rating score may be updated at periodic intervals and intimated to the registered person and also placed in the public domain in such manner as may be prescribed.

Obligation to furnish information return.

150. (1) Any person, being—

(*a*) a taxable person; or

(*b*) a local authority or other public body or association; or

(*c*) any authority of the State Government responsible for the collection of value added tax or sales tax or State excise duty or an authority of the Central Government responsible for the collection of excise duty or customs duty; or

(*d*) an income-tax authority appointed under the provisions of the Income-tax Act, 1961 (43 of 1961); or

(*e*) a banking company within the meaning of clause (*a*) of section 45A of the Reserve Bank of India Act, 1934 (2 of 1934); or

(*f*) a State Electricity Board or an electricity distribution or transmission licensee under the Electricity Act, 2003 (36 of 2003), or any other entity entrusted with such functions by the Central Government or the State Government; or

(*g*) the Registrar or Sub-Registrar appointed under section 6 of the Registration Act, 1908 (16 of 1908); or

(*h*) a Registrar within the meaning of the Companies Act, 2013 (18 of 2013); or

(*i*) the registering authority empowered to register motor vehicles under the Motor Vehicles Act, 1988 (59 of 1988); or

(*j*) the Collector referred to in clause (*g*) of section 3 of the Right to Fair Compensation and Transparency in Land Acquisition, Rehabilitation and Resettlement Act, 2013 (30 of 2013); or (*k*) the recognised stock exchange referred to in clause (*f*) of section 2 of the Securities Contracts (Regulation) Act, 1956 (42 of 1956); or

(*l*) a depository referred to in clause (*e*) of sub-section (1) of section 2 of the Depositories Act, 1996 (22 of 1996); or

(*m*) an officer of the Reserve Bank of India as constituted under section 3 of the Reserve Bank of India Act, 1934 (2 of 1934); or

(*n*) the Goods and Services Tax Network, a company registered under the Companies Act, 2013 (18 of 2013); or

(*o*) a person to whom a Unique Identity Number has been granted under sub-section (9) of section 25; or

(*p*) any other person as may be specified, on the recommendations of the Council, by the Government,

who is responsible for maintaining record of registration or statement of accounts or any periodic return or document containing details of payment of tax and other details of transaction of goods or services or both or transactions related to a bank account or consumption of electricity or transaction of purchase, sale or exchange of goods or property or right or interest in a property under any law for the time being in force, shall furnish an information return of the same in respect of such periods, within such time, in such form and manner and to such authority or agency as may be prescribed.

(2) Where the Commissioner, or an officer authorised by him in this behalf, considers that the information furnished in the information return is defective, he may intimate the defect to the person who has furnished such information return and give him an opportunity of rectifying the defect within a period of thirty days from the date of such intimation or

within such further period which, on an application made in this behalf, the said authority may allow and if the defect is not rectified within the said period of thirty days or, the further period so allowed, then, notwithstanding anything contained in any other provisions of this Act, such information return shall be treated as not furnished and the provisions of this Act shall apply.

(3) Where a person who is required to furnish information return has not furnished the same within the time specified in sub-section (1) or sub-section (2), the said authority may serve upon him a notice requiring furnishing of such information return within a period not exceeding ninety days from the date of service of the notice and such person shall furnish the information return.

[61][Power to call for information.

151. The Commissioner or an officer authorised by him may, by an order, direct any person to furnish information relating to any matter dealt with in connection with this Act, within such time, in such form, and in such manner, as may be specified therein.]

Bar on disclosure of information.

152. (1) No information [62][***] with respect to any matter given for the purposes of section 150 or section 151 shall, without the previous consent in writing of the concerned person or his authorised representative, be published in such manner so as to enable such particulars to be identified as referring to a particular person and no such information shall be used for the purpose of any proceedings under this Act [63][without giving an opportunity of being heard to the person concerned].

61. Substituted by the Finance Act, 2021, w.e.f. 1-1-2022.

62. Words "of any individual return or part thereof" omitted, *ibid.*

63. Inserted, *ibid.*

(2) [64][***]

(3) Nothing in this section shall apply to the publication of any information relating to a class of taxable persons or class of transactions, if in the opinion of the Commissioner, it is desirable in the public interest to publish such information.

Taking assistance from an expert.

153. Any officer not below the rank of Assistant Commissioner may, having regard to the nature and complexity of the case and the interest of revenue, take assistance of any expert at any stage of scrutiny, inquiry, investigation or any other proceedings before him.

Power to take samples.

154. The Commissioner or an officer authorised by him may take samples of goods from the possession of any taxable person, where he considers it necessary, and provide a receipt for any samples so taken.

Burden of proof.

155. Where any person claims that he is eligible for input tax credit under this Act, the burden of proving such claim shall lie on such person.

Persons deemed to be public servants.

156. All persons discharging functions under this Act shall be deemed to be public servants within the meaning of section 21 of the Indian Penal Code (45 of 1860).

Protection of action taken under this Act.

157. (1) No suit, prosecution or other legal proceedings shall lie against the President, State President, Members, officers or other employees of the Appellate Tribunal or any other person authorised by the said Appellate Tribunal for anything which is in good faith done or intended to be done under this Act or the rules made thereunder.

64. Omitted by the Finance Act, 2021, w.e.f. 1-1-2022.

(2) No suit, prosecution or other legal proceedings shall lie against any officer appointed or authorised under this Act for anything which is done or intended to be done in good faith under this Act or the rules made thereunder.

Disclosure of information by a public servant.

158. (1) All particulars contained in any statement made, return furnished or accounts or documents produced in accordance with this Act, or in any record of evidence given in the course of any proceedings under this Act (other than proceedings before a criminal court), or in any record of any proceedings under this Act shall, save as provided in sub-section (3), not be disclosed.

(2) Notwithstanding anything contained in the Indian Evidence Act, 1872 (1 of 1872), no court shall, save as otherwise provided in sub-section (3), require any officer appointed or authorised under this Act to produce before it or to give evidence before it in respect of particulars referred to in sub-section (1).

(3) Nothing contained in this section shall apply to the disclosure of,—

(*a*) any particulars in respect of any statement, return, accounts, documents, evidence, affidavit or deposition, for the purpose of any prosecution under the Indian Penal Code (45 of 1860) or the Prevention of Corruption Act, 1988 (49 of 1988), or any other law for the time being in force; or

(*b*) any particulars to the Central Government or the State Government or to any person acting in the implementation of this Act, for the purposes of carrying out the objects of this Act; or

(*c*) any particulars when such disclosure is occasioned by the lawful exercise under this Act of any process for the service of any notice or recovery of any demand; or (*d*) any particulars to a civil court in any suit or proceedings, to which the Government or any authority under this Act is a party, which relates to any matter arising out of any proceedings under this Act or under any other law for the time being in force authorising any such authority to exercise any powers thereunder; or

(*e*) any particulars to any officer appointed for the purpose of audit of tax receipts or refunds of the tax imposed by this Act; or

(*f*) any particulars where such particulars are relevant for the purposes of any inquiry into the conduct of any officer appointed or authorised under this Act, to any person or persons appointed as an inquiry officer under any law for the time being in force; or

(*g*) any such particulars to an officer of the Central Government or of any State Government, as may be necessary for the purpose of enabling that Government to levy or realise any tax or duty; or

(*h*) any particulars when such disclosure is occasioned by the lawful exercise by a public servant or any other statutory authority, of his or its powers under any law for the time being in force; or

(*i*) any particulars relevant to any inquiry into a charge of misconduct in connection with any proceedings under this Act against a practising advocate, a tax practitioner, a practising cost accountant, a practising chartered accountant, a practising company secretary to the authority empowered to take disciplinary action against the members practising the profession of a legal practitioner, a cost accountant, a chartered accountant or a company secretary, as the case may be; or (*j*) any particulars to any agency appointed for the purposes of data entry on any automated system or for the purpose of operating, upgrading or maintaining any automated system where such agency is contractually bound not to use or disclose such particulars except for the aforesaid purposes; or

(*k*) any particulars to an officer of the Government as may be necessary for the purposes of any other law for the time being in force; or

(*l*) any information relating to any class of taxable persons or class of transactions for publication, if, in the opinion of the Commissioner, it is desirable in the public interest, to publish such information.

[65][**Consent based sharing of information furnished by taxable person.**

158A. (1) Notwithstanding anything contained in sections 133, 152 and 158, the following details furnished by a registered person may, subject to the provisions of sub-section (2), and on the recommendations of the Council, be shared by the common portal with such other systems as may be notified by the Government, in such manner and subject to such conditions as may be prescribed, namely:—

(*a*) particulars furnished in the application for registration under section 25 or in the return filed under section 39 or under section 44;

(*b*) the particulars uploaded on the common portal for preparation of invoice, the details of outward supplies furnished under section 37 and the particulars uploaded on the common portal for generation of documents under section 68;

(*c*) such other details as may be prescribed.

65. Inserted by the Finance Act, 2023, w.e.f. 1-10-2023.

(2) For the purposes of sharing details under sub-section (1), the consent shall be obtained, of—

(*a*) the supplier, in respect of details furnished under clauses (*a*), (*b*) and (*c*) of sub-section (1); and

(*b*) the recipient, in respect of details furnished under clause (*b*) of sub-section (1), and under clause (*c*) of sub-section (1) only where such details include identity information of the recipient,

in such form and manner as may be prescribed.

(3) Notwithstanding anything contained in any law for the time being in force, no action shall lie against the Government or the common portal with respect to any liability arising consequent to information shared under this section and there shall be no impact on the liability to pay tax on the relevant supply or as per the relevant return.]

Publication of information in respect of persons in certain cases.

159. (1) If the Commissioner, or any other officer authorised by him in this behalf, is of the opinion that it is necessary or expedient in the public interest to publish the name of any person and any other particulars relating to any proceedings or prosecution under this Act in respect of such person, it may cause to be published such name and particulars in such manner as it thinks fit.

(2) No publication under this section shall be made in relation to any penalty imposed under this Act until the time for presenting an appeal to the Appellate Authority under section 107 has expired without an appeal having been presented or the appeal, if presented, has been disposed of.

Explanation.—In the case of firm, company or other association of persons, the names of the partners of the firm, directors, managing agents, secretaries and treasurers or managers of the company, or the members of the association, as the case may be, may also be published if, in the opinion of the Commissioner, or any other officer authorised by him in this behalf, circumstances of the case justify it.

Assessment proceedings, etc., not to be invalid on certain grounds.

160. (1) No assessment, re-assessment, adjudication, review, revision, appeal, rectification, notice, summons or other proceedings done, accepted, made, issued, initiated, or purported to have been done, accepted, made, issued, initiated in pursuance of any of the provisions of this Act shall be invalid or deemed to be invalid merely by reason of any mistake, defect or omission therein, if such assessment, re-assessment, adjudication, review, revision, appeal, rectification, notice, summons or other proceedings are in substance and effect in conformity with or according to the intents, purposes and requirements of this Act or any existing law.

(2) The service of any notice, order or communication shall not be called in question, if the notice, order or communication, as the case may be, has already been acted upon by the person to whom it is issued or where such service has not been called in question at or in the earlier proceedings commenced, continued or finalised pursuant to such notice, order or communication.

Rectification of errors apparent on the face of record.

161. Without prejudice to the provisions of section 160, and notwithstanding anything contained in any other provisions of this Act, any authority, who has passed or issued any decision or order or notice or certificate or any other document, may rectify any error which is apparent on the face of record in such decision or order or notice or certificate or any other document, either on its own motion or where such error is brought to its notice by any officer appointed under this Act or an officer appointed under the State Goods and Services Tax Act or an officer appointed under the Union Territory Goods and Services Tax Act or by the affected person within a period of three months from the date of issue of such decision or order or notice or certificate or any other document, as the case may be:

Provided that no such rectification shall be done after a period of six months from the date of issue of such decision or order or notice or certificate or any other document:

Provided further that the said period of six months shall not apply in such cases where the rectification is purely in the nature of correction of a clerical or arithmetical error, arising from any accidental slip or omission:

Provided also that where such rectification adversely affects any person, the principles of natural justice shall be followed by the authority carrying out such rectification.

Bar on jurisdiction of civil courts.

162. Save as provided in sections 117 and 118, no civil court shall have jurisdiction to deal with or decide any question arising from or relating to anything done or purported to be done under this Act.

Levy of fee.

163. Wherever a copy of any order or document is to be provided to any person on an application made by him for that purpose, there shall be paid such fee as may be prescribed.

Power of Government to make rules.

164. (1) The Government may, on the recommendations of the Council, by notification, make rules for carrying out the provisions of this Act.

(2) Without prejudice to the generality of the provisions of sub-section (1), the Government may make

rules for all or any of the matters which by this Act are required to be, or may be, prescribed or in respect of which provisions are to be or may be made by rules.

(3) The power to make rules conferred by this section shall include the power to give retrospective effect to the rules or any of them from a date not earlier than the date on which the provisions of this Act come into force.

(4) Any rules made under sub-section (1) or sub-section (2) may provide that a contravention thereof shall be liable to a penalty not exceeding ten thousand rupees.

Power to make regulations.

165. The Board may, by notification, make regulations consistent with this Act and the rules made thereunder to carry out the provisions of this Act.

Laying of rules, regulations and notifications.

166. Every rule made by the Government, every regulation made by the Board and every notification issued by the Government under this Act, shall be laid, as soon as may be after it is made or issued, before each House of Parliament, while it is in session, for a total period of thirty days which may be comprised in one session or in two or more successive sessions, and if, before the expiry of the session immediately following the session or the successive sessions aforesaid, both Houses agree in making any modification in the rule or regulation or in the notification, as the case may be, or both Houses agree that the rule or regulation or the notification should not be made, the rule or regulation or notification, as the case may be, shall thereafter have effect only in such modified form or be of no effect, as the case may be; so, however, that any such modification or annulment shall be without prejudice to the validity of anything previously done under that rule or regulation or notification, as the case may be.

Delegation of powers.

167. The Commissioner may, by notification, direct that subject to such conditions, if any, as may be specified in the notification, any power exercisable by any authority or officer under this Act may be exercisable also by another authority or officer as may be specified in such notification.

Power to issue instructions or directions.

168. (1) The Board may, if it considers it necessary or expedient so to do for the purpose of uniformity in the implementation of this Act, issue such orders, instructions or directions to the central tax officers as it may deem fit, and thereupon all such officers and all other persons employed in the implementation of this Act shall observe and follow such orders, instructions or directions.

(2) The Commissioner specified in clause (*91*) of section 2, sub-section (3) of section 5, clause (*b*) of sub-section (9) of section 25, sub-sections (3) and (4) of section 35, sub-section (1) of section 37, [66][***] sub-section (6) of section 39, [67][[68][section 44], sub-sections (4) and (5) of section 52,] [69][sub-section (1) of section 143, except the second proviso thereof], [70][***] clause (*l*) of sub-section (3) of section 158 and section 167 shall mean a Commissioner or Joint Secretary posted in the Board and such Commissioner or Joint Secretary shall exercise the powers specified in the said sections with the approval of the Board.

---

66. Words "sub-section (2) of section 38," omitted by the Finance Act, 2022, w.e.f. 1-10-2022.
67. Inserted by the Finance (No. 2) Act, 2019, w.e.f. 1-1-2020.
68. Substituted for "sub-section (1) of section 44" by the Finance Act, 2021, w.e.f. 1-1-2022.
69. Substituted for "sub-section (5) of section 66, sub-section (1) of section 143" by the Finance Act, 2020, w.e.f. 30-6-2020.
70. Words "sub-section (1) of section 151," omitted by the Finance Act, 2021, w.e.f. 1-1-2022.

[71][Power of Government to extend time limit in special circumstances.

168A. (1) Notwithstanding anything contained in this Act, the Government may, on the recommendations of the Council, by notification, extend the time limit specified in, or prescribed or notified under, this Act in respect of actions which cannot be completed or complied with due to *force majeure*.

(2) The power to issue notification under sub-section (1) shall include the power to give retrospective effect to such notification from a date not earlier than the date of commencement of this Act.

Explanation.—For the purposes of this section, the expression *"force majeure"* means a case of war, epidemic, flood, drought, fire, cyclone, earthquake or any other calamity caused by nature or otherwise affecting the implementation of any of the provisions of this Act.]

Service of notice in certain circumstances.

169. (1) Any decision, order, summons, notice or other communication under this Act or the rules made thereunder shall be served by any one of the following methods, namely:—

(*a*) by giving or tendering it directly or by a messenger including a courier to the addressee or the taxable person or to his manager or authorised representative or an advocate or a tax practitioner holding authority to appear in the proceedings on behalf of the taxable person or to a person regularly employed by him in connection with the business, or to any adult member of family residing with the taxable person; or

(*b*) by registered post or speed post or courier with acknowledgement due, to the person

71. Inserted by the Taxation and Other Laws (Relaxation and Amendment of Certain Provisions) Act, 2020, w.e.f. 31-3-2020.

for whom it is intended or his authorised representative, if any, at his last known place of business or residence; or

(*c*) by sending a communication to his e-mail address provided at the time of registration or as amended from time to time; or

(*d*) by making it available on the common portal; or

(*e*) by publication in a newspaper circulating in the locality in which the taxable person or the person to whom it is issued is last known to have resided, carried on business or personally worked for gain; or

(*f*) if none of the modes aforesaid is practicable, by affixing it in some conspicuous place at his last known place of business or residence and if such mode is not practicable for any reason, then by affixing a copy thereof on the notice board of the office of the concerned officer or authority who or which passed such decision or order or issued such summons or notice.

(2) Every decision, order, summons, notice or any communication shall be deemed to have been served on the date on which it is tendered or published or a copy thereof is affixed in the manner provided in sub-section (1).

(3) When such decision, order, summons, notice or any communication is sent by registered post or speed post, it shall be deemed to have been received by the addressee at the expiry of the period normally taken by such post in transit unless the contrary is proved.

Rounding off of tax, etc.

170. The amount of tax, interest, penalty, fine or any other sum payable, and the amount of refund or any other sum due, under the provisions of this Act shall be rounded off to the nearest rupee and, for this purpose, where such amount contains a part of a rupee consisting of paise, then, if such part is fifty paise or more, it shall be increased to one rupee and if such part is less than fifty paise it shall be ignored.

Anti-profiteering measure.

171. (1) Any reduction in rate of tax on any supply of goods or services or the benefit of input tax credit shall be passed on to the recipient by way of commensurate reduction in prices.

(2) The Central Government may, on recommendations of the Council, by notification, constitute an Authority, or empower an existing Authority constituted under any law for the time being in force, to examine whether input tax credits availed by any registered person or the reduction in the tax rate have actually resulted in a commensurate reduction in the price of the goods or services or both supplied by him:

[72]**[Provided** *that the Government may by notification, on the recommendations of the Council, specify the date from which the said Authority shall not accept any request for examination as to whether input tax credits availed by any registered person or the reduction in the tax rate have actually resulted in a commensurate reduction in the price of the goods or services or both supplied by him.*

Explanation.—*For the purposes of this sub-section, "request for examination" shall mean the written application filed by an applicant requesting for examination as to whether input tax credits availed by any registered person or the reduction in the tax rate have actually resulted in a commensurate reduction in the price of the goods or services or both supplied by him.*]

(3) The Authority referred to in sub-section (2) shall exercise such powers and discharge such functions as may be prescribed.

---

72. Inserted by the Finance (No. 2) Act, 2024, w.e.f. **27-9-2024.**

[73][(3A) Where the Authority referred to in sub-section (2) after holding examination as required under the said sub-section comes to the conclusion that any registered person has profiteered under sub-section (1), such person shall be liable to pay penalty equivalent to ten per cent of the amount so profiteered:

Provided that no penalty shall be leviable if the profiteered amount is deposited within thirty days of the date of passing of the order by the Authority.

Explanation [74]**[1]**.—For the purposes of this section, the expression "profiteered" shall mean the amount determined on account of not passing the benefit of reduction in rate of tax on supply of goods or services or both or the benefit of input tax credit to the recipient by way of commensurate reduction in the price of the goods or services or both.]

[74]**[**Explanation 2.—*For the purposes of this section, the expression "Authority" shall include the "Appellate Tribunal".***]**

Removal of difficulties.

172. (1) If any difficulty arises in giving effect to any provisions of this Act, the Government may, on the recommendations of the Council, by a general or a special order published in the Official Gazette, make such provisions not inconsistent with the provisions of this Act or the rules or regulations made thereunder, as may be necessary or expedient for the purpose of removing the said difficulty:

Provided that no such order shall be made after the expiry of a period of [75][five years] from the date of commencement of this Act.

---

73. Inserted by the Finance (No. 2) Act, 2019, w.e.f. 1-1-2020.
74. Inserted by the Finance (No. 2) Act, 2024, w.e.f. **27-9-2024**.
75. Substituted for "three years" by the Finance Act, 2020, w.e.f. 30-6-2020.

(2) Every order made under this section shall be laid, as soon as may be, after it is made, before each House of Parliament.

Amendment of Act 32 of 1994.

173. Save as otherwise provided in this Act, Chapter V of the Finance Act, 1994 shall be omitted.

Repeal and saving.

174. (1) Save as otherwise provided in this Act, on and from the date of commencement of this Act, the Central Excise Act, 1944 (1 of 1944) (except as respects goods included in entry 84 of the Union List of the Seventh Schedule to the Constitution), the Medicinal and Toilet Preparations (Excise Duties) Act, 1955 (16 of 1955), the Additional Duties of Excise (Goods of Special Importance) Act, 1957 (58 of 1957), the Additional Duties of Excise (Textiles and Textile Articles) Act, 1978 (40 of 1978), and the Central Excise Tariff Act, 1985 (5 of 1986) (hereafter referred to as the repealed Acts) are hereby repealed.

(2) The repeal of the said Acts and the amendment of the Finance Act, 1994 (32 of 1994) (hereafter referred to as "such amendment" or "amended Act", as the case may be) to the extent mentioned in the sub-section (1) or section 173 shall not—

(*a*) revive anything not in force or existing at the time of such amendment or repeal; or

(*b*) affect the previous operation of the amended Act or repealed Acts and orders or anything duly done or suffered thereunder; or

(*c*) affect any right, privilege, obligation, or liability acquired, accrued or incurred under the amended Act or repealed Acts or orders under such repealed or amended Acts:

Provided that any tax exemption granted as an incentive against investment through a notification shall not continue as privilege if the said notification is rescinded on or after the appointed day; or

(*d*) affect any duty, tax, surcharge, fine, penalty, interest as are due or may become due or any forfeiture or punishment incurred or inflicted in respect of any offence or violation committed against the provisions of the amended Act or repealed Acts; or

(*e*) affect any investigation, inquiry, verification (including scrutiny and audit), assessment proceedings, adjudication and any other legal proceedings or recovery of arrears or remedy in respect of any such duty, tax, surcharge, penalty, fine, interest, right, privilege, obligation, liability, forfeiture or punishment, as aforesaid, and any such investigation, inquiry, verification (including scrutiny and audit), assessment proceedings, adjudication and other legal proceedings or recovery of arrears or remedy may be instituted, continued or enforced, and any such tax, surcharge, penalty, fine, interest, forfeiture or punishment may be levied or imposed as if these Acts had not been so amended or repealed;

(*f*) affect any proceedings including that relating to an appeal, review or reference, instituted before on, or after the appointed day under the said amended Act or repealed Acts and such proceedings shall be continued under the said amended Act or repealed Acts as if this Act had not come into force and the said Acts had not been amended or repealed.

(3) The mention of the particular matters referred to in sub-sections (1) and (2) shall not be held to prejudice or affect the general application of section 6 of the General Clauses Act, 1897 (10 of 1897) with regard to the effect of repeal.

SCHEDULE I

[*See* section 7]

ACTIVITIES TO BE TREATED AS SUPPLY EVEN IF MADE WITHOUT CONSIDERATION

1. Permanent transfer or disposal of business assets where input tax credit has been availed on such assets.

2. Supply of goods or services or both between related persons or between distinct persons as specified in section 25, when made in the course or furtherance of business:

Provided that gifts not exceeding fifty thousand rupees in value in a financial year by an employer to an employee shall not be treated as supply of goods or services or both.

3. Supply of goods—

(*a*) by a principal to his agent where the agent undertakes to supply such goods on behalf of the principal; or

(*b*) by an agent to his principal where the agent undertakes to receive such goods on behalf of the principal.

4. Import of services by a [76][person] from a related person or from any of his other establishments outside India, in the course or furtherance of business.

76. Substituted for "taxable person" by the Central Goods and Services Tax (Amendment) Act, 2018, w.e.f. 1-2-2019.

SCHEDULE II

[*See* section 7]

ACTIVITIES [77][OR TRANSACTIONS] TO BE TREATED AS SUPPLY OF GOODS OR SUPPLY OF SERVICES

1. Transfer

(*a*) any transfer of the title in goods is a supply of goods;

(*b*) any transfer of right in goods or of undivided share in goods without the transfer of title thereof, is a supply of services;

(*c*) any transfer of title in goods under an agreement which stipulates that property in goods shall pass at a future date upon payment of full consideration as agreed, is a supply of goods.

2. Land and Building

(*a*) any lease, tenancy, easement, licence to occupy land is a supply of services;

(*b*) any lease or letting out of the building including a commercial, industrial or residential complex for business or commerce, either wholly or partly, is a supply of services.

3. Treatment or process

Any treatment or process which is applied to another person's goods is a supply of services.

4. Transfer of business assets

(*a*) where goods forming part of the assets of a business are transferred or disposed of by or under the directions of the person carrying on the business so as no longer to form part of

77. Inserted by the Central Goods and Services Tax (Amendment) Act, 2018, w.r.e.f. 1-7-2017.

those assets, [78][***] such transfer or disposal is a supply of goods by the person;

(*b*) where, by or under the direction of a person carrying on a business, goods held or used for the purposes of the business are put to any private use or are used, or made available to any person for use, for any purpose other than a purpose of the business, [78][***] the usage or making available of such goods is a supply of services;

(*c*) where any person ceases to be a taxable person, any goods forming part of the assets of any business carried on by him shall be deemed to be supplied by him in the course or furtherance of his business immediately before he ceases to be a taxable person, unless—

(*i*) the business is transferred as a going concern to another person; or

(*ii*) the business is carried on by a personal representative who is deemed to be a taxable person.

5. Supply of services

The following shall be treated as supply of services, namely:—

(*a*) renting of immovable property;

(*b*) construction of a complex, building, civil structure or a part thereof, including a complex or building intended for sale to a buyer, wholly or partly, except where the entire consideration has been received after issuance of completion certificate, where required, by the competent authority or after its first occupation, whichever is earlier.

---

78. Words "whether or not for a consideration," omitted by the Finance Act, 2020, w.e.f. 1-1-2021 [*vide* Finance Act, 2020, as amended by Notification No. 92/2020-Central Tax, dated 22-12-2020].

Explanation.—For the purposes of this clause—

(*1*) the expression "competent authority" means the Government or any authority authorised to issue completion certificate under any law for the time being in force and in case of non-requirement of such certificate from such authority, from any of the following, namely:—

(*i*) an architect registered with the Council of Architecture constituted under the Architects Act, 1972 (20 of 1972); or

(*ii*) a chartered engineer registered with the Institution of Engineers (India); or

(*iii*) a licensed surveyor of the respective local body of the city or town or village or development or planning authority;

(*2*) the expression "construction" includes additions, alterations, replacements or remodelling of any existing civil structure;

(*c*) temporary transfer or permitting the use or enjoyment of any intellectual property right;

(*d*) development, design, programming, customisation, adaptation, upgradation, enhancement, implementation of information technology software;

(*e*) agreeing to the obligation to refrain from an act, or to tolerate an act or a situation, or to do an act; and

(*f*) transfer of the right to use any goods for any purpose (whether or not for a specified period) for cash, deferred payment or other valuable consideration.

6. Composite supply

The following composite supplies shall be treated as a supply of services, namely:—

(*a*) works contract as defined in clause (*119*) of section 2; and

(*b*) supply, by way of or as part of any service or in any other manner whatsoever, of goods, being food or any other article for human consumption or any drink (other than alcoholic liquor for human consumption), where such supply or service is for cash, deferred payment or other valuable consideration.

7. Supply of Goods

[79][***]

---

79. Omitted by the Finance Act, 2021, w.r.e.f. 1-7-2017. [However, Notification No. 39/2021-Central Tax, dated 21-12-2021 appoints 1-1-2022 as the date of enforcement].

SCHEDULE III

[*See* section 7]

ACTIVITIES OR TRANSACTIONS WHICH SHALL BE TREATED NEITHER AS A SUPPLY OF GOODS NOR A SUPPLY OF SERVICES

1. Services by an employee to the employer in the course of or in relation to his employment.

2. Services by any court or Tribunal established under any law for the time being in force.

3. (*a*) The functions performed by the Members of Parliament, Members of State Legislature, Members of Panchayats, Members of Municipalities and Members of other local authorities;

(*b*) The duties performed by any person who holds any post in pursuance of the provisions of the Constitution in that capacity; or

(*c*) The duties performed by any person as a Chairperson or a Member or a Director in a body established by the Central Government or a State Government or local authority and who is not deemed as an employee before the commencement of this clause.

4. Services of funeral, burial, crematorium or mortuary including transportation of the deceased.

5. Sale of land and, subject to clause (*b*) of paragraph 5 of Schedule II, sale of building.

6. Actionable claims, other than [80][specified actionable claims].

[81][**7.** Supply of goods from a place in the non-taxable territory to another place in the non-taxable territory without such goods entering into India.

80. Substituted for "lottery, betting and gambling" by the Central Goods and Services Tax (Amendment) Act, 2023, w.e.f. 1-10-2023.

81. Inserted by the Central Goods and Services Tax (Amendment) Act, 2018, w.e.f. 1-2-2019. Now *vide* section 159 of the Finance Act, 2023, it shall be deemed to inserted w.e.f. 1-7-2017.

8. (*a*) Supply of warehoused goods to any person before clearance for home consumption;

(*b*) Supply of goods by the consignee to any other person, by endorsement of documents of title to the goods, after the goods have been dispatched from the port of origin located outside India but before clearance for home consumption.]

[82][**9.** *Activity of apportionment of co-insurance premium by the lead insurer to the co-insurer for the insurance services jointly supplied by the lead insurer and the co-insurer to the insured in co-insurance agreements, subject to the condition that the lead insurer pays the central tax, the State tax, the Union territory tax and the integrated tax on the entire amount of premium paid by the insured.*

10. *Services by insurer to the reinsurer for which ceding commission or the reinsurance commission is deducted from reinsurance premium paid by the insurer to the reinsurer, subject to the condition that the central tax, the State tax, the Union territory tax and the integrated tax is paid by the reinsurer on the gross reinsurance premium payable by the insurer to the reinsurer, inclusive of the said ceding commission or the reinsurance commission.*]

Explanation [83][1].—For the purposes of paragraph 2, the term "court" includes District Court, High Court and Supreme Court.

[84][*Explanation* 2.—For the purposes of paragraph 8, the expression "warehoused goods" shall have the same meaning as assigned to it in the Customs Act, 1962 (52 of 1962).]

82. Inserted by the Finance (No. 2) Act, 2024, w.e.f. **1-11-2024**.

83. *Explanation* renumbered as *Explanation 1* by the Central Goods and Services Tax (Amendment) Act, 2018, w.e.f. 1-2-2019.

84. Inserted, *ibid.* Now *vide* section 159 of the Finance Act, 2023, it shall be deemed to inserted w.e.f. 1-7-2017.

DIVISION TWO

Integrated Goods and Services Tax Act, 2017

2

INTEGRATED GOODS AND SERVICES TAX ACT, 2017

Arrangement of Sections

SECTIONS PAGE

CHAPTER I

PRELIMINARY

CHAPTER II

ADMINISTRATION

CHAPTER III

LEVY AND COLLECTION OF TAX

Integrated Goods and Services Tax Act, 2017 [13 OF 2017]*

An Act to make a provision for levy and collection of tax on inter-State supply of goods or services or both by the Central Government and for matters connected therewith or incidental thereto.

BE it enacted by Parliament in the Sixty-eighth year of the Republic of India as follows:—

CHAPTER I

PRELIMINARY

Short title, extent and commencement.

1. (1) This Act may be called the Integrated Goods and Services Tax Act, 2017.

(2) It shall extend to the whole of India [1][***].

(3) It shall come into force on such date as the Central Government may, by notification in the Official Gazette, appoint:

Provided that different dates may be appointed for different provisions of this Act and any reference in any such provision to the commencement of this Act shall be construed as a reference to the coming into force of that provision.

---

* Assented by the President of India on 12-4-2017.

1. Words "except the State of Jammu and Kashmir" omitted by the Integrated Goods and Services Tax (Extension to Jammu and Kashmir) Act, 2017, w.r.e.f. 8-7-2017.

Definitions.

2. In this Act, unless the context otherwise requires,—

(*1*) "Central Goods and Services Tax Act" means the Central Goods and Services Tax Act, 2017;

(*2*) "central tax" means the tax levied and collected under the Central Goods and Services Tax Act;

(*3*) "continuous journey" means a journey for which a single or more than one ticket or invoice is issued at the same time, either by a single supplier of service or through an agent acting on behalf of more than one supplier of service, and which involves no stopover between any of the legs of the journey for which one or more separate tickets or invoices are issued.

Explanation.—For the purposes of this clause, the term "stopover" means a place where a passenger can disembark either to transfer to another conveyance or break his journey for a certain period in order to resume it at a later point of time;

(*4*) "customs frontiers of India" means the limits of a customs area as defined in section 2 of the Customs Act, 1962 (52 of 1962);

(*5*) "export of goods" with its grammatical variations and cognate expressions, means taking goods out of India to a place outside India;

(*6*) "export of services" means the supply of any service when,—

(*i*) the supplier of service is located in India;

(*ii*) the recipient of service is located outside India;

(*iii*) the place of supply of service is outside India;

(*iv*) the payment for such service has been received by the supplier of service in convertible foreign exchange [2][or in Indian rupees wherever permitted by the Reserve Bank of India]; and

(*v*) the supplier of service and the recipient of service are not merely establishments of a distinct person in accordance with *Explanation 1* in section 8;

(7) "fixed establishment" means a place (other than the registered place of business) which is characterised by a sufficient degree of permanence and suitable structure in terms of human and technical resources to supply services or to receive and use services for its own needs;

(*8*) "Goods and Services Tax (Compensation to States) Act" means the Goods and Services Tax (Compensation to States) Act, 2017;

(*9*) "Government" means the Central Government;

(*10*) "import of goods" with its grammatical variations and cognate expressions, means bringing goods into India from a place outside India;

(*11*) "import of services" means the supply of any service, where—

(*i*) the supplier of service is located outside India;

(*ii*) the recipient of service is located in India; and

(*iii*) the place of supply of service is in India;

2. Inserted by the Integrated Goods and Services Tax (Amendment) Act, 2018, w.e.f. 1-2-2019.

(*12*) "integrated tax" means the integrated goods and services tax levied under this Act;

(*13*) "intermediary" means a broker, an agent or any other person, by whatever name called, who arranges or facilitates the supply of goods or services or both, or securities, between two or more persons, but does not include a person who supplies such goods or services or both or securities on his own account;

(*14*) "location of the recipient of services" means,—

(*a*) where a supply is received at a place of business for which the registration has been obtained, the location of such place of business;

(*b*) where a supply is received at a place other than the place of business for which registration has been obtained (a fixed establishment elsewhere), the location of such fixed establishment;

(*c*) where a supply is received at more than one establishment, whether the place of business or fixed establishment, the location of the establishment most directly concerned with the receipt of the supply; and

(*d*) in absence of such places, the location of the usual place of residence of the recipient;

(*15*) "location of the supplier of services" means,—

(*a*) where a supply is made from a place of business for which the registration has been obtained, the location of such place of business;

(*b*) where a supply is made from a place other than the place of business for which registration has been obtained (a fixed establishment elsewhere), the location of such fixed establishment;

(*c*) where a supply is made from more than one establishment, whether the place of business or fixed establishment, the location of the establishment most directly concerned with the provision of the supply; and

(*d*) in absence of such places, the location of the usual place of residence of the supplier;

[3][(*16*) "non-taxable online recipient" means any unregistered person receiving online information and database access or retrieval services located in taxable territory.

Explanation.—For the purposes of this clause, the expression "unregistered person" includes a person registered solely in terms of clause (vi) of section 24 of the Central Goods and Services Tax Act, 2017 (12 of 2017);]

(*17*) "online information and database access or retrieval services" means services whose delivery is mediated by information technology over the internet or an electronic network and the nature of which renders their supply [4][***] impossible to ensure in the absence of information technology and includes electronic services such as,—

(*i*) advertising on the internet;

(*ii*) providing cloud services;

(*iii*) provision of e-books, movie, music, software and other intangibles

---

3. Substituted by the Finance Act, 2023, w.e.f. 1-10-2023.

4. Words "essentially automated and involving minimal human intervention and" omitted, *ibid*.

through telecommunication networks or internet;

(*iv*) providing data or information, retrievable or otherwise, to any person in electronic form through a computer network;

(*v*) online supplies of digital content (movies, television shows, music and the like);

(*vi*) digital data storage; and

[5][(*vii*) online gaming, excluding the online money gaming as defined in clause (80B) of section 2 of the Central Goods and Services Tax Act, 2017 (12 of 2017);]

(*18*) "output tax", in relation to a taxable person, means the integrated tax chargeable under this Act on taxable supply of goods or services or both made by him or by his agent but excludes tax payable by him on reverse charge basis;

(*19*) "Special Economic Zone" shall have the same meaning as assigned to it in clause (*za*) of section 2 of the Special Economic Zones Act, 2005 (28 of 2005);

(*20*) "Special Economic Zone developer" shall have the same meaning as assigned to it in clause (*g*) of section 2 of the Special Economic Zones Act, 2005 (28 of 2005) and includes an Authority as defined in clause (*d*) and a Co-Developer as defined in clause (*f*) of section 2 of the said Act;

(*21*) "supply" shall have the same meaning as assigned to it in section 7 of the Central Goods and Services Tax Act;

5. Substituted by the Integrated Goods and Services Tax (Amendment) Act, 2023, w.e.f. 1-10-2023.

(*22*) "taxable territory" means the territory to which the provisions of this Act apply;

(*23*) "zero-rated supply" shall have the meaning assigned to it in section 16;

(*24*) words and expressions used and not defined in this Act but defined in the Central Goods and Services Tax Act, the Union Territory Goods and Services Tax Act and the Goods and Services Tax (Compensation to States) Act shall have the same meaning as assigned to them in those Acts;

(*25*) any reference in this Act to a law which is not in force in the State of Jammu and Kashmir, shall, in relation to that State be construed as a reference to the corresponding law, if any, in force in that State.

CHAPTER II

ADMINISTRATION

Appointment of officers.

3. The Board may appoint such central tax officers as it thinks fit for exercising the powers under this Act.

Authorisation of officers of State tax or Union territory tax as proper officer in certain circumstances.

4. Without prejudice to the provisions of this Act, the officers appointed under the State Goods and Services Tax Act or the Union Territory Goods and Services Tax Act are authorised to be the proper officers for the purposes of this Act, subject to such exceptions and conditions as the Government shall, on the recommendations of the Council, by notification, specify.

CHAPTER III

LEVY AND COLLECTION OF TAX

Levy and collection.

5. (1) Subject to the provisions of sub-section (2), there shall be levied a tax called the integrated goods and services tax on all inter-State supplies of goods or services or both, except on the supply of alcoholic liquor for human consumption [6]**[***and undenatured extra neutral alcohol or rectified spirit used for manufacture of alcoholic liquor, for human consumption***]**, on the value determined under section 15 of the Central Goods and Services Tax Act and at such rates, not exceeding forty per cent, as may be notified by the Government on the recommendations of the Council and collected in such manner as may be prescribed and shall be paid by the taxable person:

Provided that the integrated tax on goods [7][other than the goods as may be notified by the Government on the recommendations of the Council] imported into India shall be levied and collected in accordance with the provisions of section 3 of the Customs Tariff Act, 1975 (51 of 1975) on the value as determined under the said Act at the point when duties of customs are levied on the said goods under section 12 of the Customs Act, 1962 (52 of 1962).

(2) The integrated tax on the supply of petroleum crude, high speed diesel, motor spirit (commonly known as petrol), natural gas and aviation turbine fuel shall be levied with effect from such date as may be notified by the Government on the recommendations of the Council.

(3) The Government may, on the recommendations of the Council, by notification, specify categories of

---

6. Inserted by the Finance (No. 2) Act, 2024, w.e.f. **1-11-2024**.
7. Inserted by the Integrated Goods and Services Tax (Amendment) Act, 2023, w.e.f. 1-10-2023.

supply of goods or services or both, the tax on which shall be paid on reverse charge basis by the recipient of such goods or services or both and all the provisions of this Act shall apply to such recipient as if he is the person liable for paying the tax in relation to the supply of such goods or services or both.

[8][(4) The Government may, on the recommendations of the Council, by notification, specify a class of registered persons who shall, in respect of supply of specified categories of goods or services or both received from an unregistered supplier, pay the tax on reverse charge basis as the recipient of such supply of goods or services or both, and all the provisions of this Act shall apply to such recipient as if he is the person liable for paying the tax in relation to such supply of goods or services or both.]

(5) The Government may, on the recommendations of the Council, by notification, specify categories of services, the tax on inter-State supplies of which shall be paid by the electronic commerce operator if such services are supplied through it, and all the provisions of this Act shall apply to such electronic commerce operator as if he is the supplier liable for paying the tax in relation to the supply of such services:

Provided that where an electronic commerce operator does not have a physical presence in the taxable territory, any person representing such electronic commerce operator for any purpose in the taxable territory shall be liable to pay tax:

Provided further that where an electronic commerce operator does not have a physical presence in the taxable territory and also does not have a representative in the said territory, such electronic commerce operator shall appoint a person in the taxable territory

8. Substituted by the Integrated Goods and Services Tax (Amendment) Act, 2018, w.e.f. 1-2-2019.

for the purpose of paying tax and such person shall be liable to pay tax.

Power to grant exemption from tax.

6. (1) Where the Government is satisfied that it is necessary in the public interest so to do, it may, on the recommendations of the Council, by notification, exempt generally, either absolutely or subject to such conditions as may be specified therein, goods or services or both of any specified description from the whole or any part of the tax leviable thereon with effect from such date as may be specified in such notification.

(2) Where the Government is satisfied that it is necessary in the public interest so to do, it may, on the recommendations of the Council, by special order in each case, under circumstances of an exceptional nature to be stated in such order, exempt from payment of tax any goods or services or both on which tax is leviable.

(3) The Government may, if it considers necessary or expedient so to do for the purpose of clarifying the scope or applicability of any notification issued under sub-section (1) or order issued under sub-section (2), insert an *Explanation* in such notification or order, as the case may be, by notification at any time within one year of issue of the notification under sub-section (1) or order under sub-section (2), and every such *Explanation* shall have effect as if it had always been the part of the first such notification or order, as the case may be.

Explanation.—For the purposes of this section, where an exemption in respect of any goods or services or both from the whole or part of the tax leviable thereon has been granted absolutely, the registered person supplying such goods or services or both shall not collect the tax, in excess of the effective rate, on such supply of goods or services or both.

[9][**Power not to recover Goods and Services Tax not levied or short-levied as a result of general practice.**

6A. *Notwithstanding anything contained in this Act, if the Government is satisfied that—*

(a) *a practice was, or is, generally prevalent regarding levy of integrated tax (including non-levy thereof) on any supply of goods or services or both; and*

(b) *such supplies were, or are, liable to —*

(i) *integrated tax, in cases where according to the said practice, integrated tax was not, or is not being, levied; or*

(ii) *a higher amount of integrated tax than what was, or is being, levied, in accordance with the said practice,*

the Government may, on the recommendation of the Council, by notification in the Official Gazette, direct that the whole of the integrated tax payable on such supplies, or, as the case may be, the integrated tax in excess of that payable on such supplies, but for the said practice, shall not be required to be paid in respect of the supplies on which the integrated tax was not, or is not being, levied, or was, or is being, short levied, in accordance with the said practice.]

CHAPTER IV

DETERMINATION OF NATURE OF SUPPLY

Inter-State supply.

7. (1) Subject to the provisions of section 10, supply of goods, where the location of the supplier and the place of supply are in—

(*a*) two different States;

9. Inserted by the Finance (No. 2) Act, 2024, w.e.f. **1-11-2024.**

(*b*) two different Union territories; or

(*c*) a State and a Union territory,

shall be treated as a supply of goods in the course of inter-State trade or commerce.

(2) Supply of goods imported into the territory of India, till they cross the customs frontiers of India, shall be treated to be a supply of goods in the course of inter-State trade or commerce.

(3) Subject to the provisions of section 12, supply of services, where the location of the supplier and the place of supply are in—

(*a*) two different States;

(*b*) two different Union territories; or

(*c*) a State and a Union territory,

shall be treated as a supply of services in the course of inter-State trade or commerce.

(4) Supply of services imported into the territory of India shall be treated to be a supply of services in the course of inter-State trade or commerce.

(5) Supply of goods or services or both,—

(*a*) when the supplier is located in India and the place of supply is outside India;

(*b*) to or by a Special Economic Zone developer or a Special Economic Zone unit; or

(*c*) in the taxable territory, not being an intra-State supply and not covered elsewhere in this section,

shall be treated to be a supply of goods or services or both in the course of inter-State trade or commerce.

Intra-State supply.

8. (1) Subject to the provisions of section 10, supply of goods where the location of the supplier and the place of supply of goods are in the same State or same Union territory shall be treated as intra-State supply:

Provided that the following supply of goods shall not be treated as intra-State supply, namely:—

(*i*) supply of goods to or by a Special Economic Zone developer or a Special Economic Zone unit;

(*ii*) goods imported into the territory of India till they cross the customs frontiers of India; or

(*iii*) supplies made to a tourist referred to in section 15.

(2) Subject to the provisions of section 12, supply of services where the location of the supplier and the place of supply of services are in the same State or same Union territory shall be treated as intra-State supply:

Provided that the intra-State supply of services shall not include supply of services to or by a Special Economic Zone developer or a Special Economic Zone unit.

Explanation 1.—For the purposes of this Act, where a person has,—

(*i*) an establishment in India and any other establishment outside India;

(*ii*) an establishment in a State or Union territory and any other establishment outside that State or Union territory; or

(*iii*) an establishment in a State or Union territory and any other establishment [10][***] registered within that State or Union territory,

then such establishments shall be treated as establishments of distinct persons.

---

10. Words "being a business vertical" omitted by the Integrated Goods and Services Tax (Amendment) Act, 2018, w.e.f. 1-2-2019.

Explanation 2.—A person carrying on a business through a branch or an agency or a representational office in any territory shall be treated as having an establishment in that territory.

Supplies in territorial waters.

9. Notwithstanding anything contained in this Act,—

(*a*) where the location of the supplier is in the territorial waters, the location of such supplier; or

(*b*) where the place of supply is in the territorial waters, the place of supply,

shall, for the purposes of this Act, be deemed to be in the coastal State or Union territory where the nearest point of the appropriate baseline is located.

CHAPTER V

PLACE OF SUPPLY OF GOODS OR SERVICES OR BOTH

Place of supply of goods other than supply of goods imported into, or exported from India.

10. (1) The place of supply of goods, other than supply of goods imported into, or exported from India, shall be as under,—

(*a*) where the supply involves movement of goods, whether by the supplier or the recipient or by any other person, the place of supply of such goods shall be the location of the goods at the time at which the movement of goods terminates for delivery to the recipient;

(*b*) where the goods are delivered by the supplier to a recipient or any other person on the direction of a third person, whether acting as an agent or otherwise, before or during movement of goods, either by way of transfer of documents of title to the goods or otherwise, it shall be deemed that the said third person has received the goods and the place of supply of such goods shall be the principal place of business of such person;

(*c*) where the supply does not involve movement of goods, whether by the supplier or the recipient, the place of supply shall be the location of such goods at the time of the delivery to the recipient;

[11][(*ca*) where the supply of goods is made to a person other than a registered person, the place of supply shall, notwithstanding anything contrary contained in clause (*a*) or clause (*c*), be the location as per the address of the said person recorded in the invoice issued in respect of the said supply and the location of the supplier where the address of the said person is not recorded in the invoice.

Explanation.—For the purposes of this clause, recording of the name of the State of the said person in the invoice shall be deemed to be the recording of the address of the said person;]

(*d*) where the goods are assembled or installed at site, the place of supply shall be the place of such installation or assembly;

(*e*) where the goods are supplied on board a conveyance, including a vessel, an aircraft, a train or a motor vehicle, the place of supply shall be the location at which such goods are taken on board.

(2) Where the place of supply of goods cannot be determined, the place of supply shall be determined in such manner as may be prescribed.

11. Inserted by the Integrated Goods and Services Tax (Amendment) Act, 2023, w.e.f. 1-10-2023.

Place of supply of goods imported into, or exported from India.

11. The place of supply of goods,—

(*a*) imported into India shall be the location of the importer;

(*b*) exported from India shall be the location outside India.

Place of supply of services where location of supplier and recipient is in India.

12. (1) The provisions of this section shall apply to determine the place of supply of services where the location of supplier of services and the location of the recipient of services is in India.

(2) The place of supply of services, except the services specified in sub-sections (3) to (14),—

(*a*) made to a registered person shall be the location of such person;

(*b*) made to any person other than a registered person shall be,—

(*i*) the location of the recipient where the address on record exists; and

(*ii*) the location of the supplier of services in other cases.

(3) The place of supply of services,—

(*a*) directly in relation to an immovable property, including services provided by architects, interior decorators, surveyors, engineers and other related experts or estate agents, any service provided by way of grant of rights to use immovable property or for carrying out or co-ordination of construction work; or

(*b*) by way of lodging accommodation by a hotel, inn, guest house, home stay, club or campsite, by whatever name called, and including a house boat or any other vessel; or (*c*) by way of accommodation in any immovable property for organising any marriage or reception or matters related thereto, official, social, cultural, religious or business function including services provided in relation to such function at such property; or

(*d*) any services ancillary to the services referred to in clauses (*a*), (*b*) and (*c*),

shall be the location at which the immovable property or boat or vessel, as the case may be, is located or intended to be located:

Provided that if the location of the immovable property or boat or vessel is located or intended to be located outside India, the place of supply shall be the location of the recipient.

Explanation.—Where the immovable property or boat or vessel is located in more than one State or Union territory, the supply of services shall be treated as made in each of the respective States or Union territories, in proportion to the value for services separately collected or determined in terms of the contract or agreement entered into in this regard or, in the absence of such contract or agreement, on such other basis as may be prescribed.

(4) The place of supply of restaurant and catering services, personal grooming, fitness, beauty treatment, health service including cosmetic and plastic surgery shall be the location where the services are actually performed.

(5) The place of supply of services in relation to training and performance appraisal to,—

(*a*) a registered person, shall be the location of such person;

(*b*) a person other than a registered person, shall be the location where the services are actually performed.

(6) The place of supply of services provided by way of admission to a cultural, artistic, sporting, scientific, educational, entertainment event or amusement park or any other place and services ancillary thereto, shall be the place where the event is actually held or where the park or such other place is located.

(7) The place of supply of services provided by way of,—

(*a*) organisation of a cultural, artistic, sporting, scientific, educational or entertainment event including supply of services in relation to a conference, fair, exhibition, celebration or similar events; or

(*b*) services ancillary to organisation of any of the events or services referred to in clause (*a*), or assigning of sponsorship to such events,—

(*i*) to a registered person, shall be the location of such person;

(*ii*) to a person other than a registered person, shall be the place where the event is actually held and if the event is held outside India, the place of supply shall be the location of the recipient.

Explanation.—Where the event is held in more than one State or Union territory and a consolidated amount is charged for supply of services relating to such event, the place of supply of such services shall be taken as being in each of the respective States or Union territories in proportion to the value for services separately collected or determined in terms of the contract or agreement entered into in this regard or, in the absence of such contract or agreement, on such other basis as may be prescribed.

(8) The place of supply of services by way of transportation of goods, including by mail or courier to,—

(*a*) a registered person, shall be the location of such person;

(b) a person other than a registered person, shall be the location at which such goods are handed over for their transportation.

[12][***]

(9) The place of supply of passenger transportation service to,—

(a) a registered person, shall be the location of such person;

(b) a person other than a registered person, shall be the place where the passenger embarks on the conveyance for a continuous journey:

Provided that where the right to passage is given for future use and the point of embarkation is not known at the time of issue of right to passage, the place of supply of such service shall be determined in accordance with the provisions of sub-section (2).

Explanation.—For the purposes of this sub-section, the return journey shall be treated as a separate journey, even if the right to passage for onward and return journey is issued at the same time.

(10) The place of supply of services on board a conveyance, including a vessel, an aircraft, a train or a motor vehicle, shall be the location of the first scheduled point of departure of that conveyance for the journey.

(11) The place of supply of telecommunication services including data transfer, broadcasting, cable and direct to home television services to any person shall,—

(a) in case of services by way of fixed telecommunication line, leased circuits, internet leased circuit, cable or dish antenna, be the location where the telecommunication line, leased circuit or cable connection or dish antenna is installed for receipt of services;

12. Omitted by the Finance Act, 2023, w.e.f. 1-10-2023.

(*b*) in case of mobile connection for telecommunication and internet services provided on post-paid basis, be the location of billing address of the recipient of services on the record of the supplier of services;

(*c*) in cases where mobile connection for telecommunication, internet service and direct to home television services are provided on pre-payment basis through a voucher or any other means,—

(*i*) through a selling agent or a re-seller or a distributor of subscriber identity module card or recharge voucher, be the address of the selling agent or re-seller or distributor as per the record of the supplier at the time of supply; or

(*ii*) by any person to the final subscriber, be the location where such pre-payment is received or such vouchers are sold;

(*d*) in other cases, be the address of the recipient as per the records of the supplier of services and where such address is not available, the place of supply shall be location of the supplier of services:

Provided that where the address of the recipient as per the records of the supplier of services is not available, the place of supply shall be location of the supplier of services:

Provided further that if such pre-paid service is availed or the recharge is made through internet banking or other electronic mode of payment, the location of the recipient of services on the record of the supplier of services shall be the place of supply of such services.

Explanation.—Where the leased circuit is installed in more than one State or Union territory and a consolidated amount is charged for supply of services relating to such circuit, the place of supply of such services shall be taken as being in each of the respective States or Union territories in proportion to the value for services separately collected or determined in terms of the contract or agreement entered into in this regard or, in the absence of such contract or agreement, on such other basis as may be prescribed.

(12) The place of supply of banking and other financial services, including stock broking services to any person shall be the location of the recipient of services on the records of the supplier of services:

Provided that if the location of recipient of services is not on the records of the supplier, the place of supply shall be the location of the supplier of services.

(13) The place of supply of insurance services shall,—

(*a*) to a registered person, be the location of such person;

(*b*) to a person other than a registered person, be the location of the recipient of services on the records of the supplier of services.

(14) The place of supply of advertisement services to the Central Government, a State Government, a statutory body or a local authority meant for the States or Union territories identified in the contract or agreement shall be taken as being in each of such States or Union territories and the value of such supplies specific to each State or Union territory shall be in proportion to the amount attributable to services provided by way of dissemination in the respective States or Union territories as may be determined in terms of the contract or agreement entered into in this regard or, in the absence of such contract or agreement, on such other basis as may be prescribed.

Place of supply of services where location of supplier or location of recipient is outside India.

13. (1) The provisions of this section shall apply to determine the place of supply of services where the location of the supplier of services or the location of the recipient of services is outside India.

(2) The place of supply of services except the services specified in sub-sections (3) to (13) shall be the location of the recipient of services:

Provided that where the location of the recipient of services is not available in the ordinary course of business, the place of supply shall be the location of the supplier of services.

(3) The place of supply of the following services shall be the location where the services are actually performed, namely:—

(*a*) services supplied in respect of goods which are required to be made physically available by the recipient of services to the supplier of services, or to a person acting on behalf of the supplier of services in order to provide the services:

Provided that when such services are provided from a remote location by way of electronic means, the place of supply shall be the location where goods are situated at the time of supply of services:

[13][**Provided further** that nothing contained in this clause shall apply in the case of services supplied in respect of goods which are temporarily imported into India for repairs or for any other treatment or process and are exported after such repairs or treatment or process without being put to any use in

13. Substituted by the Integrated Goods and Services Tax (Amendment) Act, 2018, w.e.f. 1-2-2019.

India, other than that which is required for such repairs or treatment or process;]

(*b*) services supplied to an individual, represented either as the recipient of services or a person acting on behalf of the recipient, which require the physical presence of the recipient or the person acting on his behalf, with the supplier for the supply of services.

(4) The place of supply of services supplied directly in relation to an immovable property, including services supplied in this regard by experts and estate agents, supply of accommodation by a hotel, inn, guest house, club or campsite, by whatever name called, grant of rights to use immovable property, services for carrying out or co-ordination of construction work, including that of architects or interior decorators, shall be the place where the immovable property is located or intended to be located.

(5) The place of supply of services supplied by way of admission to, or organisation of a cultural, artistic, sporting, scientific, educational or entertainment event, or a celebration, conference, fair, exhibition or similar events, and of services ancillary to such admission or organisation, shall be the place where the event is actually held.

(6) Where any services referred to in sub-section (3) or sub-section (4) or sub-section (5) is supplied at more than one location, including a location in the taxable territory, its place of supply shall be the location in the taxable territory.

(7) Where the services referred to in sub-section (3) or sub-section (4) or sub-section (5) are supplied in more than one State or Union territory, the place of supply of such services shall be taken as being in each of the respective States or Union territories and the value of such supplies specific to each State or Union territory shall be in proportion to the value for services separately collected or determined in terms of

the contract or agreement entered into in this regard or, in the absence of such contract or agreement, on such other basis as may be prescribed.

(8) The place of supply of the following services shall be the location of the supplier of services, namely:—

(*a*) services supplied by a banking company, or a financial institution, or a non-banking financial company, to account holders;

(*b*) intermediary services;

(*c*) services consisting of hiring of means of transport, including yachts but excluding aircrafts and vessels, up to a period of one month.

Explanation.—For the purposes of this sub-section, the expression,—

(*a*) "account" means an account bearing interest to the depositor, and includes a non-resident external account and a non-resident ordinary account;

(*b*) "banking company" shall have the same meaning as assigned to it under clause (*a*) of section 45A of the Reserve Bank of India Act, 1934 (2 of 1934);

(*c*) "financial institution" shall have the same meaning as assigned to it in clause (*c*) of section 45-I of the Reserve Bank of India Act, 1934 (2 of 1934);

(*d*) "non-banking financial company" means,—

(*i*) a financial institution which is a company;

(*ii*) a non-banking institution which is a company and which has as its principal business the receiving of deposits, under any scheme or arrangement or in any other manner, or lending in any manner; or (*iii*) such other non-banking institution or class of such institutions, as the Reserve Bank of India may, with the previous approval of the Central Government and by notification in the Official Gazette, specify.

(9) [14][***]

(10) The place of supply in respect of passenger transportation services shall be the place where the passenger embarks on the conveyance for a continuous journey.

(11) The place of supply of services provided on board a conveyance during the course of a passenger transport operation, including services intended to be wholly or substantially consumed while on board, shall be the first scheduled point of departure of that conveyance for the journey.

(12) The place of supply of online information and database access or retrieval services shall be the location of the recipient of services.

Explanation.—For the purposes of this sub-section, person receiving such services shall be deemed to be located in the taxable territory, if any two of the following non-contradictory conditions are satisfied, namely:—

(*a*) the location of address presented by the recipient of services through internet is in the taxable territory;

(*b*) the credit card or debit card or store value card or charge card or smart card or any other card by which the recipient of services settles payment has been issued in the taxable territory;

(*c*) the billing address of the recipient of services is in the taxable territory;

14. Omitted by the Finance Act, 2023, w.e.f. 1-10-2023.

(*d*) the internet protocol address of the device used by the recipient of services is in the taxable territory;

(*e*) the bank of the recipient of services in which the account used for payment is maintained is in the taxable territory;

(*f*) the country code of the subscriber identity module card used by the recipient of services is of taxable territory;

(*g*) the location of the fixed land line through which the service is received by the recipient is in the taxable territory.

(13) In order to prevent double taxation or non-taxation of the supply of a service, or for the uniform application of rules, the Government shall have the power to notify any description of services or circumstances in which the place of supply shall be the place of effective use and enjoyment of a service.

Special provision for payment of tax by a supplier of online information and database access or retrieval services.

14. (1) On supply of online information and database access or retrieval services by any person located in a non-taxable territory and received by a non-taxable online recipient, the supplier of services located in a non-taxable territory shall be the person liable for paying integrated tax on such supply of services :

Provided that in the case of supply of online information and database access or retrieval services by any person located in a non-taxable territory and received by a non-taxable online recipient, an intermediary located in the non-taxable territory, who arranges or facilitates the supply of such services, shall be deemed to be the recipient of such services from the supplier of services in non-taxable territory and supplying such services to the non-taxable online recipient except when such intermediary satisfies the following conditions, namely:—

(*a*) the invoice or customer's bill or receipt issued or made available by such intermediary taking part in the supply clearly identifies the service in question and its supplier in non-taxable territory;

(*b*) the intermediary involved in the supply does not authorise the charge to the customer or take part in its charge which is that the intermediary neither collects or processes payment in any manner nor is responsible for the payment between the non-taxable online recipient and the supplier of such services;

(*c*) the intermediary involved in the supply does not authorise delivery; and

(*d*) the general terms and conditions of the supply are not set by the intermediary involved in the supply but by the supplier of services.

(2) The supplier of online information and database access or retrieval services referred to in sub-section (1) shall, for payment of integrated tax, take a single registration under the Simplified Registration Scheme to be notified by the Government:

Provided that any person located in the taxable territory representing such supplier for any purpose in the taxable territory shall get registered and pay integrated tax on behalf of the supplier :

Provided further that if such supplier does not have a physical presence or does not have a representative for any purpose in the taxable territory, he may appoint a person in the taxable territory for the purpose of paying integrated tax and such person shall be liable for payment of such tax.

[15][Special provision for specified actionable claims supplied by a person located outside taxable territory.

14A. (1) A supplier of online money gaming as defined in clause (*80B*) of section 2 of the Central Goods and Services Tax Act, 2017 (12 of 2017), not located in the taxable territory, shall in respect of the supply of online money gaming by him to a person in the taxable territory, be liable to pay integrated tax on such supply.

(2) For the purposes of complying with provisions of sub-section (1), the supplier of online money gaming shall obtain a single registration under the Simplified Registration Scheme referred to in sub-section (2) of section 14 of this Act:

Provided that any person located in the taxable territory representing such supplier for any purpose in the taxable territory shall get registered and pay the integrated tax on behalf of the supplier:

Provided further that if such supplier does not have a physical presence or does not have a representative for any purpose in the taxable territory, he shall appoint a person in the taxable territory for the purpose of paying integrated tax and such person shall be liable for payment of such tax.

(3) In case of failure to comply with provisions of sub-section (1) or sub-section (2) by the supplier of the online money gaming or a person appointed by such supplier or both, notwithstanding anything contained in section 69A of the Information Technology Act, 2000 (21 of 2000), any information generated, transmitted, received or hosted in any computer resource used for supply of online money gaming by such supplier shall be liable to be blocked for access by the public in such manner as specified in the said Act.]

15. Inserted by the Integrated Goods and Services Tax (Amendment) Act, 2023, w.e.f. 1-10-2023.

CHAPTER VI

REFUND OF INTEGRATED TAX TO INTERNATIONAL TOURIST

Refund of integrated tax paid on supply of goods to tourist leaving India.

15. The integrated tax paid by tourist leaving India on any supply of goods taken out of India by him shall be refunded in such manner and subject to such conditions and safeguards as may be prescribed.

Explanation.—For the purposes of this section, the term "tourist" means a person not normally resident in India, who enters India for a stay of not more than six months for legitimate non-immigrant purposes.

CHAPTER VII

ZERO RATED SUPPLY

Zero rated supply.

16. (1) "Zero rated supply" means any of the following supplies of goods or services or both, namely:—

(*a*) export of goods or services or both; or

(*b*) supply of goods or services or both [16][for authorised operations] to a Special Economic Zone developer or a Special Economic Zone unit.

(2) Subject to the provisions of sub-section (5) of section 17 of the Central Goods and Services Tax Act, credit of input tax may be availed for making zero-rated supplies, notwithstanding that such supply may be an exempt supply.

[17][(3) A registered person making zero rated supply shall be eligible to claim refund of unutilised input tax credit on supply of goods or services or both, without payment of integrated tax, under bond or Letter of Undertaking, in accordance with the provisions of

---

16. Inserted by the Finance Act, 2021, w.e.f. 1-10-2023.

17. Sub-sections (3) and (4) substituted for sub-section (3), *ibid*.

section 54 of the Central Goods and Services Tax Act or the rules made thereunder, subject to such conditions, safeguards and procedure as may be prescribed:

Provided that the registered person making zero rated supply of goods shall, in case of non-realisation of sale proceeds, be liable to deposit the refund so received under this sub-section along with the applicable interest under section 50 of the Central Goods and Services Tax Act within thirty days after the expiry of the time limit prescribed under the Foreign Exchange Management Act, 1999 (42 of 1999) for receipt of foreign exchange remittances, in such manner as may be prescribed.

(4) The Government may, on the recommendation of the Council, and subject to such conditions, safeguards and procedures, by notification, specify—

(*i*) a class of persons who may make zero rated supply on payment of integrated tax and claim refund of the tax so paid [18]**[***in accordance with the provisions of section 54 of the Central Goods and Services Tax Act or the rules made thereunder***]***;*

(*ii*) a class of goods or services [19]**[***or both, on zero rated supply of which, the supplier may pay integrated tax and claim the refund of tax so paid, in accordance with the provisions of section 54 of the Central Goods and Services Tax Act or the rules made thereunder***]**.]

[18]**[***(5) Notwithstanding anything contained in sub-sections (3) and (4), no refund of unutilised input tax credit on account of zero rated supply of goods or of integrated tax paid on account of zero rated supply of goods shall be allowed where such zero rated supply of goods are subjected to export duty.***]**

18. Inserted by the Finance (No. 2) Act, 2024, w.e.f. **1-11-2024.**

19. Substituted for "which may be exported on payment of integrated tax and the supplier of such goods or services may claim the refund of tax so paid", *ibid.*

CHAPTER VIII

APPORTIONMENT OF TAX AND SETTLEMENT OF FUNDS

Apportionment of tax and settlement of funds.

17. (1) Out of the integrated tax paid to the Central Government,—

(*a*) in respect of inter-State supply of goods or services or both to an unregistered person or to a registered person paying tax under section 10 of the Central Goods and Services Tax Act;

(*b*) in respect of inter-State supply of goods or services or both where the registered person is not eligible for input tax credit;

(*c*) in respect of inter-State supply of goods or services or both made in a financial year to a registered person, where he does not avail of the input tax credit within the specified period and thus remains in the integrated tax account after expiry of the due date for furnishing of annual return for such year in which the supply was made;

(*d*) in respect of import of goods or services or both by an unregistered person or by a registered person paying tax under section 10 of the Central Goods and Services Tax Act;

(*e*) in respect of import of goods or services or both where the registered person is not eligible for input tax credit;

(*f*) in respect of import of goods or services or both made in a financial year by a registered person, where he does not avail of the said credit within the specified period and thus remains in the integrated tax account after expiry of the due date for furnishing of annual return for such year in which the supply was received,

the amount of tax calculated at the rate equivalent to the central tax on similar intra-State supply shall be apportioned to the Central Government.

(2) The balance amount of integrated tax remaining in the integrated tax account in respect of the supply for which an apportionment to the Central Government has been done under sub-section (1) shall be apportioned to the,—

(*a*) State where such supply takes place; and

(*b*) Central Government where such supply takes place in a Union territory:

Provided that where the place of such supply made by any taxable person cannot be determined separately, the said balance amount shall be apportioned to,—

(*a*) each of the States; and

(*b*) Central Government in relation to Union territories,

in proportion to the total supplies made by such taxable person to each of such States or Union territories, as the case may be, in a financial year:

Provided further that where the taxable person making such supplies is not identifiable, the said balance amount shall be apportioned to all States and the Central Government in proportion to the amount collected as State tax or, as the case may be, Union territory tax, by the respective State or, as the case may be, by the Central Government during the immediately preceding financial year.

[20][(2A) The amount not apportioned under sub-section (1) and sub-section (2) may, for the time being, on the recommendations of the Council, be apportioned at the rate of fifty per cent to the Central Government and fifty per cent to the State Governments or the Union territories, as the case may be, on *ad hoc* basis and shall be adjusted against the amount apportioned under the said sub-sections.]

(3) The provisions of sub-sections (1) and (2) relating to apportionment of integrated tax shall, *mutatis mutandis,* apply to the apportionment of interest,

---

20. Inserted by the Integrated Goods and Services Tax (Amendment) Act, 2018, w.e.f. 1-2-2019.

penalty and compounding amount realised in connection with the tax so apportioned.

(4) Where an amount has been apportioned to the Central Government or a State Government under sub-section (1) or sub-section (2) or sub-section (3), the amount collected as integrated tax shall stand reduced by an amount equal to the amount so apportioned and the Central Government shall transfer to the central tax account or Union territory tax account, an amount equal to the respective amounts apportioned to the Central Government and shall transfer to the State tax account of the respective States an amount equal to the amount apportioned to that State, in such manner and within such time as may be prescribed.

(5) Any integrated tax apportioned to a State or, as the case may be, to the Central Government on account of a Union territory, if subsequently found to be refundable to any person and refunded to such person, shall be reduced from the amount to be apportioned under this section, to such State, or Central Government on account of such Union territory, in such manner and within such time as may be prescribed.

[21][**Transfer of certain amounts.**

17A. Where any amount has been transferred from the electronic cash ledger under this Act to the electronic cash ledger under the State Goods and Services Tax Act or the Union Territory Goods and Services Tax Act, the Government shall transfer to the State tax account or the Union territory tax account, an amount equal to the amount transferred from the electronic cash ledger, in such manner and within such time, as may be prescribed.]

Transfer of input tax credit.

18. On utilisation of credit of integrated tax availed under this Act for payment of,—

(*a*) Central tax in accordance with the provisions of sub-section (5) of section 49 of the Central

---

21. Inserted by the Finance (No. 2) Act, 2019, w.e.f. 1-1-2020.

Goods and Services Tax Act, the amount collected as integrated tax shall stand reduced by an amount equal to the credit so utilised and the Central Government shall transfer an amount equal to the amount so reduced from the integrated tax account to the central tax account in such manner and within such time as may be prescribed;

(*b*) Union territory tax in accordance with the provisions of section 9 of the Union Territory Goods and Services Tax Act, the amount collected as integrated tax shall stand reduced by an amount equal to the credit so utilised and the Central Government shall transfer an amount equal to the amount so reduced from the integrated tax account to the Union territory tax account in such manner and within such time as may be prescribed;

(*c*) State tax in accordance with the provisions of the respective State Goods and Services Tax Act, the amount collected as integrated tax shall stand reduced by an amount equal to the credit so utilised and shall be apportioned to the appropriate State Government and the Central Government shall transfer the amount so apportioned to the account of the appropriate State Government in such manner and within such time as may be prescribed.

Explanation.—For the purposes of this Chapter, "appropriate State" in relation to a taxable person, means the State or Union territory where he is registered or is liable to be registered under the provisions of the Central Goods and Services Tax Act.

Tax wrongfully collected and paid to Central Government or State Government.

19. (1) A registered person who has paid integrated tax on a supply considered by him to be an inter-State supply, but which is subsequently held to be an intra-State supply, shall be granted refund of the amount of integrated tax so paid in such manner and subject to such conditions as may be prescribed.

(2) A registered person who has paid central tax and State tax or Union territory tax, as the case may be, on a transaction considered by him to be an intra-State supply, but which is subsequently held to be an inter-State supply, shall not be required to pay any interest on the amount of integrated tax payable.

CHAPTER IX

MISCELLANEOUS

Application of provisions of Central Goods and Services Tax Act.

20. Subject to the provisions of this Act and the rules made thereunder, the provisions of Central Goods and Services Tax Act relating to,—

(*i*) scope of supply;

(*ii*) composite supply and mixed supply;

(*iii*) time and value of supply;

(*iv*) input tax credit;

(*v*) registration;

(*vi*) tax invoice, credit and debit notes;

(*vii*) accounts and records;

(*viii*) returns, other than late fee;

(*ix*) payment of tax;

(*x*) tax deduction at source;

(*xi*) collection of tax at source;

(*xii*) assessment;

(*xiii*) refunds;

(*xiv*) audit;

(*xv*) inspection, search, seizure and arrest;

(*xvi*) demands and recovery;

(*xvii*) liability to pay in certain cases;

(*xviii*) advance ruling;

(*xix*) appeals and revision;

(*xx*) presumption as to documents;

(*xxi*) offences and penalties;

(*xxii*) job work;

(*xxiii*) electronic commerce;

(*xxiv*) transitional provisions; and

(*xxv*) miscellaneous provisions including the provisions relating to the imposition of interest and penalty,

shall, *mutatis mutandis,* apply, so far as may be, in relation to integrated tax as they apply in relation to central tax as if they are enacted under this Act:

Provided that in the case of tax deducted at source, the deductor shall deduct tax at the rate of two per cent from the payment made or credited to the supplier:

Provided further that in the case of tax collected at source, the operator shall collect tax at such rate not exceeding two per cent, as may be notified on the recommendations of the Council, of the net value of taxable supplies:

Provided also that for the purposes of this Act, the value of a supply shall include any taxes, duties, cesses, fees and charges levied under any law for the time being in force other than this Act, and the Goods and Services Tax (Compensation to States) Act, if charged separately by the supplier:

Provided also that in cases where the penalty is leviable under the Central Goods and Services Tax Act and the State Goods and Services Tax Act or the Union Territory Goods and Services Tax Act, the penalty leviable under this Act shall be the sum total of the said penalties:

[22]**[Provided also** *that a maximum amount of forty crore rupees shall be payable for each appeal to be filed before the Appellate Authority or the Appellate Tribunal.***]**

Import of services made on or after the appointed day.

21. Import of services made on or after the appointed day shall be liable to tax under the provisions of this Act regardless of whether the transactions for

22. Substituted by the Finance (No. 2) Act, 2024, w.e.f. **1-11-2024**.

such import of services had been initiated before the appointed day:

Provided that if the tax on such import of services had been paid in full under the existing law, no tax shall be payable on such import under this Act:

Provided further that if the tax on such import of services had been paid in part under the existing law, the balance amount of tax shall be payable on such import under this Act.

Explanation.—For the purposes of this section, a transaction shall be deemed to have been initiated before the appointed day if either the invoice relating to such supply or payment, either in full or in part, has been received or made before the appointed day.

Power to make rules.

22. (1) The Government may, on the recommendations of the Council, by notification, make rules for carrying out the provisions of this Act.

(2) Without prejudice to the generality of the provisions of sub-section (1), the Government may make rules for all or any of the matters which by this Act are required to be, or may be, prescribed or in respect of which provisions are to be or may be made by rules.

(3) The power to make rules conferred by this section shall include the power to give retrospective effect to the rules or any of them from a date not earlier than the date on which the provisions of this Act come into force.

(4) Any rules made under sub-section (1) may provide that a contravention thereof shall be liable to a penalty not exceeding ten thousand rupees.

Power to make regulations.

23. The Board may, by notification, make regulations consistent with this Act and the rules made thereunder to carry out the provisions of this Act.

Laying of rules, regulations and notifications.

24. Every rule made by the Government, every regulation made by the Board and every notification issued by the Government under this Act, shall be laid, as soon as may be, after it is made or issued, before each House of Parliament, while it is in session, for a total period of thirty days which may be comprised in one session or in two or more successive sessions, and if, before the expiry of the session immediately following the session or the successive sessions aforesaid, both Houses agree in making any modification in the rule or regulation or in the notification, as the case may be, or both Houses agree that the rule or regulation or the notification should not be made, the rule or regulation or notification, as the case may be, shall thereafter have effect only in such modified form or be of no effect, as the case may be; so, however, that any such modification or annulment shall be without prejudice to the validity of anything previously done under that rule or regulation or notification, as the case may be.

Removal of difficulties.

25. (1) If any difficulty arises in giving effect to any provision of this Act, the Government may, on the recommendations of the Council, by a general or a special order published in the Official Gazette, make such provisions not inconsistent with the provisions of this Act or the rules or regulations made thereunder, as may be necessary or expedient for the purpose of removing the said difficulty:

Provided that no such order shall be made after the expiry of a period of [23][five years] from the date of commencement of this Act.

(2) Every order made under this section shall be laid, as soon as may be, after it is made, before each House of Parliament.

23. Substituted for "three years" by the Finance Act, 2020, w.e.f. 30-6-2020.

DIVISION THREE

Union Territory Goods and Services Tax Act, 2017

3

UNION TERRITORY GOODS AND SERVICES TAX ACT, 2017

Arrangement of Sections

SECTIONS PAGE

CHAPTER I

PRELIMINARY

CHAPTER II

ADMINISTRATION

SECTIONS PAGE

CHAPTER III

LEVY AND COLLECTION OF TAX

CHAPTER IV

PAYMENT OF TAX

CHAPTER V

INSPECTION, SEARCH, SEIZURE AND ARREST

CHAPTER VI

DEMANDS AND RECOVERY

CHAPTER VII

ADVANCE RULING

CHAPTER VIII

TRANSITIONAL PROVISIONS

CHAPTER IX

MISCELLANEOUS

Union Territory Goods and Services Tax Act, 2017 [14 OF 2017]*

An Act to make a provision for levy and collection of tax on intra-State supply of goods or services or both by the Union territories and the matter connected therewith or incidental thereto.

BE it enacted by Parliament in the Sixty-eighth Year of the Republic of India as follows:—

CHAPTER I

PRELIMINARY

Short title, extent and commencement.

1. (1) This Act may be called the Union Territory Goods and Services Tax Act, 2017.

(2) It extends to the Union territories of the Andaman and Nicobar Islands, Lakshadweep, [1][Dadra and Nagar Haveli and Daman and Diu, Ladakh], Chandigarh and other territory.

(3) It shall come into force on such date as the Central Government may, by notification in the Official Gazette, appoint:

Provided that different dates may be appointed for different provisions of this Act and any reference in

*Assented by the President of India on 12-4-2017.

1. Substituted for "Dadra and Nagar Haveli and Daman and Diu" by the Finance Act, 2020, w.e.f. 27-3-2020.

any such provision to the commencement of this Act shall be construed as a reference to the coming into force of that provision.

Definitions.

2. In this Act, unless the context otherwise requires,—

(*1*) "appointed day" means the date on which the provisions of this Act shall come into force;

(*2*) "Commissioner" means the Commissioner of Union territory tax appointed under section 3;

(*3*) "designated authority" means such authority as may be notified by the Commissioner;

(*4*) "exempt supply" means supply of any goods or services or both which attracts *nil* rate of tax or which may be exempt from tax under section 8, or under section 6 of the Integrated Goods and Services Tax Act, and includes non-taxable supply;

(*5*) "existing law" means any law, notification, order, rule or regulation relating to levy and collection of duty or tax on goods or services or both passed or made before the commencement of this Act by Parliament or any Authority or person having the power to make such law, notification, order, rule or regulation;

(*6*) "Government" means the Administrator or any authority or officer authorised to act as Administrator by the Central Government;

(7) "output tax" in relation to a taxable person, means the Union territory tax chargeable under this Act on taxable supply of goods or services or both made by him or by his agent but excludes tax payable by him on reverse charge basis;

(*8*) "Union territory" means the territory of,—

(*i*) the Andaman and Nicobar Islands;

(*ii*) Lakshadweep;

[2][(*iii*) Dadra and Nagar Haveli and Daman and Diu;]

[3][(*iv*) Ladakh;]

(*v*) Chandigarh; or

(*vi*) other territory.

Explanation.—For the purposes of this Act, each of the territories specified in sub-clauses (*i*) to (*vi*) shall be considered to be a separate Union territory;

(*9*) "Union territory tax" means the tax levied under this Act;

(*10*) words and expressions used and not defined in this Act but defined in the Central Goods and Services Tax Act, the Integrated Goods and Services Tax Act, the State Goods and Services Tax Act, and the Goods and Services Tax (Compensation to States) Act, shall have the same meaning as assigned to them in those Acts.

CHAPTER II

ADMINISTRATION

Officers under this Act.

3. The Administrator may, by notification, appoint Commissioners and such other class of officers as may be required for carrying out the purposes of this

2. Substituted by the Finance Act, 2020, w.e.f. 27-3-2020.
3. Inserted, *ibid*.

Act and such officers shall be deemed to be proper officers for such purposes as may be specified therein:

Provided that the officers appointed under the existing law shall be deemed to be the officers appointed under the provisions of this Act.

Authorisation of officers.

4. The Administrator may, by order, authorise any officer to appoint officers of Union territory tax below the rank of Assistant Commissioner of Union territory tax for the administration of this Act.

Powers of officers.

5. (1) Subject to such conditions and limitations as the Commissioner may impose, an officer of the Union territory tax may exercise the powers and discharge the duties conferred or imposed on him under this Act.

(2) An officer of a Union territory tax may exercise the powers and discharge the duties conferred or imposed under this Act on any other officer of a Union territory tax who is subordinate to him.

(3) The Commissioner may, subject to such conditions and limitations as may be specified in this behalf by him, delegate his powers to any other officer subordinate to him.

(4) Notwithstanding anything contained in this section, an Appellate Authority shall not exercise the powers and discharge the duties conferred or imposed on any other officer of Union territory tax.

Authorisation of officers of central tax as proper officer in certain circumstances.

6. (1) Without prejudice to the provisions of this Act, the officers appointed under the Central Goods and Services Tax Act are authorised to be the proper officers for the purposes of this Act, subject to such conditions as the Government shall, on the recommendations of the Council, by notification, specify.

(2) Subject to the conditions specified in the notification issued under sub-section (1),—

(*a*) where any proper officer issues an order under this Act, he shall also issue an order under the Central Goods and Services Tax Act, as authorised by the said Act under intimation to the jurisdictional officer of central tax;

(*b*) where a proper officer under the Central Goods and Services Tax Act has initiated any proceedings on a subject matter, no proceedings shall be initiated by the proper officer under this Act on the same subject matter.

(3) Any proceedings for rectification, appeal and revision, wherever applicable, of any order passed by an officer appointed under this Act, shall not lie before an officer appointed under the Central Goods and Services Tax Act.

CHAPTER III

LEVY AND COLLECTION OF TAX

Levy and collection.

7. (1) Subject to the provisions of sub-section (2), there shall be levied a tax called the Union territory tax on all intra-State supplies of goods or services or both, except on the supply of alcoholic liquor for human consumption [4]**[***and undenatured extra neutral alcohol or rectified spirit which is used for manufacture of alcoholic liquor, for human consumption***]**, on the value determined under section 15 of the Central Goods and Services Tax Act and at such rates, not

4. Inserted by the Finance (No. 2) Act, 2024, w.e.f. **1-11-2024.**

exceeding twenty per cent as may be notified by the Central Government on the recommendations of the Council and collected in such manner as may be prescribed and shall be paid by the taxable person.

(2) The Union territory tax on the supply of petroleum crude, high speed diesel, motor spirit (commonly known as petrol), natural gas and aviation turbine fuel shall be levied with effect from such date as may be notified by the Central Government on the recommendations of the Council.

(3) The Central Government may, on the recommendations of the Council, by notification, specify categories of supply of goods or services or both, the tax on which shall be paid on reverse charge basis by the recipient of such goods or services or both and all the provisions of this Act shall apply to such recipient as if he is the person liable for paying the tax in relation to the supply of such goods or services or both.

[5][(4) The Government may, on the recommendations of the Council, by notification, specify a class of registered persons who shall, in respect of supply of specified categories of goods or services or both received from an unregistered supplier, pay the tax on reverse charge basis as the recipient of such supply of goods or services or both, and all the provisions of this Act shall apply to such recipient as if he is the person liable for paying the tax in relation to such supply of goods or services or both.]

(5) The Central Government may, on the recommendations of the Council, by notification, specify categories of services the tax on intra-State supplies of which shall be paid by the electronic commerce operator if such services are supplied through it,

5. Substituted by the Union Territory Goods and Services Tax (Amendment) Act, 2018, w.e.f. 1-2-2019.

and all the provisions of this Act shall apply to such electronic commerce operator as if he is the supplier liable for paying the tax in relation to the supply of such services:

Provided that where an electronic commerce operator does not have a physical presence in the taxable territory, any person representing such electronic commerce operator for any purpose in the taxable territory shall be liable to pay tax:

Provided further that where an electronic commerce operator does not have a physical presence in the taxable territory and also he does not have a representative in the said territory, such electronic commerce operator shall appoint a person in the taxable territory for the purpose of paying tax and such person shall be liable to pay tax.

Power to grant exemption from tax.

8. (1) Where the Central Government is satisfied that it is necessary in the public interest so to do, it may, on the recommendations of the Council, by notification, exempt generally either absolutely or subject to such conditions as may be specified therein, goods or services or both of any specified description from the whole or any part of the tax leviable thereon with effect from such date as may be specified in such notification.

(2) Where the Central Government is satisfied that it is necessary in the public interest so to do, it may, on the recommendations of the Council, by special order in each case, under circumstances of an exceptional nature to be stated in such order, exempt from payment of tax any goods or services or both on which tax is leviable.

(3) The Central Government may, if it considers necessary or expedient so to do for the purpose of clarifying the scope or applicability of any notification

issued under sub-section (1) or order issued under sub-section (2), insert an explanation in such notification or order, as the case may be, by notification at any time within one year of issue of the notification under sub-section (1) or order under sub-section (2), and every such explanation shall have effect as if it had always been the part of the first such notification or order, as the case may be.

(4) Any notification issued by the Central Government under sub-section (1) of section 11 or order issued under sub-section (2) of the said section of the Central Goods and Services Tax Act shall be deemed to be a notification or, as the case may be, an order issued under this Act.

Explanation.—For the purposes of this section, where an exemption in respect of any goods or services or both from the whole or part of the tax leviable thereon has been granted absolutely, the registered person supplying such goods or services or both shall not collect the tax, in excess of the effective rate, on such supply of goods or services or both.

[6][Power not to recover Goods and Services Tax not levied or short-levied as a result of general practice.

8A. *Notwithstanding anything contained in this Act, if the Government is satisfied that—*

(a) *a practice was, or is, generally prevalent regarding levy of Union territory tax (including non-levy thereof) on any supply of goods or services or both; and*

(b) *such supplies were, or are, liable to—*

(i) *Union territory tax, in cases where according to the said practice, Union territory tax was not, or is not being, levied; or*

6. Inserted by the Finance (No. 2) Act, 2024, w.e.f. **1-11-2024**.

(ii) *a higher amount of Union territory tax than what was, or is being, levied, in accordance with the said practice,*

*the Government may, on the recommendation of the Council, by notification in the Official Gazette, direct that the whole of the Union territory tax payable on such supplies, or, as the case may be, the Union territory tax in excess of that payable on such supplies, but for the said practice, shall not be required to be paid in respect of the supplies on which the Union territory tax was not, or is not being, levied, or was, or is being, short-levied, in accordance with the said practice.***]**

CHAPTER IV

PAYMENT OF TAX

Payment of tax.

9. The amount of input tax credit available in the electronic credit ledger of the registered person on account of,—

(*a*) integrated tax shall first be utilised towards payment of integrated tax and the amount remaining, if any, may be utilised towards the payment of Central tax and State tax, or as the case may be, Union territory tax, in that order;

(*b*) the Union territory tax shall first be utilised towards payment of Union territory tax and the amount remaining, if any, may be utilised towards payment of integrated tax:

[6a][**Provided** that the input tax credit on account of Union territory tax shall be utilised towards payment of integrated tax only where the balance of the input tax credit on account of central tax is not available for payment of integrated tax;]

6a. Inserted by the Union Territory Goods and Services Tax (Amendment) Act, 2018, w.e.f. 1-2-2019.

(*c*) the Union territory tax shall not be utilised towards payment of Central tax.

[7][Utilisation of input tax credit.

9A. Notwithstanding anything contained in section 9, the input tax credit on account of Union territory tax shall be utilised towards payment of integrated tax or Union territory tax, as the case may be, only after the input tax credit available on account of integrated tax has first been utilised towards such payment.

Order of utilisation of input tax credit.

9B. Notwithstanding anything contained in this Chapter and subject to the provisions of clause (*c*) of section 9, the Government may, on the recommendations of the Council, prescribe the order and manner of utilisation of the input tax credit on account of integrated tax, central tax, State tax or Union territory tax, as the case may be, towards payment of any such tax.]

Transfer of input tax credit.

10. On utilisation of input tax credit of Union territory tax for payment of tax dues under the Integrated Goods and Services Tax Act in accordance with the provisions of sub-section (5) of section 49 of the Central Goods and Services Tax Act, as reflected in the valid return furnished under sub-section (1) of section 39 of the Central Goods and Services tax Act, the amount collected as Union territory tax shall stand reduced by an amount equal to such credit so utilised and the Central Government shall transfer an amount equal to the amount so reduced from the Union territory tax account to the integrated tax account in such manner and within such time as may be prescribed.

7. Inserted by the Union Territory Goods and Services Tax (Amendment) Act, 2018, w.e.f. 1-2-2019.

CHAPTER V

INSPECTION, SEARCH, SEIZURE AND ARREST

Officers required to assist proper officers.

11. (1) All officers of Police, Railways, Customs, and those officers engaged in the collection of land revenue, including village officers, and officers of Central tax and officers of the State tax shall assist the proper officers in the implementation of this Act.

(2) The Government may, by notification, empower and require any other class of officers to assist the proper officers in the implementation of this Act when called upon to do so by the Commissioner.

CHAPTER VI

DEMANDS AND RECOVERY

Tax wrongfully collected and paid to Central Government or Union Territory Government.

12. (1) A registered person who has paid the Central tax and the Union territory tax on a transaction considered by him to be an intra-State supply, but which is subsequently held to be an inter-State supply, shall be refunded the amount of taxes so paid in such manner and subject to such conditions as may be prescribed.

(2) A registered person who has paid integrated tax on a transaction considered by him to be an inter-State supply, but which is subsequently held to be an intra-State supply, shall not be required to pay any interest on the amount of the Central tax and the Union territory tax payable.

Recovery of tax.

13. (1) Where any amount of tax, interest or penalty is payable by a person to the Government under any of the provisions of this Act or the rules made thereunder and which remains unpaid, the proper officer of Central tax, during the course of recovery of said tax arrears, may recover the amount from the said person as if it were an arrear of Central tax and credit the amount so recovered to the account of the Government under the appropriate head of Union territory tax.

(2) Where the amount recovered under sub-section (1) is less than the amount due to the Government under this Act and the Central Goods and Services Tax Act, the amount to be credited to the account of the Government shall be in proportion to the amount due as Union territory tax and Central tax.

CHAPTER VII

ADVANCE RULING

Definitions.

14. In this Chapter, unless the context otherwise requires,—

(*a*) "advance ruling" means a decision provided by the Authority or the Appellate Authority to an applicant on matters or on questions specified in sub-section (2) of section 97 or sub-section (1) of section 100 of the Central Goods and Services Tax Act, in relation to the supply of goods or services or both being undertaken or proposed to be undertaken by the applicant;

(*b*) "Appellate Authority" means the Appellate Authority for Advance Ruling constituted under section 16;

(*c*) "applicant" means any person registered or desirous of obtaining registration under this Act;

(*d*) "application" means an application made to the Authority under sub-section (1) of section 97 of the Central Goods and Services Tax Act;

(*e*) "Authority" means the Authority for Advance Ruling, constituted under section 15.

Constitution of Authority for Advance Ruling.

15. (1) The Central Government shall, by notification, constitute an Authority to be known as the (name of the Union territory) Authority for Advance Ruling:

Provided that the Central Government may, on the recommendations of the Council, notify any Authority located in any State or any other Union territory to act as the Authority for the purposes of this Act.

(2) The Authority shall consist of—

(*i*) one member from amongst the officers of Central tax; and

(*ii*) one member from amongst the officers of Union territory tax,

to be appointed by the Central Government.

(3) The qualifications, the method of appointment of the members and the terms and conditions of their service shall be such as may be prescribed.

Constitution of Appellate Authority for Advance Ruling.

16. (1) The Central Government shall, by notification, constitute an Appellate Authority to be known as the (name of the Union territory) Appellate Authority for Advance Ruling for Goods and Services Tax for hearing appeals against the advance ruling pronounced by the Advance Ruling Authority:

Provided that the Central Government may, on the recommendations of the Council, notify any Appellate Authority located in any State or any other Union territory to act as the Appellate Authority for the purposes of this Act.

(2) The Appellate Authority shall consist of—

(*i*) the Chief Commissioner of Central tax as designated by the Board; and

(*ii*) the Commissioner of Union territory tax having jurisdiction over the applicant.

CHAPTER VIII

TRANSITIONAL PROVISIONS

Migration of existing taxpayers.

17. (1) On and from the appointed day, every person registered under any of the existing laws and having a valid Permanent Account Number shall be issued a certificate of registration on provisional basis, subject to such conditions and in such form and manner as may be prescribed, which unless replaced by a final certificate of registration under sub-section (2), shall be liable to be cancelled if the conditions so prescribed are not complied with.

(2) The final certificate of registration shall be granted in such form and manner and subject to such conditions as may be prescribed.

(3) The certificate of registration issued to a person under sub-section (1) shall be deemed to have not been issued if the said registration is cancelled in pursuance of an application filed by such person that he was not liable to registration under section 22 or section 24 of the Central Goods and Services Tax Act.

Transitional arrangements for input tax credit.

18. (1) A registered person, other than a person opting to pay tax under section 10 of the Central Goods and Services Tax Act, shall be entitled to take, in his electronic credit ledger, credit of the amount of Value Added Tax and Entry Tax, if any, carried forward in the return relating to the period ending with the day immediately preceding the appointed day, furnished by him under the existing law, not later than ninety days after the said day, in such manner as may be prescribed:

Provided that the registered person shall not be allowed to take credit in the following circumstances, namely:—

(*i*) where the said amount of credit is not admissible as input tax credit under this Act; or (*ii*) where he has not furnished all the returns required under the existing law for the period of six months immediately preceding the appointed day; or

(*iii*) where the said amount of credit relates to goods sold under such exemption notifications as are notified by the Government:

Provided further that so much of the said credit as is attributable to any claim related to section 3, sub-section (3) of section 5, section 6 or section 6A or sub-section (8) of section 8 of the Central Sales Tax Act, 1956 (74 of 1956) that is not substantiated in the manner, and within the period, prescribed in rule 12 of the Central Sales Tax (Registration and Turnover) Rules, 1957 shall not be eligible to be credited to the electronic credit ledger:

Provided also that an amount equivalent to the credit specified in the second proviso shall be refunded under the existing law when the said claims are substantiated in the manner prescribed in rule 12 of the Central Sales Tax (Registration and Turnover) Rules, 1957.

(2) A registered person, other than a person opting to pay tax under section 10 of the Central Goods and Services Tax Act, shall be entitled to take, in his electronic credit ledger, credit of the unavailed input tax credit in respect of capital goods, not carried forward in a return, furnished under the existing law by him, for the period ending with the day immediately preceding the appointed day in such manner as may be prescribed:

Provided that the registered person shall not be allowed to take credit unless the said credit was admissible as input tax credit under the existing law and is also admissible as input tax credit under this Act.

Explanation.—For the purposes of this section, the expression "unavailed input tax credit" means the amount that remains after subtracting the amount of input tax credit already availed in respect of capital goods by the taxable person under the existing law from the aggregate amount of input tax credit to which the said person was entitled in respect of the said capital goods under the existing law.

(3) A registered person, who was not liable to be registered under the existing law or who was engaged in the sale of exempted goods or tax free goods or goods which have suffered tax at first point of their sale in the Union territory and the subsequent sales of which are not subject to tax in the Union territory under the existing law but which are liable to tax under this Act or where the person was entitled to the credit of input tax at the time of sale of goods, shall be entitled to take, in his electronic credit ledger, credit of the value added tax and entry tax, if any, in respect of inputs held in stock and inputs contained in semi-finished or finished goods held in stock on the appointed day subject to the following conditions, namely:—

- (*i*) such inputs or goods are used or intended to be used for making taxable supplies under this Act;
- (*ii*) the said registered person is eligible for input tax credit on such inputs under this Act;
- (*iii*) the said registered person is in possession of invoice or other prescribed documents evidencing payment of tax under the existing law in respect of such inputs; and
- (*iv*) such invoices or other prescribed documents were issued not earlier than twelve months immediately preceding the appointed day:

Provided that where a registered person, other than a manufacturer or a supplier of services, is not in possession of an invoice or any other documents evidencing payment of tax in respect of inputs, then, such registered person shall, subject to such conditions, limitations and safeguards as may be prescribed, including that the said taxable person shall pass on the benefit of such credit by way of reduced prices to the recipient, be allowed to take credit at such rate and in such manner as may be prescribed.

(4) A registered person, who was engaged in the sale of taxable goods as well as exempted goods or tax free goods under the existing law but which are liable to tax under this Act, shall be entitled to take, in his electronic credit ledger,—

(*a*) the amount of credit of the value added tax and entry tax, if any, carried forward in a return furnished under the existing law by him in accordance with the provisions of sub-section (1); and

(*b*) the amount of credit of the value added tax and entry tax, if any, in respect of inputs held in stock and inputs contained in semi-finished or finished goods held in stock on the appointed day, relating to such exempted goods or tax free goods in accordance with the provisions of sub-section (3).

(5) A registered person shall be entitled to take, in his electronic credit ledger, credit of value added tax and entry tax, if any, in respect of inputs received on or after the appointed day but the tax in respect of which has been paid by the supplier under the existing law, subject to the condition that the invoice or any other tax paying document of the same was recorded in the books of account of such person within a period of thirty days from the appointed day:

Provided that the period of thirty days may, on sufficient cause being shown, be extended by the Commissioner for a further period not exceeding thirty days:

Provided further that the said registered person shall furnish a statement, in such manner as may be prescribed, in respect of credit that has been taken under this sub-section.

(6) A registered person, who was either paying tax at a fixed rate or paying a fixed amount in lieu of the tax payable under the existing law shall be entitled to take, in his electronic credit ledger, credit of value added tax in respect of inputs held in stock and inputs contained in semi-finished or finished goods held in stock on the appointed day subject to the following conditions, namely:—

(*i*) such inputs or goods are used or intended to be used for making taxable supplies under this Act;

(*ii*) the said registered person is not paying tax under section 10 of the Central Goods and Services Tax Act;

(*iii*) the said registered person is eligible for input tax credit on such inputs under this Act;

(*iv*) the said registered person is in possession of invoice or other prescribed documents evidencing payment of tax under the existing law in respect of inputs; and

(*v*) such invoices or other prescribed documents were issued not earlier than twelve months immediately preceding the appointed day.

(7) The amount of credit under sub-sections (3), (4) and (6) shall be calculated in such manner as may be prescribed.

Transitional provisions relating to job work.

19. (1) Where any inputs received at a place of business had been despatched as such or despatched after being partially processed to a job worker for further processing, testing, repair, reconditioning or any other purpose in accordance with the provisions of existing law prior to the appointed day and such inputs are returned to the said place on or after the appointed day, no tax shall be payable if such inputs, after completion of the job work or otherwise, are returned to the said place within six months from the appointed day:

Provided that the period of six months may, on sufficient cause being shown, be extended by the Commissioner for a further period not exceeding two months:

Provided further that if such inputs are not returned within a period of six months or the extended period from the appointed day, the input tax credit shall be liable to be recovered in accordance with the provisions of clause (*a*) of sub-section (8) of section 142 of the Central Goods and Services Tax Act.

(2) Where any semi-finished goods had been despatched from any place of business to any other premises for carrying out certain manufacturing processes in accordance with the provisions of existing law prior to the appointed day and such goods (hereinafter in this section referred to as "the said goods") are returned to the said place on or after the appointed day, no tax shall be payable if the said goods, after undergoing manufacturing processes or otherwise, are returned to the said place within six months from the appointed day:

Provided that the period of six months may, on sufficient cause being shown, be extended by the Commissioner for a further period not exceeding two months:

Provided further that if the said goods are not returned within a period specified in this sub-section, the input tax credit shall be liable to be recovered in accordance with the provisions of clause (*a*) of sub-section (8) of section 142 of the Central Goods and Services Tax Act:

Provided also that the person despatching the goods may, in accordance with the provisions of the existing law, transfer the said goods to the premises of any registered person for the purpose of supplying therefrom on payment of tax in India or without payment of tax for exports within six months or the extended period, as the case may be, from the appointed day.

(3) Where any goods had been despatched from the place of business without payment of tax for carrying out tests or any other process to any other premises, whether registered or not, in accordance with the provisions of existing law prior to the appointed day and such goods are returned to the said place of business on or after the appointed day, no tax shall be payable if the said goods, after undergoing tests or any other process, are returned to such place within six months from the appointed day:

Provided that the period of six months may, on sufficient cause being shown, be extended by the Commissioner for a further period not exceeding two months:

Provided further that if the said goods are not returned within the period specified in this sub-section, the input tax credit shall be liable to be recovered in accordance with the provisions of clause (*a*) of sub-section (8) of section 142 of the Central Goods and Services Tax Act:

Provided also that the person despatching the goods may, in accordance with the provisions of the existing law, transfer the said goods from the said other premises on payment of tax in India or without payment of tax for exports within six months or the extended period, as the case may be, from the appointed day.

(4) The tax under sub-sections (1), (2) and (3) shall not be payable only if the person despatching the goods and the job worker declare the details of the inputs or goods held in stock by the job worker on behalf of the said person on the appointed day in such form and manner and within such time as may be prescribed.

Miscellaneous transitional provisions.

20. (1) Where any goods on which tax, if any, had been paid under the existing law at the time of sale thereof, not being earlier than six months prior to the appointed day, are returned to any place of business on or after the appointed day, the registered person shall be eligible for refund of the tax paid under the existing law where such goods are returned by a person, other than a registered person, to the said place of business within a period of six months from the appointed day and such goods are identifiable to the satisfaction of the proper officer:

Provided that if the said goods are returned by a registered person, the return of such goods shall be deemed to be a supply.

(2) (*a*) Where, in pursuance of a contract entered into prior to the appointed day, the price of any goods is revised upwards on or after the appointed day, the registered person who had sold such goods shall issue to the recipient a supplementary invoice or debit note, containing such particulars as may be prescribed, within thirty days of such price revision and for the purposes of this Act, such supplementary invoice or debit note shall be deemed to have been issued in respect of an outward supply made under this Act.

(*b*) Where, in pursuance of a contract entered into prior to the appointed day, the price of any goods is revised downwards on or after the appointed day, the registered person who had sold such goods may issue to the recipient a credit note, containing such particulars as may be prescribed, within thirty days of such price revision and for the purposes of this Act such credit note shall be deemed to have been issued in respect of an outward supply made under this Act:

Provided that the registered person shall be allowed to reduce his tax liability on account of issue of the credit note only if the recipient of the credit note has reduced his input tax credit corresponding to such reduction of tax liability.

(3) Every claim for refund filed by any person before, on or after the appointed day, for refund of any amount of input tax credit, tax, interest or any other amount paid under the existing law, shall be disposed of in accordance with the provisions of existing law

and any amount eventually accruing to him shall be refunded to him in cash in accordance with the provisions of the said law:

Provided that where any claim for refund of the amount of input tax credit is fully or partially rejected, the amount so rejected shall lapse:

Provided further that no refund shall be allowed of any amount of input tax credit where the balance of the said amount as on the appointed day has been carried forward under this Act.

(4) Every claim for refund filed after the appointed day for refund of any tax paid under the existing law in respect of the goods exported before or after the appointed day shall be disposed of in accordance with the provisions of the existing law:

Provided that where any* for refund of input tax credit is fully or partially rejected, the amount so rejected shall lapse:

Provided further that no refund shall be allowed of any amount of input tax credit where the balance of the said amount as on the appointed day has been carried forward under this Act.

(5) (*a*) Every proceeding of appeal, revision, review or reference relating to a claim for input tax credit initiated whether before, on or after the appointed day, under the existing law shall be disposed of in accordance with the provisions of the existing law, and any amount of credit found to be admissible to the claimant shall be refunded to him in cash in accordance with the provisions of the existing law and the amount rejected, if any, shall not be admissible as input tax credit under this Act:

Provided that no refund shall be allowed of any amount of input tax credit where the balance of the said amount as on the appointed day has been carried forward under this Act.

---

*Word "claim" should occur after the word "any".

(*b*) Every proceeding of appeal, revision, review or reference relating to recovery of input tax credit initiated whether before, on or after the appointed day, under the existing law shall be disposed of in accordance with the provisions of the existing law, and if any amount of credit becomes recoverable as a result of such appeal, revision, review or reference, the same shall, unless recovered under the existing law, be recovered as an arrear of tax under this Act and the amount so recovered shall not be admissible as input tax credit under this Act.

(6) (*a*) Every proceeding of appeal, revision, review or reference relating to any output tax liability initiated whether before, on or after the appointed day under the existing law, shall be disposed of in accordance with the provisions of the existing law, and if any amount becomes recoverable as a result of such appeal, revision, review or reference, the same shall, unless recovered under the existing law, be recovered as an arrear of tax under this Act and amount so recovered shall not be admissible as input tax credit under this Act.

(*b*) Every proceeding of appeal, revision, review or reference relating to any output tax liability initiated whether before, on or after the appointed day under the existing law, shall be disposed of in accordance with the provisions of the existing law, and any amount found to be admissible to the claimant shall be refunded to him in cash in accordance with the provisions of the existing law and the amount rejected, if any, shall not be admissible as input tax credit under this Act.

(7) (*a*) Where in pursuance of an assessment or adjudication proceedings instituted, whether before, on or after the appointed day, under the existing law, any amount of tax, interest, fine or penalty becomes recoverable from the person, the same shall, unless recovered under the existing law, be recovered as an arrear of tax under this Act and the amount so

recovered shall not be admissible as input tax credit under this Act.

(*b*) Where in pursuance of an assessment or adjudication proceedings instituted, whether before, on or after the appointed day under the existing law, any amount of tax, interest, fine or penalty becomes refundable to the taxable person, the same shall be refunded to him in cash under the said law and the amount rejected, if any, shall not be admissible as input tax credit under this Act.

(8) (*a*) Where any return, furnished under the existing law, is revised after the appointed day and if, pursuant to such revision, any amount is found to be recoverable or any amount of input tax credit is found to be inadmissible, the same shall, unless recovered under the existing law, be recovered as an arrear of tax under this Act and the amount so recovered shall not be admissible as input tax credit under this Act.

(*b*) Where any return, furnished under the existing law, is revised after the appointed day but within the time limit specified for such revision under the existing law and if, pursuant to such revision, any amount is found to be refundable or input tax credit is found to be admissible to any taxable person, the same shall be refunded to him in cash under the existing law and the amount rejected, if any, shall not be admissible as input tax credit under this Act.

(9) Save as otherwise provided in this Chapter, the goods or services or both supplied on or after the appointed day in pursuance of a contract entered into prior to the appointed day shall be liable to tax under the provisions of this Act.

(10) (*a*) Notwithstanding anything contained in section 12 of the Central Goods and Services Tax Act, no tax shall be payable on goods under this Act to the extent the tax was leviable on the said goods under the existing law.

(*b*) Notwithstanding anything contained in section 13 of the Central Goods and Services Tax Act, no tax shall be payable on services under this Act to the extent the tax was leviable on the said services under Chapter V of the Finance Act, 1994 (32 of 1994).

(*c*) Where tax was paid on any supply, both under any existing law relating to sale of goods and under Chapter V of the Finance Act, 1994 (32 of 1994), tax shall be leviable under this Act and the taxable person shall be entitled to take credit of value added tax or service tax paid under the existing law to the extent of supplies made after the appointed day and such credit shall be calculated in such manner as may be prescribed.

(11) Where any goods sent on approval basis, not earlier than six months before the appointed day, are rejected or not approved by the buyer and returned to the seller on or after the appointed day, no tax shall be payable thereon if such goods are returned within six months from the appointed day:

Provided that the said period of six months may, on sufficient cause being shown, be extended by the Commissioner for a further period not exceeding two months:

Provided further that the tax shall be payable by the person returning the goods if such goods are liable to tax under this Act and are returned after the period specified in this sub-section:

Provided also that tax shall be payable by the person who has sent the goods on approval basis if such goods are liable to tax under this Act, and are not returned within the period specified in this sub-section.

(12) Where a supplier has made any sale of goods in respect of which tax was required to be deducted at source under any existing law relating to sale of goods and has also issued an invoice for the same before the appointed day, no deduction of tax at source under section 51 of the Central Goods and Services Tax Act,

as made applicable to this Act, shall be made by the deductor under the said section where payment to the said supplier is made on or after the appointed day.

Explanation.—For the purposes of this Chapter, the expression "capital goods" shall have the same meaning as assigned to it in any existing law relating to sale of goods.

CHAPTER IX

MISCELLANEOUS

Application of provisions of Central Goods and Services Tax Act.

21. Subject to the provisions of this Act and the rules made thereunder, the provisions of the Central Goods and Services Tax Act, relating to,—

(*i*) scope of supply;

(*ii*) composition levy;

(*iii*) composite supply and mixed supply;

(*iv*) time and value of supply;

(*v*) input tax credit;

(*vi*) registration;

(*vii*) tax invoice, credit and debit notes;

(*viii*) accounts and records;

(*ix*) returns;

(*x*) payment of tax;

(*xi*) tax deduction at source;

(*xii*) collection of tax at source;

(*xiii*) assessment;

(*xiv*) refunds;

(*xv*) audit;

(*xvi*) inspection, search, seizure and arrest;

(*xvii*) demands and recovery;

(*xviii*) liability to pay in certain cases;

(*xix*) advance ruling;

(*xx*) appeals and revision;

(*xxi*) presumption as to documents;

(*xxii*) offences and penalties;

(*xxiii*) job work;

(*xxiv*) electronic commerce;

(*xxv*) settlement of funds;

(*xxvi*) transitional provisions; and

(*xxvii*) miscellaneous provisions including the provisions relating to the imposition of interest and penalty,

shall, *mutatis mutandis*, apply,—

(*a*) so far as may be, in relation to Union territory tax as they apply in relation to central tax as if they were enacted under this Act;

(*b*) subject to the following modifications and alterations which the Central Government considers necessary and desirable to adapt those provisions to the circumstances, namely:—

(*i*) references to "this Act" shall be deemed to be references to the Union Territory Goods and Services Tax Act, 2017;

(*ii*) references to "Commissioner" shall be deemed to be references to "Commissioner" of Union territory tax as defined in clause (*2*) of section 2 of this Act;

(*iii*) references to "officers of central tax" shall be deemed to be references to "officers of Union territory tax";

(*iv*) references to "central tax" shall be deemed to be reference to "Union territory tax" and *vice versa*;

(*v*) references to "Commissioner of State tax or Commissioner of Union territory tax" shall be deemed to be references to "Commissioner of central tax";

(*vi*) references to "State Goods and Services Tax Act or Union Territory Goods and Services Tax Act" shall be deemed to be references to "Central Goods and Services Tax Act";

(*vii*) references to "State tax or Union territory tax" shall be deemed to be references to "central tax".

Power to make rules.

22. (1) The Central Government may, on the recommendations of the Council, by notification, make rules for carrying out the provisions of this Act.

(2) Without prejudice to the generality of the provisions of sub-section (1), the Central Government may make rules for all or any of the matters which by this Act are required to be, or may be, prescribed or in respect of which provisions are to be or may be made by rules.

(3) The power to make rules conferred by this section shall include the power to give retrospective effect to the rules or any of them from a date not earlier than the date on which the provisions of this Act come into force.

(4) Any rules made under sub-section (1) may provide that a contravention thereof shall be liable to a penalty not exceeding ten thousand rupees.

General power to make regulations.

23. The Board may, by notification, make regulations consistent with this Act and the rules made thereunder to carry out the purposes of this Act.

Laying of rules, regulations and notifications.

24. Every rule made by the Central Government, every regulation made by the Board and every notification issued by the Central Government under this Act, shall be laid, as soon as may be, after it is made or issued, before each House of Parliament, while it is in session, for a total period of thirty days which may be comprised in one session or in two or more successive sessions, and if, before the expiry of the session immediately following the session or the successive sessions aforesaid, both Houses agree in making any modification in the rule or regulation or in the notification, as the case may be, or both Houses agree that the rule or regulation or the notification should not be made, the rule or regulation or notification, as the case may be, shall thereafter have effect only in such modified form or be of no effect, as the case may be; so, however, that any such modification or annulment shall be without prejudice to the validity of anything previously done under that rule or regulation or notification, as the case may be.

Power to issue instructions or directions.

25. The Commissioner may, if he considers it necessary or expedient so to do for the purpose of uniformity in the implementation of this Act, issue such orders, instructions or directions to the Union territory tax officers as he may deem fit, and thereupon all such officers and all other persons employed in the implementation of this Act shall observe and follow such orders, instructions or directions.

Removal of difficulties.

26. (1) If any difficulty arises in giving effect to any provision of this Act, the Central Government may, on the recommendations of the Council, by a general or a special order published in the Official Gazette, make such provisions not inconsistent with the provisions of this Act or the rules or regulations made thereunder, as may be necessary or expedient for the purpose of removing the said difficulty:

Provided that no such order shall be made after the expiry of a period of [8][five years] from the date of commencement of this Act.

(2) Every order made under this section shall be laid, as soon as may be, after it is made, before each House of Parliament.

8. Substituted for "three years" by the Finance Act, 2020, w.e.f. 27-3-2020.

DIVISION FOUR

Goods and Services Tax (Compensation to States) Act, 2017

4

GOODS AND SERVICES TAX (COMPENSATION TO STATES) ACT, 2017

Arrangement of Sections

Goods and Services Tax (Compensation to States) Act, 2017
[15 OF 2017]*

An Act to provide for compensation to the States for the loss of revenue arising on account of implementation of the goods and services tax in pursuance of the provisions of the Constitution (One Hundred and First Amendment) Act, 2016.

BE it enacted by Parliament in the Sixty-eighth Year of the Republic of India as follows:—

Short title, extent and commencement.

1. (1) This Act may be called the Goods and Services Tax (Compensation to States) Act, 2017.

(2) It extends to the whole of India.

(3) It shall come into force on such date as the Central Government may, by notification in the Official Gazette, appoint.

Definitions.

2. (1) In this Act, unless the context otherwise requires,—

(*a*) "central tax" means the central goods and services tax levied and collected under the Central Goods and Services Tax Act;

(*b*) "Central Goods and Services Tax Act" means the Central Goods and Services Tax Act, 2017;

* Assented by the President of India on 12-4-2017.

(*c*) "cess" means the goods and services tax compensation cess levied under section 8;

(*d*) "compensation" means an amount, in the form of goods and services tax compensation, as determined under section 7;

(*e*) "Council" means the Goods and Services Tax Council constituted under the provisions of article 279A of the Constitution;

(*f*) "Fund" means the Goods and Services Tax Compensation Fund referred to in section 10;

(*g*) "input tax" in relation to a taxable person, means,—

(*i*) cess charged on any supply of goods or services or both made to him;

(*ii*) cess charged on import of goods and includes the cess payable on reverse charge basis;

(*h*) "Integrated Goods and Services Tax Act" means the Integrated Goods and Services Tax Act, 2017;

(*i*) "integrated tax" means the integrated goods and services tax levied and collected under the Integrated Goods and Services Tax Act;

(*j*) "prescribed" means prescribed by rules made, on the recommendations of the Council, under this Act;

(*k*) "projected growth rate" means the rate of growth projected for the transition period as per section 3;

(*l*) "Schedule" means the Schedule appended to this Act;

(*m*) "State" means,—

(*i*) for the purposes of sections 3, 4, 5, 6 and 7 the States as defined under the Central Goods and Services Tax Act; and

and retained by the concerned State Government under the erstwhile article 268 of the Constitution;

(*g*) any cess or surcharge or fee leviable under entry 66 read with entries 52, 54, 55 and 62 of List II of the Seventh Schedule to the Constitution by the State Government under any Act notified under sub-section (4),

prior to the commencement of the provisions of the Constitution (One Hundred and First Amendment) Act, 2016:

Provided that the revenue collected during the base year in a State, net of refunds, under the following taxes shall not be included in the calculation of the base year revenue for that State, namely:—

(*a*) any taxes levied under any Act enacted under the erstwhile entry 54 of List II (State List) of the Seventh Schedule to the Constitution, prior to the coming into force of the provisions of the Constitution (One Hundred and First Amendment) Act, 2016, on the sale or purchase of petroleum crude, high speed diesel, motor spirit (commonly known as petrol), natural gas, aviation turbine fuel and alcoholic liquor for human consumption;

(*b*) tax levied under the Central Sales Tax Act, 1956 (74 of 1956), on the sale or purchase of petroleum crude, high speed diesel, motor spirit (commonly known as petrol), natural gas, aviation turbine fuel and alcoholic liquor for human consumption;

(*c*) any cess imposed by the State Government on the sale or purchase of petroleum crude, high speed diesel, motor spirit (commonly known as petrol), natural gas, aviation turbine fuel and alcoholic liquor for human consumption; and (*d*) the entertainment tax levied by the State but collected by local bodies, under any Act enacted under the erstwhile entry 62 of List II (State List) of the Seventh Schedule to the Constitution, prior to coming into force of the provisions of the Constitution (One Hundred and First Amendment) Act, 2016.

(2) In respect of the State of Jammu and Kashmir, the base year revenue shall include the amount of tax collected on sale of services by the said State Government during the base year.

(3) In respect of the States mentioned in sub-clause (*g*) of clause (*4*) of article 279A of the Constitution, the amount of revenue foregone on account of exemptions or remission given by the said State Governments to promote industrial investment in the State, with respect to such specific taxes referred to in sub-section (1), shall be included in the total base year revenue of the State, subject to such conditions as may be prescribed.

(4) The Acts of the Central Government and State Governments under which the specific taxes are being subsumed into the goods and services tax shall be such as may be notified.

(5) The base year revenue shall be calculated as per sub-sections (1), (2), (3) and (4) on the basis of the figures of revenue collected and net of refunds given in that year, as audited by the Comptroller and Auditor-General of India.

(6) In respect of any State, if any part of revenues mentioned in sub-sections (1), (2), (3) and (4) are not credited in the Consolidated Fund of the respective State, the same shall be included in the total base year revenue of the State, subject to such conditions as may be prescribed.

Projected revenue for any year.

6. The projected revenue for any year in a State shall be calculated by applying the projected growth rate over the base year revenue of that State.

Illustration—If the base year revenue for 2015-16 for a concerned State, calculated as per section 5 is one hundred rupees, then the projected revenue for financial year 2018-19 shall be as follows—

Projected Revenue for 2018-19—100 $(1+14/100)^3$

Calculation and release of compensation.

7. (1) The compensation under this Act shall be payable to any State during the transition period.

(2) The compensation payable to a State shall be provisionally calculated and released at the end of every two months period, and shall be finally calculated for every financial year after the receipt of final revenue figures, as audited by the Comptroller and Auditor-General of India:

Provided that in case any excess amount has been released as compensation to a State in any financial year during the transition period, as per the audited figures of revenue collected, the excess amount so released shall be adjusted against the compensation amount payable to such State in the subsequent financial year.

(3) The total compensation payable for any financial year during the transition period to any State shall be calculated in the following manner, namely:—

(*a*) the projected revenue for any financial year during the transition period, which could have accrued to a State in the absence of the goods and services tax, shall be calculated as per section 6;

(*b*) the actual revenue collected by a State in any financial year during the transition period shall be—

(*i*) the actual revenue from State tax collected by the State, net of refunds given by the said State under Chapters XI and XX of the State Goods and Services Tax Act;

(*ii*) the integrated goods and services tax apportioned to that State; and

(*iii*) any collection of taxes on account of the taxes levied by the respective State under the Acts specified in sub-section (4) of section 5, net of refund of such taxes,

as certified by the Comptroller and Auditor-General of India;

(*c*) the total compensation payable in any financial year shall be the difference between the projected revenue for any financial year and the actual revenue collected by a State referred to in clause (*b*).

(4) The loss of revenue at the end of every two months period in any year for a State during the transition period shall be calculated, at the end of the said period, in the following manner, namely:—

(*a*) the projected revenue that could have been earned by the State in absence of the goods and services tax till the end of the relevant two months period of the respective financial year shall be calculated on a *pro rata* basis as a percentage of the total projected revenue for any financial year during the transition period, calculated in accordance with section 6.

Illustration—If the projected revenue for any year calculated in accordance with section 6 is one hundred rupees, for calculating the projected revenue that could be earned till the end of the period of ten months for the purpose of this sub-section shall be : (100 × (5/6) = ₹ 83.33);

(*b*) the actual revenue collected by a State till the end of relevant two months period in any financial year during the transition period shall be–

(*i*) the actual revenue from State tax collected by the State, net of refunds given by the State under Chapters XI and XX of the State Goods and Services Tax Act;

(*ii*) the integrated goods and services tax apportioned to that State, as certified by the Principal Chief Controller of Accounts of the [1][Central Board of Indirect Taxes and Customs]; and

(*iii*) any collection of taxes levied by the said State, under the Acts specified in sub-section (4) of section 5, net of refund of such taxes;

(*c*) the provisional compensation payable to any State at the end of the relevant two months period in any financial year shall be the difference between the projected revenue till the end of the relevant period in accordance with clause (*a*) and the actual revenue collected by a State in the said period as referred to in clause (*b*), reduced by the provisional compensation paid to a State till the end of the previous two months period in the said financial year during the transition period.

(5) In case of any difference between the final compensation amount payable to a State calculated in accordance with the provisions of sub-section (3)

---

1. Substituted for "Central Board of Excise and Customs" by the Goods and Services Tax (Compensation to States) Amendment Act, 2018, w.e.f. 1-2-2019.

upon receipt of the audited revenue figures from the Comptroller and Auditor-General of India, and the total provisional compensation amount released to a State in the said financial year in accordance with the provisions of sub-section (4), the same shall be adjusted against release of compensation to the State in the subsequent financial year.

(6) Where no compensation is due to be released in any financial year, and in case any excess amount has been released to a State in the previous year, this amount shall be refunded by the State to the Central Government and such amount shall be credited to the Fund in such manner as may be prescribed.

Levy and collection of cess.

8. (1) There shall be levied a cess on such intra-State supplies of goods or services or both, as provided for in section 9 of the Central Goods and Services Tax Act, and such inter-State supplies of goods or services or both as provided for in section 5 of the Integrated Goods and Services Tax Act, and collected in such manner as may be prescribed, on the recommendations of the Council, for the purposes of providing compensation to the States for loss of revenue arising on account of implementation of the goods and services tax with effect from the date from which the provisions of the Central Goods and Services Tax Act is brought into force, for a period of five years or for such period as may be prescribed on the recommendations of the Council:

Provided that no such cess shall be leviable on supplies made by a taxable person who has decided to opt for composition levy under section 10 of the Central Goods and Services Tax Act.

(2) The cess shall be levied on such supplies of goods and services as are specified in column (2) of the Schedule, on the basis of value, quantity or on such basis at such rate not exceeding the rate set forth in the corresponding entry in column (4) of the

Schedule, as the Central Government may, on the recommendations of the Council, by notification in the Official Gazette, specify:

Provided that where the cess is chargeable on any supply of goods or services or both with reference to their value, for each such supply the value shall be determined under section 15 of the Central Goods and Services Tax Act for all intra-State and inter-State supplies of goods or services or both:

Provided further that the cess on goods imported into India shall be levied and collected in accordance with the provisions of section 3 of the Customs Tariff Act, 1975 (51 of 1975), at the point when duties of customs are levied on the said goods under section 12 of the Customs Act, 1962 (52 of 1962), on a value determined under the Customs Tariff Act, 1975.

[2][Power not to recover cess not levied or short-levied as a result of general practice.

8A. *Notwithstanding anything contained in this Act, if the Government is satisfied that—*

(a) *a practice was, or is, generally prevalent regarding levy of cess (including non-levy thereof) on any supply of goods or services or both; and*

(b) *such supplies were, or are, liable to,–*

(i) *cess, in cases where according to the said practice, cess was not, or is not being, levied; or*

(ii) *a higher amount of cess than what was, or is being, levied, in accordance with the said practice,*

the Government may, on the recommendation of the Council, by notification in the Official Gazette, direct that the whole of the cess payable on such supplies, or, as the case may be, the cess in excess of that payable on such supplies, but for the said practice, shall

2. Inserted by the Finance (No. 2) Act, 2024, w.e.f. **1-11-2024.**

not be required to be paid in respect of the supplies on which the cess was not, or is not being, levied, or was, or is being, short-levied, in accordance with the said practice.]

Returns, payments and refunds.

9. (1) Every taxable person, making a taxable supply of goods or services or both, shall—

(*a*) pay the amount of cess as payable under this Act in such manner;

(*b*) furnish such returns in such forms, along with the returns to be filed under the Central Goods and Services Tax Act; and

(*c*) apply for refunds of such cess paid in such form,

as may be prescribed.

(2) For all purposes of furnishing of returns and claiming refunds, except for the form to be filed, the provisions of the Central Goods and Services Tax Act and the rules made thereunder, shall, as far as may be, apply in relation to the levy and collection of the cess leviable under section 8 on all taxable supplies of goods or services or both, as they apply in relation to the levy and collection of central tax on such supplies under the said Act or the rules made thereunder.

Crediting proceeds of cess to Fund.

10. (1) The proceeds of the cess leviable under section 8 and such other amounts as may be recommended by the Council, shall be credited to a non-lapsable Fund known as the Goods and Services Tax Compensation Fund, which shall form part of the public account of India and shall be utilised for purposes specified in the said section.

(2) All amounts payable to the States under section 7 shall be paid out of the Fund.

(3) Fifty per cent of the amount remaining unutilised in the Fund at the end of the transition period shall

be transferred to the Consolidated Fund of India as the share of Centre, and the balance fifty per cent shall be distributed amongst the States in the ratio of their total revenues from the State tax or the Union territory goods and services tax, as the case may be, in the last year of the transition period.

[3][(3A) Notwithstanding anything contained in sub-section (3), fifty per cent of such amount, as may be recommended by the Council, which remains unutilised in the Fund, at any point of time in any financial year during the transition period shall be transferred to the Consolidated Fund of India as the share of Centre, and the balance fifty per cent shall be distributed amongst the States in the ratio of their base year revenue determined in accordance with the provisions of section 5:

Provided that in case of shortfall in the amount collected in the Fund against the requirement of compensation to be released under section 7 for any two months' period, fifty per cent of the same, but not exceeding the total amount transferred to the Centre and the States as recommended by the Council, shall be recovered from the Centre and the balance fifty per cent from the States in the ratio of their base year revenue determined in accordance with the provisions of section 5.]

(4) The accounts relating to Fund shall be audited by the Comptroller and Auditor-General of India or any person appointed by him at such intervals as may be specified by him and any expenditure in connection with such audit shall be payable by the Central Government to the Comptroller and Auditor-General of India.

---

3. Inserted by the Goods and Services Tax (Compensation to States) Amendment Act, 2018, w.e.f. 1-2-2019.

(5) The accounts of the Fund, as certified by the Comptroller and Auditor-General of India or any other person appointed by him in this behalf together with the audit report thereon shall be laid before each House of Parliament.

Other provisions relating to cess.

11. (1) The provisions of the Central Goods and Services Tax Act, and the rules made thereunder, including those relating to assessment, input tax credit, non-levy, short-levy, interest, appeals, offences and penalties, shall, as far as may be, *mutatis mutandis,* apply, in relation to the levy and collection of the cess leviable under section 8 on the intra-State supply of goods and services, as they apply in relation to the levy and collection of central tax on such intra-State supplies under the said Act or the rules made thereunder.

(2) The provisions of the Integrated Goods and Services Tax Act, and the rules made thereunder, including those relating to assessment, input tax credit, non-levy, short-levy, interest, appeals, offences and penalties, shall, *mutatis mutandis,* apply in relation to the levy and collection of the cess leviable under section 8 on the inter-State supply of goods and services, as they apply in relation to the levy and collection of integrated tax on such inter State supplies under the said Act or the rules made thereunder:

Provided that the input tax credit in respect of cess on supply of goods and services leviable under section 8, shall be utilised only towards payment of said cess on supply of goods and services leviable under the said section.

Power to make rules.

12. (1) The Central Government shall, on the recommendations of the Council, by notification in the Official Gazette, make rules for carrying out the provisions of this Act.

(2) In particular, and without prejudice to the generality of the foregoing power, such rules may provide for all or any of the following matters, namely:—

(*a*) the conditions which were included in the total base year revenue of the States, referred to in sub-clause (*g*) of clause (*4*) of article 279A of the Constitution, under sub-section (3) of section 5;

(*b*) the conditions subject to which any part of revenues not credited in the Consolidated Fund of the respective State shall be included in the total base year revenue of the State, under sub-section (6) of section 5;

(*c*) the manner of refund of compensation by the States to the Central Government under sub-section (6) of section 7;

(*d*) the manner of levy and collection of cess and the period of its imposition under sub-section (1) of section 8;

(*e*) the manner and forms for payment of cess, furnishing of returns and refund of cess under sub-section (1) of section 9; and

(*f*) any other matter which is to be, or may be, prescribed, or in respect of which provision is to be made, by rules.

Laying of rules before Parliament.

13. Every rule made under this Act by the Central Government shall be laid, as soon as may be after it is made, before each House of Parliament, while it is in session, for a total period of thirty days which may be comprised in one session or in two or more successive sessions, and if, before the expiry of the session immediately following the session or successive sessions aforesaid, both Houses agree in making any modification in the rule or both Houses agree that the rule should not be made, the rule shall thereafter have effect only in such modified form or be of no effect, as the case may be; so, however, that any such modification or annulment shall be without prejudice to the validity of anything previously done under that rule.

Power to remove difficulties.

14. (1) If any difficulty arises in giving effect to the provisions of this Act, the Central Government may, on the recommendations of the Council, by order published in the Official Gazette, make such provisions, not inconsistent with the provisions of this Act, as appear to it to be necessary or expedient for removing the difficulty:

Provided that no order shall be made under this section after the expiry of [4][five years] from the commencement of this Act.

(2) Every order made under this section shall, as soon as may be after it is made, be laid before each House of Parliament.

SCHEDULE

[*See* section 8(2)]

1. In this Schedule, reference to a "tariff item", "heading", "sub-heading" and "Chapter", wherever they occur, shall mean respectively a tariff item, heading, sub-heading and Chapter in the First Schedule to the Customs Tariff Act, 1975 (51 of 1975).

2. The rules for the interpretation of the First Schedule to the Customs Tariff Act, 1975 (51 of 1975), the section and Chapter Notes and the General Explanatory Notes of the First Schedule shall, so far as may be, apply to the interpretation of this Schedule.

4. Substituted for "three years" by the Finance Act, 2020, w.e.f. 27-3-2020.

S. No.	*Description of supply of goods or services*	*Tariff item, heading, sub-heading, Chapter, or supply of goods or services, as the case may be*	*The maximum rate at which goods and services tax compensation cess may be collected*
(1)	*(2)*	*(3)*	*(4)*
1.	Pan Masala.	2106 90 20	[5][Fifty-one per cent of retail sale price per unit].
2.	Tobacco and manufactured tobacco substitutes, including tobacco products.	24	[6][Four thousand one hundred and seventy rupees per thousand sticks or two hundred and ninety per cent *ad valorem* or a combination thereof, but not exceeding four thousand one hundred and seventy rupees per thousand sticks plus two hundred and ninety per cent *ad valorem* or hundred per cent of retail sale price per unit].

5. Substituted for "One hundred and thirty-five per cent *ad valorem*" by the Finance Act, 2023, w.e.f. 1-4-2023.
6. Substituted for "Four thousand one hundred and seventy rupees per thousand sticks or two hundred and ninety per cent *ad valorem* or a combination thereof, but not exceeding four thousand one hundred and seventy rupees per thousand sticks plus two hundred and ninety per cent *ad valorem*", *ibid.*

S. No.	*Description of supply of goods or services*	*Tariff item, heading, sub-heading, Chapter, or supply of goods or services, as the case may be*	*The maximum rate at which goods and services tax compensation cess may be collected*
(1)	*(2)*	*(3)*	*(4)*
3.	Coal, briquettes, ovoids and similar solid fuels manufactured from coal, lignite, whether or not agglomerated, excluding jet, peat (including peat litter), whether or not agglomerated.	2701, 2702 or 2703	Four hundred rupees per tonne.
4.	Aerated waters.	2202 10 10	Fifteen per cent *ad valorem*.
[7][4A.	Motor vehicles for the transport of not more than thirteen persons, including the driver.	8702 10, 8702 20, 8702 30 or 8702 90	Twenty-five per cent *ad valorem*.]
5.	Motor cars and other motor vehicles principally designed for the transport of persons (other than motor vehicles for the transport of ten	8703	[8][Twenty-five per cent *ad valorem*.]

7. Inserted by the Goods and Services Tax (Compensation to States) Amendment Act, 2017, w.r.e.f. 2-9-2017.
8. Substituted for "Fifteen per cent *ad valorem*.", *ibid.*

S. No.	Description of supply of goods or services	Tariff item, heading, sub-heading, Chapter, or supply of goods or services, as the case may be	The maximum rate at which goods and services tax compensation cess may be collected
(1)	(2)	(3)	(4)
	or more persons, including the driver), including station wagons and racing cars.		
6.	Any other supplies.		Fifteen per cent *ad valorem*.

[9][*Explanation*.—For the purposes of this Schedule,—

(*i*) "retail sale price" means the maximum price at which the concerned goods in packaged form may be sold to the ultimate consumer and includes all taxes, local or otherwise, freight, transport charges, commission payable to dealers, and all charges towards advertisement, delivery, packing, forwarding and the like and the price is the sole consideration for such sale:

Provided that where the provisions of the Legal Metrology Act, 2009 (1 of 2010) or the rules made thereunder or any other law for the time being in force require to declare on the package, the retail sale price excluding any taxes, local or otherwise, the retail sale price shall be construed accordingly;

9. Inserted by the Finance Act, 2023, w.e.f. 1-4-2023.

(*ii*) where on the package of any concerned goods more than one retail sale price is declared, the maximum of such retail sale price shall be deemed to be the retail sale price;

(*iii*) where the retail sale price, declared on the package of any concerned goods at the time of its clearance from the place of manufacture, is altered to increase the retail sale price, such altered retail sale price shall be deemed to be the retail sale price;

(*iv*) where different retail sale prices are declared on different packages for the sale of any concerned goods in packaged form in different areas, each such retail sale price shall be the retail sale prices for the purposes of determination of the rate of cess for the said goods intended to be sold in the area to which the retail sale price relates.]